The History of the
JEWISH PEOPLE

Volume II
The Early Middle Ages

Books by Moses A. Shulvass

Die Juden in Würzburg während des Mittelalters 1934

Rome and Jerusalem (Hebrew) 1944

Chapters from the life of Samuel David Luzzatto
(Hebrew) 1951

The Jews in the World of the Renaissance
(Hebrew Version) 1955

In the Grip of Centuries (Hebrew) 1960

Between the Rhine and the Bosporus 1964

From East to West 1971

The Jews in the World of the Renaissance
(English Version) 1973

Jewish Culture in Eastern Europe 1975

The History of the Jewish People 1982–

The History of the
JEWISH PEOPLE

Moses A. Shulvass

Volume II
The Early Middle Ages

REGNERY GATEWAY

Chicago

Library of Congress Catalog Card Number 81-85564
ISBN 0-89526-657-1 (Vol. II)
ISBN 0-89526-652-0 (5-vol. set)

Regnery Gateway
360 West Superior Street
Chicago, Illinois 60610

To the memory of my father-in-law
Jacob Cemach
of Warsaw, Poland
(1886–1943)
Died as a Martyr of the Holocaust on
5 Heshwan, 5704–November 3, 1943

CONTENTS

SECTION XIII   IN THE ORBIT OF ISLAM DURING
THE EARLY MIDDLE AGES   1

Chapter 1   **The New Situation**   1
The Emergence of the Muslim Empire, 1;
The Status of the Jew as an Unbeliever, 3

Chapter 2   **In the Caliphate**   5
The Jewish Population, 5; Political
Conditions and Taxation, 8; The
Economic Scene, 11

Chapter 3   **In the Breakaway States**   13
The General Scene, 13; The Jewish
Population, 15; Political Conditions, 18;
The Economic Scene, 25

Chapter 4   **Community Government**   28
Exilarchal Administration in the Caliphate,
28; The Rule of Negidim in the Breakaway
States, 32; Local Community Administration, 34

Chapter 5   **The Cultural Scene**   35
The Growth of Culture, 35; Linguistic
Conditions, 37; The Academies and the
Geonim, 40; Saadiah Gaon (882–942), 44;
Other Schools and Scholars, 48;
Rabbinic Literature, 51; Moses Maimonides
(1135–1204), 53; The Other Philosophers, 62;
Sherira's Epistle, 64; Exegesis of the Bible, 65;
The Golden Age, 66; The Sciences, 76

Chapter 6   **The Religious Life**   80
Religious Leadership, 80; Religious Practice
and Prayer, 83; Religious Unrest, 86

Chapter 7   **Karaism and the Karaites**   **88**
The Emergence of the Sect, 88; Religious
Doctrine and Practice, 90; Karaite-Rabbanite
Relations, 93; The Karaites in the Orbit
of Islam, 95; The Karaites in Byzantium-
Turkey and in Eastern Europe, 98;
In the Holocaust and After, 103

SECTION XIV IN THE ORBIT OF EASTERN CHRISTIANITY
DURING THE EARLY MIDDLE AGES   **107**

Chapter 1   **In the Byzantine Empire**   **107**
The Jewish Population, 107; Political
and Economic Conditions, 109; Culture
and Religious Life, 110

Chapter 2   **The Khazars**   **113**
The Khazars and Their Land, 113;
Conversion to Judaism, 114; Jewish
Khazaria, 116

Chapter 3   **In Russia**   **118**

SECTION XV   IN THE ORBIT OF WESTERN CHRISTENDOM
DURING THE EARLY MIDDLE AGES   **121**

Chapter 1   **The General Scene**   **121**

Chapter 2   **The Jewish Population**   **127**

Chapter 3   **Jewish Political Destiny**   **134**
General Developments, 134; On the
Iberian Peninsula, 136; In Frankland, 139;
In France, 140; In Germany, 142; In Italy,
145; In England, 146; In Bohemia-Moravia,
Hungary, and Poland, 148

Chapter 4   **The Church and the Jews**   **150**
The Theological Image of the Jew and its
Consequences, 150; Attitudes of the
Church Councils, 153; The Attitude of

the Popes, 155; Religious Disputations and
the Offensive Against Jewish Books, 157

Chapter 5   **In the Crucible of the Crusades**   **158**
On the Threshold of the Crusades, 158; The
First Crusade, 160; The Later Crusades, 163;
The Jews in the Crusader Kingdom of
Jerusalem, 166; Sanctification of the Holy
Name, 168

Chapter 6   **The Accusations**   **171**
The Blood Libel, 171; Other Libels, 174

Chapter 7   **Community Government**   **175**
Jewish Communal Autonomy, 175;
Community Administration, 178

Chapter 8   **The Economic Scene**   **181**
Major Trends, 181; The Jews in
Commerce, 184; Jews in the Crafts, 187;
Jews in Agriculture, 188; The
Jewish Moneylenders, 189

Chapter 9   **The Cultural Experience**   **193**
General Developments, 193; Linguistic
Conditions, 198; Talmudic Studies and
Talmudic Literature, 202; Biblical Exegesis,
208; Hebrew Poetry and Belles-Lettres, 212;
Chronology and History, 213; Geography
and Travel, 215; Philosophy, 218; The
Sciences, 221

Chapter 10   **The Religious Life**   **224**
The Question of Religious Authority, 225;
Ritual and Prayer, 226; The Pious Men of
Ashkenaz, 230; Mysticism and the Mystics, 232;
Facing Christianity, 234

INDEX   **239**

ACKNOWLEDGMENTS

I wish to express my profound gratitude to my wife and co-worker Celia A. Shulvass, of blessed memory. Her encouragement and support in all phases of writing this work were immensely helpful. And so were her opinions in our many discussions on the problems and challenges that I confronted as an author.

As before, Benita Masters, Sharon Swanson, my daughter Phyllis Gelman, and Samuel Cherniak made many felicitous linguistic and stylistic suggestions. Several grants from the Rosaline Cohn Scholars Fund of Spertus College of Judaica provided technical assistance in the collection of source material. Jacqueline Bocian and Maryse Manelli prepared the index. Leon A. Pasko and David G. Singer assisted in the proofreading. To all of them go my sincere thanks.

IN THE ORBIT OF ISLAM DURING THE EARLY MIDDLE AGES

Chapter 1

The New Situation

The Emergence of the Muslim Empire

Mohammed's original idea was to create a new monotheistic religion which would render obsolete the struggle between Judaism and Christianity and allow both Jews and Christians to join his Arab compatriots in one great unity. He soon realized that neither Jews nor Christians were willing to respond to his message. He then began to build his new religious community on a purely nationalistic Arab basis. Nonetheless, later Muslim theologians continued to pursue Mohammed's idea of monotheistic unity and developed the principle of spreading the new faith, Islam, with the power of the sword. Mohammed himself rejoiced in leading his followers into battle against nonbelievers, and so created for the Muslims a practical example for an attempt at world conquest.

While Mohammed was still alive, his forces began to break out of the Arabian peninsula into Palestine and to clash with the Byzantine forces stationed there. But, it was not until 633, about one year after Mohammed's death, that the Muslim drive

1

began to gain real momentum. From then on, the conquest of territories in Asia and North Africa proceeded rapidly. Damascus was captured in 635. The Byzantine defeat at the Yarmuk River, in Transjordan, in 636, and the defeat of the Persian army the following year, opened for the Muslims the way to large areas hitherto part of the Byzantine and Persian empires. Jerusalem fell in 637 or 638, and by 640 the entire Holy Land was in the hands of the Muslims. About the same time, the Muslims extended their control over Egypt and large parts of the Persian empire. By the middle of the seventh century the conquest of the Persian empire was complete. Libya, Tripolitania, and Tunisia were subsequently conquered without noticeable opposition.

The leader of the Muslims who succeeded Mohammed as ruler of the Arabs, but not as the "messenger of God," carried the title of caliph. Most of the original conquests were achieved under the first two caliphs, Abu Bakr and Umar I, especially the latter. But it was not until 661 that the first dynasty of the caliphate, that of the Umayyads, was established by Muawiya I (661–80), with its capital in Damascus.

The caliphate-empire continued to expand throughout the second half of the seventh and the first decades of the eighth centuries. After having vanquished serious opposition in today's Algeria under the Jewish woman leader Dahya al-Kahina (cf. Vol. I, Sec. X, Chap. 2), Arab rule became firmly established in all of northwest Africa, and the conquerors were now ready to invade Europe. This occurred in the year 711, when they invaded Spain. They occupied most of the country within a few months, and later easily conquered the rest of the peninsula. A few years later the Arabs crossed the Pyrenees and occupied the southern regions of France. Although beaten by the ruler of Frankland, Charles Martel, in 732 in the battle of Tours and Poitiers, they still retained a foothold in the province of Septimania, including the city of Narbonne till 759.

As a result of all these conquests the Jewish people found itself in a totally new situation. Instead of living under pagan Persian emperors and a multiplicity of Christian rulers, the overwhelming majority of the Jewish people was now living within the confines of the caliphate. We shall see later that these developments had a far-reaching impact on the economic role of the

Jews in the period of the Early Middle Ages. But of even greater significance was the change which took place in the general situation of the Jewish people.

The Status of the Jew as an Unbeliever

Despite the hostile confrontation between the Jews and Mohammed in North Arabia (cf. Vol. I, Sec. IX, Chap. 3), the Jews of Palestine, Syria, and Babylonia possibly helped the Arabs in the conquest of these countries. Byzantium's treatment of the Jews after re-conquering Palestine from the Persians (cf. Vol. I, Sec. VIII, Chap. 5), and the generally chaotic situation in the Persian empire, placed the Jews of these countries on the side of the Arab conquerors. Furthermore, the fact that the Muslims in these countries were at the beginning a relatively small group of military men and administrators created a natural alliance between them and the Jewish minorities.

In subsequent years, when Muslim religious thinkers began to formulate the attitude of the new faith to the unbelievers, the framework for Jewish existence that evolved was quite different from that developed by Christian theologians and statesmen. To begin with, among the Muslims, the idea that the Jews were aliens never took hold. Thus, the expulsion of the Jews from cities and entire countries, so characteristic of the history of the Jews under Medieval Christendom, only rarely occurred in Muslim countries. Another factor in the preservation of Jewish existence was the concept implied in the Quran (9:29), that unbelievers should carry the main burden of financially maintaining the state. This concept worked not only against the expulsion of the Jews but tacitly also against attempting forcibly to convert them on a large scale. But, although the Jew thus became an important factor in the maintenance of the financial stability of the state, he nevertheless was given the social status of a second-class subject. The countless statements in the Quran condemning the unbelievers could not help but create an atmosphere in which the Muslim was considered as favored by God and the unbeliever as despised by Him.

These anti-Jewish feelings were greatly strengthened when

Christians in the conquered countries began to convert to Islam en masse and brought along into the new faith the violent hatred of the Jews developed in the Church, both in the Near East and in Spain, during the centuries preceding the Arab conquests. True, Muslim religious literature is also full of attacks against Judaism. But, both in normative Islam and its sects, these never even approached in intensity the venom and anger heaped upon Jews and Judaism in the writings of the Fathers of the Church. A further mitigating influence on the Muslim attitude to the Jews may have resulted from the similarity of the Muslim law and the Jewish Oral Law. The extent of this similarity is a matter of debate. But such a similarity does exist, even though limited and not always easily discernible.

The earliest legal document regulating the relationship of the Muslim state with the Jews (as well as other unbelievers) is the so-called Pact of Umar, most probably a forgery. In this document, which is essentially of a contractual nature, the state promised protection to a given non-Muslim community, while at the same time assigning to it a social status distinctly lower than that of the Muslims, an attitude already indicated in the above-mentioned verse of the Quran. This was accompanied by a variety of restrictions, including some on dress. Most conspicuous among these were the prohibitions against bearing arms and riding on horses. Under favorable conditions, these restrictions were more often honored in the breach rather than in the observance. But even when fully executed, the Pact of Umar still provided the Jew with more bearable conditions than those accorded to him under Christendom. Even the burden of taxation was in the final analysis more bearable than that under Christendom, since the economic opportunities extended to the Jew were incomparably more varied and much less restrictive than those given to him in Christian countries. Under the general conditions of insecurity prevalent in the Middle Ages, coupled with the basic structural weakness of the medieval state, the status of the Jews as *ahl al-dhimma* (or, in short, *dhimmi*), people of the pact, was not at all unfavorable.

Chapter 2

In the Caliphate

The Jewish Population

Against the backdrop of the favorable political conditions, the Jewish population in the caliphate underwent a process of growth. The old large communities, such as that of Babylonia, continued to harbor masses of Jews. Countries and cities, previously devoid of Jews, or whose Jewish population underwent drastic cuts in pre-Mohammedan times, became areas of Jewish settlement again. Unlike the Christians and pagans, who converted to Islam in ever-growing numbers, only few Jews joined the faith of the new conqueror for the time being. To be sure, right after the conquests a certain number of Jews did convert to Islam. But by the time the first rush was over, only few Jews had become Muslims. Thus, at first defection did not constitute a serious factor in determining the size of the Jewish population within the orbit of Islam.

To begin with, a certain number of Jews remained in North Arabia after Mohammed's and Umar's actions designed to liquidate its large Jewish community. There is also evidence of the presence of Jews in this area in the tenth and eleventh centuries. As for Yemen, practically nothing is known of a Jewish settlement until the tenth century. If there were any Jews, they constituted a "silent community" (cf. Vol. I, Sec. IX, Chap. 3). There is, of course, a possibility that the Jewish community which existed in the tenth century in Yemen was descended directly from Jews living there prior to the country's Islamization. Be this as it may, Yemen's Jewish community in the tenth century was numerically not insignificant, and it included larger aggregations of Jews in the cities of Sana and Aden.

The Jewish community in the Holy Land underwent a process of remarkable growth. At the time of the Arab conquest some Jewish settlements existed in the Negev and farther north on both sides of the Jordan. An important community existed in Gaza, which, after the exclusion of Jews from Jerusalem, had become the major Jewish center in the south of the country. Still larger numbers of Jews lived in Galilee, where Tiberias was the leading community.

Jerusalem had remained uninhabited by Jews, as we have seen, since the unhappy end of the Second Revolt (135 C.E.). With the advent of the Muslims, the country's Jewish population began to grow steadily. Already between the years 624 and 628 refugees from the Jewish tribes in northern Arabia began to augment the Jewish population. Additional refugees arrived from Arabia a few years later when Umar I broke his agreement with the Jews of Khaibar and expelled them. Later Jewish immigrants arrived in Palestine from other countries as well. The fact that Christians and Samaritans were still the overwhelming majority in the country must have made Jewish immigration rather welcome to the Muslim authorities. Soon opposition to Jewish settlement in Jerusalem was dropped.

Once permission was given, many Jews settled in the city, attracted by its religious character. Conspicuous among them were the "mourners of Zion," mostly Babylonian Rabbanite Jews and Karaites, whose only goal in life was to pray at the Western Wall for the speedy coming of the Messiah. Ramleh, too, established in 716, and serving as the seat of the caliph's governor, became the home of a sizable Jewish community. In time, larger Jewish communities also came into being in Haifa and Ashkelon. The only area in the Holy Land which did not attract new Jewish settlers was its southernmost region, the Negev. Under the caliphs, the Negev lost the significance it had under Roman and Byzantine rule as a major caravan route, and ceased to be an area of dense settlement.

The Jewish communities in Syria grew as well. Jewish immigrants arrived from various countries, and settled partly in the old Jewish communities and partly in towns and sections of towns abandoned by fleeing Christians. Tyre, Tripoli, Aleppo, and Damascus had sizable Jewish communities. The latter had a Jewish population of several thousand. Palmyra too continued to harbor several thousand Jews. Jews were also found in the Caucasus, on the northwestern frontier of the caliphate.

The bulk of the caliphate's Jewish population continued to live in the territories of the former Persian empire, that is, Iraq (still called Babylonia by the Jews), Iran, and Khorasan. The latter consisted of northeastern Persia, Afghanistan, and parts of Turkestan. As in pre-Mohammedan times, Jews continued to live in massive concentrations in Iraq-Babylonia. Their presence is attested to in at least 20 cities. Some cities, such as Sura, were still overwhelmingly Jewish. But even in cities where the Jews were not the majority their number was considerable. Basra, for instance, had a Jewish population of no less than 10,000. Jews also had been living in that suburb of Ctesiphon which became the city of Baghdad, and since 762–63 the capital of the caliphate. Baghdad, naturally, attracted many Jews, and its Jewish community continuously numbered about 40,000. Although some of the caliphs attempted to limit the non-Muslim population of the city, the number of Jews did not diminish, and remained about the same until the Mongol conquest in 1258.

Jewish settlement in Persia proper underwent a great expansion. The communities of Isfahan, Ahwaz, and Shiraz counted among the important Jewish centers in the caliphate. In Khorasan and the rest of Muslim Central Asia Jews are known to have been present beginning with the early eighth century. Most of them were Babylonian and Persian Jews who either immigrated voluntarily, or were deported there by the exilarchal authorities from the areas of Jewish mass settlement as an undesirable element. In time, the number of Jews in Khorasan became quite considerable.

After the Muslim conquest of North Africa its Jewish population also began to grow rapidly. We have seen (Vol. I, Sec. X) how under the rule of the Christian emperors the Jewish population steadily diminished. Now its number began to rise again in Egypt, Libya, and in the rest of North Africa. It is impossible to determine which of the Jewish communities in North Africa in the seventh and eighth centuries were new and which had survived the Christian oppression and were now augmented in size. Jews were also to be found everywhere in the new cities established by the Muslims, such as Kairuwan in today's Tunisia, and Fez in Morocco. But the real growth of the Jewish communities in North Africa took place at a later time, when these countries had broken away from the caliphate.

Muslim Spain too had a very large Jewish population. As we

have seen (Vol. I, Sec. XI, Chap. 3), it must be assumed that most of the Jews made slaves by the Visigothic government only a few short years before the Arab conquest, now could openly profess Judaism again. Here too the number of Jews grew in later times. But already in the first half century of Muslim rule, before Spain declared itself independent from the caliphate, this—its westernmost province—had a Jewish population second in number only to that of Iraq. Jewish concentration in the cities was conspicuous. Some cities, such as Seville or Lucena, were considered "Jewish cities," even though non-Jews probably lived there as well.

Political Conditions and Taxation

The status of the Jews as *dhimmis* remained unchanged in principle during the entire period of the rule of the Umayyads (661—750), whose capital was in Damascus, and the Abassids (750–1258), who resided in the new capital Baghdad. In practice, however, the fate of the Jews depended on the individual caliphs. Most of them treated the Jews well, while exacting from them in taxes as much money as possible. Some of the caliphs, in addition, issued anti-Jewish ordinances, often modeled after similar Byzantine legislation. Such laws usually remained in force for a limited period, until abolished or forgotten. Other caliphs created difficulties for their Jewish subjects by pitting them and the Christian population against each other. Curiously, Harun-ar-Rashid (786–809), so famous in the western world for his chivalry, was one of the Baghdad caliphs less friendly to the Jews. Ordinances about special garments for the Jews were issued by several caliphs, but it is doubtful that the law was ever enforced in the manner later customary in Christian countries. The existence of Jewish quarters in the cities did not result from a governmental plan to separate the Jews from the rest of the population, but rather from the Arab custom of assigning to each tribe a separate area. The poll tax (*jizya*) paid by the Jews as *dhimmis* was burdensome, but was offset by the greatly expanded economic opportunities accorded to them. The land tax particularly must have been a heavy burden, since it often ran as high as 20 percent of the crop.

The fact that many of the caliphate's Jews, especially in the area of mass settlement in Iraq, still tilled the soil, turned this tax into a serious hardship. Characteristic of the situation is the opinion issued by Sheshna Gaon, Babylonian Jewry's religious leader in the 680s, absolving his coreligionists from any ban imposed in matters of taxation by the Jewish communal authorities under governmental pressure. No doubt, in matters of taxation the caliphs were often harsh on their Jewish subjects.

The attitude of the caliphs to the question of the employment of Jews in governmental service was ambiguous. The Pact of Umar clearly intended to keep Jews out of positions of authority. In practice, however, Jews were employed in various services, and especially in the financial administration, as early as the second half of the seventh century. A Jew, for example, was connected with the mint late in the seventh century under caliph Abd al-Malik. Several decades later, however, Umar II (717–20) purged all infidels, including Jews, from all governmental offices. In the tenth century we find Jews again playing a conspicuous role in the financial administration. By and large, Jewish officials in the Baghdad caliphate never wielded as much authority as the Jewish officials in the Cordova caliphate and successor states, after they broke away from the Baghdad caliphate (cf. the next chapter).

Between the middle of the tenth and the middle of the twelfth centuries, the Abassid caliphs reigned under the control of various invaders. In the middle of the tenth century Persian sectarian (Shiite) Muslims occupied Baghdad, and their emirs ruled the country for over a hundred years. Under their rule the situation of the Jews deteriorated considerably, and the exilarch was stripped of his power. The Jews seem to have been better treated by the Seljuk Turks who later occupied Baghdad for a period of about 80 years. When the Abassid caliphs regained their full power close to the middle of the twelfth century, they re-activated the traditional Jewish policy of the caliphate. This policy then remained in force till the end of the Abassid dynasty in 1258.

Close to the middle of the twelfth century, the Jewry of the caliphate witnessed an attempt by a group of Jews, inspired by messianic hopes, to reconquer the Holy Land, then under the rule of the Crusaders, for the Jewish people. What really happened is not very clear. It seems that shortly after 1140 a man, popularly known as David Alroy, re-kindled a movement begun some decades earlier by his father. His plan was possibly to utilize the ever-weakening position of the Crusader states in order to break through to the Holy Land and re-establish there the Jewish state. It seems that in the beginning the Muslim authorities viewed David's plan of displacing the Christians from Palestine with favor, since it was in line with their political goals. Later, however, the attitude of the authorities changed, for reasons unclear to us. Possibly in line with this, the exilarch and the Jewish religious leadership also turned against David. The movement came to an end soon thereafter when David died, or was assassinated, under uncertain circumstances. As in the case of other "messiahs," David's memory survived among a group of Jews who tenaciously believed in his messiahship.

The Jewish policy of the caliphs in Palestine, Syria, North Africa, and Spain was basically not much different. Some variations could be noticed, however. In Syria, for example, the fate of the Jews deteriorated somewhat after the Abassids took over from the Umayyads. This may have been caused by the change in the religious balance in the country, where the number of Muslims was on a constant rise, with a corresponding diminution in the number of Christians. The Jews were thus losing ground as an "ally" of the caliphate. The attitude of the Abassids may have also resulted from a resentment against the inhabitants of Syria, the seat of the former dynasty. The Jewish situation was further aggravated, in Palestine even more than in Syria, by the perpetual strife between rival Bedouin tribes. With the transfer of the capital from Damascus to Baghdad, Syria and Palestine had become areas remote from the center of the government, and even a friendly and caring caliphal authority was unable to properly maintain a state of law and order there. When the Seljuks captured Syria in the second half of the eleventh century, they treated the Jews in the same benign manner accorded by them to the Jews of Iraq.

In North Africa too the caliphate extended protection to the Jews in return for the poll tax paid by them as *dhimmis*. Characteristic of the determination of the Muslims to protect the Jewish group is the fact that upon conquering Egypt they rejected a demand of the Christian patriarch of Alexandria that they keep the

Jews out of the city. Whether there is truth to the tradition that upon founding the city of Kairuwan, in today's Tunisia, in the 670s the caliphs had transferred there about 1,000 Jewish families from Egypt, is impossible to determine. But it should be assumed that at least the nucleus of the Kairuwan Jewish community, later so numerous and affluent, came into being while North Africa was still under caliphal control.

In Spain even more than elsewhere the Arab conquerors established a close alliance with the Jewish minority. Jewish assistance in the conquest was widespread. There may be some truth in the tradition that Jews opened the gates of the capital city of Toledo to the Arabs. If certain medieval chronicles can be believed, the Muslim conquerors placed Jewish garrisons in a number of southern cities, including Granada and Seville, in order to free their forces to continue their march to the north of the peninsula. Thus, from the first moment, the foundation was laid for that Jewish-Arab cooperation and unequaled cultural symbiosis which developed in a later period.

The Economic Scene

The Arab conquests and the emergence of the caliphate created great economic opportunities for the Jews. Restrictions on Jewish economic activities were almost nonexistent. Even caliphs who did curtail the Jews' political and civil rights, rarely, if at any time, attempted to limit their economic opportunities. These generally favorable conditions were further enhanced by a number of other factors. To begin with, the territorial vastness of the caliphate created special trade opportunities for a people living in all its corners. The Hebrew language, common to all Jews, and the uniform Jewish civil law made it easy for Jews to communicate, to draw up legal documents, and to settle conflicts between trading parties. Also, in a world sharply divided between Christians and Muslims, the Jews were tacitly recognized by both sides as a neutral element. This gave Jewish traders much mobility, which was further strengthened by the confidence that if they were captured on the high seas by pirates, the nearest Jewish community would consider their ransom a religious duty.

Thus, more and more Jews abandoned agriculture and flocked to the urban centers to enter the caliphate's mercantilistic economy. This movement received additional impetus from the fiscal policy of the caliphs, who imposed very heavy taxes on land-ownership. The growing Jewish merchant class traded in slaves, spices, pharmaceuticals, metals, and textiles. Partnerships between Jews and Muslims or Jews and Christians were no rarity. But, despite the ideal conditions under which they traded, the Jewish merchants never became a decisive element in the caliphate's economy. This was simply precluded by their insignificant numerical proportion within the general population of the caliphate. The same holds true of the role of Jewish bankers, although their enterprises were ever-expanding. Some of them, such as the Netira family in tenth-century Baghdad, were important bankers, but even they never achieved a controlling position in the economy.

It could even be argued that Jewish banking as such did not exist, but rather was merely a sideline of moneychanging and trading. Many of the Jewish banking transactions had the nature of pawnbroking. It was mainly this which was responsible for the prominent role played by Jewish bankers in the trade of precious stones, for in those times more often than not pawns, mostly jewelry, were left unredeemed and were sold by the lender. The combined nature of this business and banking activity was a new phenomenon in the economic life of the Jews and called for certain religio-legal adjustments. True, what could be called a specific Jewish economic literature was not produced by the Jews of the caliphate, but the Rabbis with their profound knowledge of the talmudic religious and civil law, did find ways to make it possible for the Jewish merchants to transact their business and at the same time avoid coming into conflict with the rigid Jewish usury laws.

As in every medieval society, the Jewish merchants were a group limited in number. Despite the unfavorable conditions, many more Jews still made a living from agriculture, with more and more of them working their land with slaves or hired labor. The number of Jewish craftsmen and laborers was still larger. The multitude and variety of crafts practiced by Jews attest both to their heavy concentration in this sector of the economy and to their impressive specialization. Some crafts, such as dyeing, were almost exclusively Jewish. Wherever production was conducted on a larger scale, Jews were found both as entrepreneurs and laborers. It is also worth noting that Jewish merchants tended to trade in articles mostly produced by Jewish craftsmen. It may be assumed that Jewish craftsmen often succeeded in amassing enough capital to join the ranks of the merchants.

In the tenth century the economic situation of the Jews began to deteriorate, due to a decline which set in in the general economic well-being of the caliphate. The caliphate was basically a wealth-consuming, not a wealth-producing, entity. Therefore, as long as the Abassids kept on adding territories to their dominions, an endless stream of wealth taken from the subjugated countries flowed into the center in Iraq. Once expansion gave way to stagnation, however, and even shrinkage, an inevitable economic decline set in. The Jews, like all other citizens, became its victims. By then, however, as will be seen, the Jewish communities in North Africa and Spain, which had broken away from the caliphate, had begun to experience a period of economic ascendance not much different from that of their Iraqi brethren in the immediate past.

Chapter 3

In the Breakaway States

The General Scene

The existence of the caliphate as an empire stretching over three continents, and from Central Asia to Spain, was of relatively short duration. Naturally, it was difficult for the caliphal government to maintain effective control over such a vast area under the conditions of poor communications characteristic of the Middle Ages. But as long as the Arab conquerors constituted only a small group of warriors and officials in the subjugated countries, they clung to the caliph and the power concentrated in his hands. Thus, a certain degree of unity was maintained in the empire. Later, however, when the masses of Christians had converted to Islam, and the Muslims began to feel more secure everywhere, a process of dissolution of the caliphate naturally began. The different political and economic interests, coupled with the ambitions of local commanders and governors, became a centrifugal force which steadily worked for the loosening of the ties binding the outlying areas to the center in Baghdad. The centrifugal forces were further strengthened by claims to a share in the rule of the Muslim world made by various men who were descended from the prophet or from his relatives, as well as by the sectarian movements which developed within Islam in connection with these claims.

The ascent of the Abassids to power in 750 was accompanied by the secession of Spain, whose Muslims preferred to remain loyal to an Umayyad prince, Abd ar-Rahman, who had miraculously escaped the Abbasid attempt to exterminate the preceding dynasty. About half a century later, separatist forces developed in North Africa, and the Aghlabid dynasty entrenched itself to rule most of the area for a period of over 100 years. Early in the tenth century the Aghlabids were replaced by the Fatimid dynasty, which claimed descent from Mohammed's daughter Fatima. Within a period of about 60 years the Fatimids wrested Tripolitania and Libya from the caliphs.

Meanwhile, in 868, Ahmad ibn Tulun, a lieutenant of the governor of Egypt, made himself practically the independent ruler of the country. His grip over Egypt was so firm that less than ten years later he was able to gain control over Palestine and Syria as well. Henceforth these two countries remained most of the time under Egyptian rule until the arrival of the Crusaders in 1098–99. Only for a short period in the last quarter of the eleventh century did the Turkish Seljuks, then the actual rulers in Baghdad, recapture Palestine and Syria for the caliphate.

In 969 the Fatimids under Al-Muizz (952–75) set out on their most ambitious conquest, that of Egypt. Al-Muizz overthrew the Tulun dynasty, founded the city of Cairo, and transferred thither his capital in 972. From here the Fatimids ruled over a considerable part of what was originally the caliphate. Close to the middle of the eleventh century the Fatimids' governor in *Ifriqiya* (present-day Tunisia) rebelled against them. In revenge, the Fatimids unleashed against him hordes of Arabic nomads from Upper Egypt, and these brought utter destruction to most of the area. The magnificent city of Kairuwan was sacked, and never regained its previous position of importance. Following these events the fanatical Muslim tribes of the Almoravids and Almohades successively ruled Northwest Africa. The rule of the latter lasted till 1269.

In the eleventh century the power of the Fatimid dynasty also began to decline in Egypt. Its end came in 1174 when the Seljuk Saladin usurped the throne and established the Ayyubid dynasty. The Ayyubid dynasty then ruled Egypt until replaced by another regime in 1250.

Yemen too detached itself from the caliphate, simultaneously undergoing a process of partition, with regional rulers residing in Sana, Aden, and a few other towns. In 897 a leader of a Muslim sect known as the Zaydi conquered a city in northern Yemen. His successors then began to expand their possessions, and gradually became the rulers of most of Yemen. They ruled the country over a millennium, although with temporary interruptions, until they were overthrown in 1960.

Early in the ninth century, over 100 years after the Arab invasion of Spain, another invasion into Europe was underway. Beginning in 827, Arab forces from both North Africa and Spain made several thrusts into Sicily, until almost the entire island was under their control by the year 902. Arab domination extended also over the southernmost region of the Italian peninsula. This area remained under Arab control for a period of about 200 years. Muslim Sicily too was independent of the caliph in Baghdad.

The Jewish Population

Jews continued to live in all the states which broke away from the caliphate. In fact, the number of Jews in all these areas increased steadily due to natural growth and to immigration from the economically declining eastern parts of the caliphate. Even distant Spain received a number of immigrants from Babylonia. Numerous Jewish communities existed in most parts of Spain, except the extreme northwest, where they were very sparse. Of course, with the progress of the Christian re-conquest of Spain (see further, Sec. XV, Chap. 1) the number of Jews and Jewish communities in Muslim Spain was decreasing. But this did not affect the totality of the Jewish population on the entire peninsula, which was large and compact. By the middle of the eleventh century, just before the *Reconquista* began to proceed with great rapidity, about 40 Jewish communities can be identified as having existed in Muslim Spain. It must be assumed that an additional number of communities had existed and are now unidentifiable. Of course, such unidentifiable communities must have been of small size.

Most of the Jewish communities were concentrated in the south, in the part of the country known as Andalusia. Another area of Jewish concentration was in the northeast, in regions adjacent to Christian Spain. The south-central part of the peninsula, identical with the southern part of Castile, had a smaller concentration of Jewish communities. It has been estimated that the Jews constituted less than 1 percent of the entire population. In the urban centers, however, their percentage was larger. But even in each of the major cities there rarely seems to have been a Jewish community with a population in excess of 10,000. In Granada, for example, although the Jews constituted a majority of the population, their number was 7,000 to 8,000 in 1066. Toledo harbored only about 4,000 Jews. Other major communities existed in Lucena, Seville, and Saragossa. Cordova, at an earlier period, must have had a somewhat larger Jewish community. In the first half of the twelfth century the Jewish population in Muslim Spain was drastically reduced due to the flight of many Jews, and the conversion of many others to Islam, as a result of the occupation of the country by the fanatical Almoravids and Almohades.

The Jewish community was also at first growing in number under the Muslims in North Africa. Certain Jewish communities, especially those in the Berber regions to the south, had survived Christian oppression in the late Antiquity and the turmoil of the

Arab conquest (cf. Vol. I, Sec. X, Chap. 2). With the restoration of peace under the caliphate, the Jewish population increased. The same holds true of the later period when North Africa severed its ties with the caliphate. Not only did sizable Jewish communities exist in the old cities, such as Tripoli, but—even more important—communities came into being in the new cities, such as Kairuwan in Tunisia, and Fez in Morocco.

All in all, some 50 Jewish communities can be identified as having existed about the year 1100 in the area between the Atlantic coast and the borders of Egypt. Characteristically, these communities were almost evenly divided among Morocco, Algeria, Tunisia, and Tripolitania-Libya. Here, too, in time the Jewish population began to undergo a process of decline. The onslaught of the hordes of Arab nomads on the area west of the Egyptian border in the middle of the eleventh century drove many, many Jews, including those of Kairuwan, into flight. But North African Jewry was reduced even more drastically in number when in the middle of the twelfth century the Almohades spread their rule over the entire area. It is, however, noteworthy that the Almohade oppression did not result in the complete elimination of the Jewish population.

The Jewish population in Egypt was more dense than in the rest of North Africa. Good economic conditions and a growing affluence of the Jewish community attracted immigrants from other parts of North Africa, from Sicily, and even from far-off Central Asia. Curiously, the Fatimid attack by hordes of nomads on its former possessions in Tunisia resulted in the flight of large numbers of Jews from Kairuwan to Egypt, thus further enlarging Egypt's Jewish community. Attempts at charting a map of the Egyptian Jewish communities under Fatimid rule identified as many as 90.

As was the case in Antiquity, Jewish settlement was most dense in the area of the Nile Delta. Over 30 communities were identified as having existed there. But even south of the Delta major Jewish communities existed, including Aswan in the far south. Estimates of the total Jewish population run between 12,000 and 35,000. Be it, however, noted that the general picture of Egypt's Jewish community, as it emerges from the available sources, suggests that its size was possibly substantially larger. As in Muslim Spain, here too the Jews constituted a tiny minority of less than 1 percent. In the cities, however, the Jewish population was proportionately much larger. Closely connected with North African Jewry were the Jewish communities in Sicily during the period of Muslim control over the island from the first half of the ninth to the second half of the eleventh century. All this time quite a number of Jewish communities existed there whose total population was not inconsiderable.

A large number of Jewish communities existed in the eleventh century also in Yemen, on the southern edge of the Muslim world. But, except for those in Sana and Aden, these were in all likelihood tiny communities. The total number of the Jews in Yemen was no doubt far below that of Egypt.

Political Conditions

The severance of Spain's ties with the caliphate did not visibly affect the general situation of the Jews. If anything, their situation can be said to have improved. Nothing perhaps attests as well to the favorable political situation of the Jews as the fact that the first 200 years of Umayyad rule were clearly an uneventful period in the life of the Jews. Furthermore, the event which did break the "monotony" in the political situation of the Jews was the rise to high office of Hisdai ibn Shaprut. Hisdai was the first in a galaxy of high Jewish officials so characteristic in the later history of the Jews both in Muslim and Christian Spain. He was by profession a physician and was possibly originally called to the court in this capacity. It was probably his knowledge of languages which later earned him the position of chief of customs and foreign trade and the task of welcoming foreign embassies. We shall see later that, simultaneously, Hisdai also played a leading role in the life of the Jewish community, and that this was made possible in part by his position as a high government official.

In the first half of the eleventh century Muslim Spain had become a cluster of small states in which the Jews continued to be treated as favorably as before. In fact, more opportunities were now open to Jews to attain high office in the courts of the many petty rulers. Saragossa, for example, had a Jewish vizier in the eleventh century. But no Jewish official could boast of as spectacular a career as Samuel ibn Nagrela, mostly known by his Hebrew appellation Samuel ha-Nagid. Born in 993 in Cordova, he settled in Malaga, in the territory of the kingdom of Granada, where he lived in modest circumstances as a shopkeeper. He became acquainted by chance with the vizier, whose home was also in Malaga. The vizier soon became aware of the extraordinary wisdom and political insight of the Jewish shopkeeper, and made him his chief, although informal, adviser. After the vizier's death, Samuel was officially given the former's position. It soon became clear that this Jewish statesman could also ably command the king's army. Samuel held his dual position of vizier and commander-in-chief for about 20 years, until his death c. 1056. We shall see later that he, even more than Hisdai ibn Shaprut about 100 years earlier, excelled as a leader of the Jewish community. He was also one of the leading Hebrew poets and talmudic scholars in Spain.

Samuel ibn Nagrela managed to remain in the king's service for two decades, or possibly longer, despite many court intrigues directed against him. This was not only due to his ability to weather many storms, but also to the fact that King Badis, of Berber origin, had little confidence in his Arab subjects, and felt more secure with a Jewish vizier. This may also have been the reason why, upon Samuel's death, the king appointed the latter's son Joseph (Yehoseph) as the new vizier. Joseph held the office for about ten years. Then, in the year 1066, popular opposition to his rule developed to such a degree that he was assassinated. The populace also turned against the vizier's Jewish coreligionists, and several thousand of them were massacred.

The reason for the outbreak is not very clear. The chronicler Abraham ibn Daud, who recorded the event about 100 years later, ascribed Joseph's ill fate to his lack of humility, which goaded the Berber princes to attack him. There were probably deeper causes for the downfall of the Jewish vizier and this first anti-Jewish riot in Muslim Spain. Jewish officials in other Muslim states also brought down from time to time through their conduct the wrath of the populace upon their Jewish coreligionists. It may possibly be argued that the benefit the Jewish community derived from the elevation of some of its members to high office was sometimes outweighed by the resentment those members evoked in the Muslim population.

By the end of the eleventh century the Jewish situation in Muslim Spain began to deteriorate somewhat. Frightened by the fall of Toledo in 1085, the rulers of Spain's Muslim states extended a call to the Almoravids of North Africa to come to their aid. The Almoravids were a Berber people, who professed a form of puritanical Islam. A few decades earlier they had extended their rule over Morocco and Algeria, where they established an orderly and vigorous regime. They responded to the call of the Spanish Muslims, and won an initial victory over a *Reconquista* army. Soon, however, they decided to remove all the Muslim petty rulers, and between 1090 and 1094 won control over all Muslim Spain. Under them the Jews were not as free as before. The number of Jewish high officials declined, and religious and ethnic tensions became more articulate.

By and large, however, Jewish life continued along the lines of former times. In fact, somewhat later Jewish high officials again began to appear in the court. But, the new tolerance was short-lived. The Almoravids began to show signs of religious laxity, and their military successes became rare and less spectacular. This evoked a fanatical Islamic revolt in the heartland of their dominion in North Africa. The rebellion was carried out by another Berber group, known as the Almohades. The Almohades invaded Spain in 1146 and set out on a policy of forcibly converting the Jews to Islam. Many Jews fled northward to the Christian possessions. Many others accepted Islam, and attempted to practice their Judaism clandestinely. It is impossible to say to what degree these Moslem *Marranos* succeeded in retaining their Judaism. Many of the Jewish children were surely lost to their parents forever, having been taken away by the Almohades to be raised as Muslims.

An attempt in 1162 by Jews and Christians to oust the Almohades from the city of Granada ended in failure. The degree of suffering brought down upon Muslim Spain's Jewry by the Almohade persecution is well exemplified by the vicissitudes of the Cordovan rabbi Maimon and his family. First the family, including the then 12-year-old Moses Maimonides, fled to Christian Spain. They, however, soon returned to the Muslim South; from there they went to Morocco. It is obvious that both in Muslim Spain and Morocco they could not identify themselves as Jews, and were compelled to practice their religion in secret. They therefore left for the Near East, and after a short stay in the Holy Land, found permanent refuge in Egypt. By 1172 the Almohades were in control of almost all of Muslim Spain, and Jewish existence in the country virtually came to an end.

After the turn of the century, the Almohades too began to lose out in their fight against the Christian re-conquerors of Spain. In 1212 they suffered a resounding defeat in the battle at Las Navas de Tolosa, after which they no longer played any role in the defense of Muslim Spain. The Christian conquest of Cordova in 1235–36 and of Seville in 1248 practically concluded the history of the Jews in Muslim Spain.

The history of the Jews in North Africa is generally not different from that of the Jews in Muslim Spain. The fact that often Spain and Northwest Africa were controlled by the same rulers lent additional similarity to the destiny of the Jews in both countries. However, the lack of political stability in North Africa often caused sudden upheavals in the life of the Jews, to a degree unknown in Muslim Spain. As long as the Aghlabids and Fatimids ruled North Africa, the Jewish communities lived fairly peacefully. Some of them, such as Fez in Morocco and Kairuwan in Tunisia, experienced a period of extraordinary grandeur.

When the Fatimids transferred the center of their empire to Egypt, however, the general situation, and with it the situation of the Jews, became less stable. By the middle of the eleventh century, as we have seen, much devastation was brought to Tunisia, as a result of which Kairuwan, the most outstanding among the Jewish communities, was almost totally destroyed. Late in the eleventh century, and during the first half of the twelfth century, North Africa experienced its own version of a *"Reconquista"* when the Normans (i.e., Vikings), who had wrested Sicily from the Muslims, attacked North Africa and occupied parts of it for a certain period of time. True, the Normans generally manifested a benevolent attitude to the Jews, but the turmoil caused by their attacks was an additional blow to the shattered Jewry of *Ifriqiya* (Tunisia).

The situation of the Jews, of course, deteriorated with the

spread of Almohade rule in the second half of the twelfth century. As in Spain, the Jews of North Africa were exposed to repeated Almohade attempts to convert them forcibly to the Muslim faith. Many fled to Christian Spain. But even those who chose to stay and convert were subjected to much discrimination, including the wearing of distinguishing garments. Several massacres of Jews also took place. And yet, although the North African Jewish communities largely lay in ruins, the Jews were not fully uprooted. Not only did vestiges of Jewish life survive in such an outlying area as Libya, but even in the Almohade heartland of Morocco a number of Jews withstood the persecutions. Thus, in 1269, when Almohade rule in North Africa came to an end, a nucleus for a Jewish revival remained in North Africa.

We have seen (cf. above, Chap. 2) how under caliphal rule Egypt's Jewish community began to emerge from the state of oppression and depression in which it lived under the Byzantines. The situation of the Jews became still better when Egypt broke away from the caliphate and became a major power under Tulunid and Fatimid rule. There is a likelihood that Jews were of help to the Fatimids in the conquest of Egypt. It is thus not surprising that employment in the government was open to Jews, probably not less than in Muslim Spain. The same holds true of Syria. In fact, a Jew even served as the Fatimid governor of this country. Also, Jewish physicians were no rarity in the court of the Fatimid rulers in Cairo. How friendly the Fatimids were to their Jewish subjects can best be demonstrated by the fact that at the recommendation of one of their Jewish officials, they extended financial support to the *yeshivah* of the Holy Land.

A sole exception among the Fatimid rulers was Al-Hakim (996–1021). Being of an eccentric and erratic mind, he broke with the traditional Muslim policy of toleration towards the *dhimmis*. He first began to persecute the Copts, and in 1009 also the Jews. The course of the events is not fully clear. It seems that Muslim mobs, knowing of Al-Hakim's unfriendly attitude to the Jews, attacked the Jewish quarter in Fustat. This was followed by actions resulting in the forcible conversion to Islam of many Jews, in the confiscation of Jewish property, and in the demolition or confiscation of synagogues. While Fustat, the Jewish section of Cairo, was the main scene of the persecution, it is certain that provincial Jewry and the Jews of Palestine and Syria were affected by it as well.

In the last year of his reign, al-Hakim, again for reasons unknown to us, rescinded his policy and permitted the Jews who had become Muslims to return to the Jewish faith. Confiscated synagogues were restored to the Jews and permission was given to build new ones. Thus, the persecution of the years 1009–20 remained a mere episode. Further anti-Jewish riots under the Fatimids either did not occur at all or were not serious enough to leave traces in the records. The Ayyubids, too, treated the Jews with tolerance, though formally a new emphasis was put on the disabilities to which infidels ought to be subjected in a Muslim country. The situation of the Egyptian Jews further improved when Moses Maimonides, their undisputed though unofficial leader, served for decades as physician to the royal house and high officialdom.

Egypt followed a similar policy of toleration with regard to the Jews of Palestine and Syria. This indeed became one of the better periods in the life of medieval Syrian Jewry. The communities of Damascus, Tyre, and Aleppo continued to count among the important Jewish communities of the time. Less fortunate, however, were the Jews of Palestine, whose tranquility, as in the caliphal times, was repeatedly disturbed by intertribal strife and an unceasing war of the Bedouins against the Fatimid army. The situation was further aggravated by a series of devastating earthquakes, the strongest of which occurred in 1016, 1034, and 1068. The situation did not essentially change under the Seljuks. Seljuk rule, as we have seen, was short-lived, and in 1098–99 Palestine and parts of Syria were occupied by the Crusaders. The advent of the Crusaders removed the Holy Land and parts of Syria from the orbit of Islam and tied their destiny to the new eastern outpost of Western Christendom for a period of almost 200 years.

Little is known directly about the political destiny of the Jews in Yemen after the Zaydi dynasty established itself in the last years of the ninth century. The close relationship they established with Egyptian Jewry and the role the Jewish merchant princes of Aden played in the country's economy in the eleventh century and the first half of the twelfth century would suggest that by and large they lived under conditions of relative tranquility. After the middle of the twelfth century, however, stormy times arrived for the Yemenite Jews. Like many other episodes in the history of medieval Jewry, the events in Yemen cannot be reconstructed with full clarity. It is fairly certain that in 1165 the ruler undertook to convert the Jews to Islam forcibly and that about the same time a man appeared who claimed to be the Messiah. A leader of the Yemenite Jews then turned for advice and succor to Moses Maimonides, whom the Yemenite Jews then and thereafter revered more than did any other Jewish community. Maimonides replied in a series of responsa, out of which grew his *Epistle to Yemen,* one of the great works of the "Great Eagle." The *Epistle* was written with much warmth and was clearly designed to lift the depressed spirits of the Jews in Yemen. Be it also noted that about the same time Maimonides implored the court of Cairo to intervene against heavy fiscal oppression to which the Yemenite Jews were subjected. The persecution of 1165 was the first in a long line of tribulations suffered by the Jews of Yemen down to our own times. Thus, Yemen already then had acquired the sad distinction of subjecting its Jewish community to persecution more severe than any other Muslim state prior to the outbreak of the Israeli-Arab conflict in our own times.

Far better than in Yemen, but less benign than elsewhere, was the way the Jews were treated in the other outlying area of the Muslim world, Sicily. For reasons not fully clear, the Arab authorities here insisted on a more rigid application of the restrictions laid down in the Pact of Umar. In addition, taxation was very heavy, and between 1015 and 1020 almost drove the Jewish community to ruin. But, in general, the Jewish condition was still much better than in the preceding period of Byzantine rule. Being part of the Muslim world made it possible for Sicilian Jewry to establish close contacts with the other Jewish communities in Muslim lands, and thus to participate, as we shall see, in the great upsurge of their cultural experience.

The Economic Scene

The breakup of the caliphate, though unfavorable to the economic life of the Jews in the Muslim countries, harmed it only moderately. The instruments of trade established in the seventh and eighth centuries emerged basically unscathed. Furthermore, some of the successor states, as for example that of the Fatimids, stretched over such large parts of what was formerly the Abassid caliphate, that a comfortable base for trade continued to exist in the orbit of Islam all through the period of the Early Middle Ages. In fact, the limitations now encountered by Jews in their economic endeavors were mostly caused by external circumstances. Thus, beginning with the ninth century, direct trade relations developed between Muslim and Christian countries, and the Jews began to lose their role of sole intermediary between the two warring camps. The Jewish role in the maritime trade further decreased in the twelfth and thirteenth centuries, when the Italian merchant republics usurped for themselves the lion's share of this trade.

Nonetheless, the Jews continued to prosper economically in all the breakaway states. This was certainly the case in Umayyad Spain, where the government devoted much concern to the development and protection of trade. The Jews derived full advantage from this governmental protection, since all avenues of economic endeavor were open to them. It should, however, be stressed that the bulk of the Jewish population belonged to the lower economic strata. Probably most of them were either laborers or craftsmen. A sort of Jewish agricultural "middle class" also existed in Spain, where suburban farming was in vogue and quite remunerative. There, Jewish owners of farmland and vineyards increasingly withdrew from working the soil personally, and more and more relied on the labor of others.

Of less variety were the occupations of the Jews in North Africa. Here, it seems, most were engaged in some form of commerce. When North Africa severed its ties with the caliphate and experienced a period of extraordinary prosperity, Jews fully benefited from it. Symbolic of the prosperity of the Jewish population was the affluent community of Kairuwan, located to the south of the city of Tunis. The Jewish merchants of Kairuwan and of

Tunisia at large exported metals, hides, and agricultural products. Their imports included perfumes, jewelry, linen, and especially silk. Their business contacts reached as far as southern Arabia, India, and China. The sources indicate that all this international trade was conducted by a tightly knit group of merchants, which possibly consisted of as few as 20 families. It is, however, safe to assume that many more Jewish families were economically dependent on the main entrepreneurs. Only such an assumption could explain why North African Jewry gave the impression of a very affluent society. As we have seen, the economic prosperity of North African Jewry came to an abrupt end when, in 1057, the entire area was overrun and devastated by hordes of Arab nomads who came from Upper Egypt.

Another corner of North Africa, Morocco, possibly served as the base of a group of Jewish entrepreneurs known as *Radhaniya*. According to the sources, they conducted an extensive trade between countries of the West, especially Morocco and France, and a number of countries in the East, including China, during the eighth, and possibly the first half of the ninth, century. Their caravans crossed the deserts of North Africa and the mountains of southern Europe and they sailed the Mediterranean to Byzantium, the Muslim Near East, India, and China. They brought to the eastern countries slaves and a variety of products. Their returning caravans carried loads of rare spices grown in the East. The Arab authors who recorded their activities ascribe much of the success of the *Radhaniya* to their extensive knowledge of languages, which included besides Arabic and French also Persian, Greek, and Slavonic. Curiously, they do not mention the Hebrew language, which, as we have seen, was an important instrument in the international trade conducted by Jews in those times. Modern research, much intrigued by this uncommon Jewish economic phenomenon, has not yet succeeded in explaining the meaning of the name "Radhaniya" or unveiling the true character of these Jewish medieval merchant princes. But the picture of the Jewish medieval economy cannot be complete without mentioning the Radhanites.

Egypt, too, after its breakaway from the caliphate, provided a friendly climate for Jewish economic activity. To begin with, no Jewish proletariat seems to have existed. Jews who performed manual labor were practically always independent craftsmen who belonged to the middle class. Jews who owned land were rarely tilling it themselves and mostly relied on the labor of others. Here again it was the class of the Jewish merchants which mainly left its traces in the contemporary records. Quite a number of them could be classed as merchant princes, and they gave the Jewish communities of Fustat and Alexandria the character of extreme affluence. One of them, for example, had business interests and owned real estate in such distant places as Morocco and Sicily. Of course, much of this activity was made possible by, and much of the wealth derived from, the transit trade among Tunisia and India and China. Egypt, simply, was geographically destined to become a major beneficiary of this trade. Moneylending too had become a distinct profession among the Egyptian Jews, if judged by the existence of a Jewish moneylenders' guild in Fustat in 973.

Syria too, during the period of its independence from Baghdad and dependence on Egypt gave its Jews opportunities similar to those available to the Egyptian Jews, both in business and the crafts. It is worth noting here that Jews played an important role in Syria's famous glass blowing industry. Less fortunate economically were the Jews in the Holy Land. The perpetual tribal warfare and the frequent natural disasters there neutralized the otherwise favorable conditions, and led the country decisively down the road to economic decline. True, the earlier prosperity gave way only slowly, but the ultimate impoverishment of later times could not be prevented. As for Yemen, here too the bulk of the Jewish population made a living as craftsmen who socially probably belonged to a lower class than their Jewish peers in Egypt. But at least in Aden, again an important transit station on the India-China route, a class of international Jewish merchants did exist. We find one of them, for example, traveling to India and westward to Morocco and Spain. Another established a virtual dynasty of merchant princes which controlled much of the transit trade for several generations, to the middle of the twelfth century.

All in all, the Jews fared well economically in the breakaway states. Even those who did not have substantial capital at their disposal could make a living and even prosper. It was Jewish mobility and the close contacts among Jewish communities which made the specific Jewish role in international trade possible. Not only were the Near Eastern Jewish merchants at home in the well-established India-China trade, but it is likely that they transacted business even with Korea and Japan as early as 1,000 years ago. But, in the final analysis, it was the geographic position of the Muslim world and the encouragement of the Muslim governments which served as the all-important backdrop for this golden age in the economic history of the Jewish people.

Chapter 4

Community Government

Exilarchal Administration in the Caliphate

When the caliphate was established in the middle of the seventh century, it had among its inhabitants vast numbers of people who professed religions other than Islam. We have seen that these various religious groups were given the status of protected communities. And it was in line with this policy that the caliphs permitted them to organize their inner life along lines of denominational self-government.

In accordance with this policy, the caliphs extended recognition to the office of the Jewish exilarch, which had already existed in Parthian and Sassanian times. In fact, the office of the exilarch which had had a stormy history in the later Sassanian period (cf. Vol. I, Sec. IX, Chap. 2), obtained a new lease on life under the Muslims. A member of the exilarchal family by the name of Bustanai seems to have held the office at the time of the Arab conquest. He now became the first in a dynasty of about 30 exilarchs who ruled the Jewry of the caliphate till the Tartar conquest of Baghdad in 1258 and beyond. The status of the office was now enhanced by the fairly justified claim of the exilarchs to be of Davidic descent, since King David was recognized by Islam as a prophet. Official documents, in fact, call the exilarch "son of

David." The exilarch, like the leaders of other important religious communities, was a member of the supreme caliphal council. The exilarch continued to live in much luxury and splendor, first in his residence in Mahoza, near Ctesiphon, and after 767 in Baghdad. The veneration given to him by his Jewish subjects was seemingly unlimited. In the ninth century a special prayer in his honor (*Yequm purqan*) was introduced to be recited during the Sabbath service. Curiously, countless Jews even today recite this prayer every Saturday. Even more significant was the fact that instead of the exilarch being called to the Torah, the Torah scroll was brought to the place where he was seated. There hardly could be a more conspicuous way of honoring a leader, even a descendant of King David.

While the office was hereditary in Bustanai's family, the principle of succession of the first-born was not always followed. The caliph usually appointed to the office that exilarchal prince who was popular in the Jewish community and had the support of Baghdad's Jewish grandees and the geonim, that is, the heads of the academies at Sura and Pumbedita (see the next chapter).

Not at all clear is the nature of the authority vested in the exilarch, and this has been a matter of debate among modern Jewish scholars. What seems certain is that the exilarchs were considered by the caliphs the official leaders and representatives of the Jewish community in the caliphate. They probably played a certain, though limited, role in the collection of the poll tax from the Jewish community and its delivery to the caliphal treasury. More important was their role in the Jewish judiciary. They appointed judges in the local Jewish communities in Babylonia, Persia, and the adjacent countries. In the early period of the caliphate they did it on their own authority. Later, however, they could do it only with the consent of the geonim. In addition to the local courts, the exilarchal judiciary also included a supreme court known as "the exilarch's court," or "the sovereign's court." This court, already functioning in Sassanian times, was presided over by the exilarch if he possessed proper legal training, or by a qualified jurist.

At a non-determinable time, the geonim began to interfere with the prerogatives of the exilarch and to usurp for themselves some of his powers. With this the geonim continued the old drive of the scholarly class to control Jewish life. We have no clear knowledge of the course of this process, but the sources leave no doubt that the geonim had much success in this undertaking. This was made possible by the fact that the administration of the exilarch was based on the Jewish law, and the geonim, as heads of the two major Jewish law schools, were universally considered competent interpreters of this law. Furthermore, the geonim—as the religious leaders—often had a wider appeal in the Jewish communities than the exilarch, whose role was mainly political and administrative.

As a result, the geonim, as we have seen, not only became party to the appointment of local judges, but also came to share in the revenue, whatever it may have been, that the exilarchs received from the local communities in Iraq, Persia, Khorasan, and possibly other provinces. By the year 900 the geonim had succeeded in bringing about an arrangement whereby the revenue from some provinces now went directly to the two schools, instead of the exilarchal treasury. An attempt by the exilarch Uqva to reverse the process in 913 ended in failure and in his removal from office and expulsion from Iraq. Nothing could better have demonstrated the weakness of the exilarchs in their relations with the geonim than the fact that a powerful personality like the exilarch David ben Zakai did not win his feud with the gaon Saadiah, even though he had the full support of the caliph (see further, Chap. 6).

These developments ultimately led to a major change in the administration of the caliphate's Jewish community. While originally all the powers of the centralized leadership were concentrated in the hands of the exilarch, these were now vested in the dual leadership of the exilarchs and the geonim. Whether it was legal procedure or not, the exilarchs appointed, or influenced the appointment, of geonim, and the latter in turn influenced the appointment of the former. Furthermore, in times of conflict exilarchs used to depose geonim, and these used to strike back by deposing their deposers. All this resulted in the emergence of a system of checks and balances in the administration of Jewish communal affairs which must have been quite beneficial to the Jewish population.

The actual power of the exilarch was quite real, even though its scope varied from time to time. At his disposal was a system of penalties, including that of banishment to remote areas in Central Asia. But, even in times when the caliphal government curtailed the authority of the exilarchs in enforcing their ordinances, they still retained the power of imposing the ban (herem), the ultimate weapon at the disposal of Jewish communal authorities.

The ninth century seems to have been the heyday of exilarchal power and glory, and then it began to decline. Various factors united to promote the decline. To begin with, the severe schism which resulted from the emergence of the Karaite sect under the leadership of a member of the exilarchal family in the second half of the eighth century (see further, Chap. 7) dealt a severe blow to the exilarchate. In addition, the legitimacy of the exilarchal dynasty was repeatedly questioned because of persistent rumors about its alleged descent from a Persian princess, who was Bustanai's concubine. No less harmful was the perpetual rivalry of the geonim, which seriously undermined the office. But more than anything else it was the dissolution of the caliphate and the waning power of the caliphs in the remote regions of the empire that contributed to the simultaneous decline of the exilarchate. It has even been suggested that there were times when the authority of the exilarchs dwindled into relative insignificance and was limited to the Jews in the city of Baghdad and its immediate environs.

Characteristic of the decline of the exilarchate was the emigration of many princes of the exilarchal family to other cities and to countries that began to break away from the caliphate. To be sure, some of them made attempts to establish themselves as rulers of their host communities. By and large, these attempts ended in failure, and the immigrant princes had to content themselves with a status of prestige and financial support given to them as descendants of the House of David. Only in the city of Mosul, in northern Iraq, did a branch of the exilarchal family establish itself in the first half of the eleventh century to rule the Jewish community over a period of about 300 years. In the breakaway countries, local Jewish leaders established themselves as rulers of their communities along the lines of the exilarchal administration in Baghdad. They usually assumed the title of nagid.

The Rule of Negidim in the
Breakaway States

As in the case of the exilarchate, the origins of the office of
nagid are still obscure. One theory has it that the office first came
into being in Egypt, and later in other countries which had broken
away from the caliphate. Another theory maintains that a nagid
had appeared for the first time in Tunisia in 1015 and that he was
appointed by the gaon Hai of Babylonia. According to this theory,
the office of nagid was established in Egypt about half a century
later. Be this as it may, it is certain that the nagid, a regional
Jewish chief, wherever and whenever he functioned, wielded over
the Jewish community powers more or less similar to those of the
Babylonian exilarch. The nagid's authority, like that of the
exilarch's, was subject to variations conditioned by the time and
the country in which he held office.

The difference between the negidim and the exilarchs was
that the former never claimed Davidic origin, nor authority over
all the Jewish communities in the orbit of Islam. They usually
attained their position due to their personal merit, status, or
wealth. Like that of the exilarchs, the authority of the negidim
was reinforced by governmental recognition. As in the caliphate,
the rulers of the breakaway states customarily tolerated autonomous self-government by the non-Muslim religious communities.
To the outside world the nagid was known under the title of *rais
al-yahud,* chief of the Jews. Except for Egypt, where the office
existed hundreds of years under several dynasties, the negidim
appeared only sporadically in Spain, Tunisia, Palestine, Syria, and
Yemen. There were also negidim whose authority was limited to
a single community, such as those of Aleppo, in Syria. No doubt,
the authority of such local negidim was quite limited.

It is still a matter of debate whether Hisdai ibn Shaprut, who
was sometimes called *nasi,* held any position as official leader of
the Jews of Andalusia. The only two men who clearly held the
position of nagid in Spain were Samuel ibn Nagrela and his son
Joseph. Samuel, and after him his son, were possibly appointed as
negidim by Babylonian geonim. But at any rate their authority
was clearly limited to the Jews in the rather small kingdom of
Granada. What the real scope of their authority was is hard to

determine. In fact, it is impossible to say whether they performed some of their Jewish activities by virtue of being negidim, or as magnanimous philanthropists. The same holds true of three men who resided in Kairuwan in the course of the eleventh century, and whose authority as negidim probably was recognized in Tunisia and parts of Algeria. As for Yemen, the office of nagid was first held through several generations by a family of wealthy merchants in Aden in the eleventh and twelfth centuries. The negidim of Aden too seem to have derived their authority, whatever it may have been, from investiture or recognition by Babylonian geonim. Various other negidim functioned later in Aden, down to the beginning of the fourteenth century.

As we have mentioned, the question of how and when the office of nagid emerged in Egypt, the only country in which it existed almost continuously for several hundred years, is still unclear. One theory has it that a certain Paltiel, who supplied Al-Muizz' army during the conquest of Egypt in 969 (cf. above, Chap. 3), became the first nagid in this country. Other theories maintain that it was not until the 1060s that the office came into being. The available sources leave no doubt that the office became stable and to a certain degree hereditary only at this late date. The question also remains unanswered whether the Egyptian nagid required the approval of the exilarch in Babylonia. In Egypt the authority over Jewish communal affairs vested in the negidim was more real than in either Spain, Tunisia, or Yemen. Their authority was further enhanced by the fact that although always Rabbanites, the Egyptian negidim also represented the sectarian Jewish communities of Samaritans and Karaites before the government. It was this importance of the office, precisely at a time when the Babylonian exilarchate was clearly declining in power and prestige, that made it worthwhile for members of the exilarchal family to attempt repeatedly, beginning with 1078, to usurp the negiduth. These attempts remained largely unsuccessful, and the local negidim "dynasty" continued to rule until about 1140. During the subsequent several decades, a court physician Samuel ben Hananiah, and later a certain Zuta, held the office. But with the arrival of Moses Maimonides, and the constant growth of his prestige, Zuta's authority began to decline, and he was deposed about the year 1175.

Whether Moses Maimonides then assumed the office of nagid is still a matter of debate. But with his demise in 1204, his son Abraham Maimuni became the founder of the second negidim dynasty, several generations of which solidly ruled Egyptian Jewry. After the Maimuni dynasty, various other negidim headed Egyptian Jewry, and the office survived well into the sixteenth century, decades after Egypt's occupation by the Ottoman Turks. All in all, over 20 negidim stood at the head of Egypt's Jewish community between the eleventh and sixteenth centuries.

It seems that after Saladin's conquest of parts of the Holy Land and Syria in 1187, the rule of the Egyptian negidim was extended to these territories as well. Be it, however, noted that here and there certain individuals are described in the sources as "negidim of Erets Israel and Judah." It is quite possible that these were only honorific titles given to men of importance. Repeated attempts by both Rabbanites and Karaites to revive the Palestinian patriarchate of old remained unsuccessful.

Local Community Administration

The centralized Jewish communal leadership of an exilarch or nagid addressed itself, by its nature, to general issues confronting the totality of the Jewish population in the area of his control. The day-to-day administration of local Jewish affairs had of necessity to be conducted by local leaders. The fact that Jews lived, at least in the larger cities of the caliphate and the breakaway states, in separate quarters and often were immigrants from different countries, broadened the scope of the activities of the local leadership. A review of these activities reveals that the local kehillah administration conducted a variety of religious, educational, and social programs, not much different from those of a modern Jewish community. True, in times and places where the authority of an exilarch or nagid was conspicuous, the regulation of most of these affairs was in the hands of a judge and a bureaucracy appointed by them. No doubt, under such circumstances not much room was left to local leadership or local democratic tendencies. One theory even maintains that the control of communal affairs by the local judges increased precisely at the time when the authority of the exilarchs and the negidim began to wane, much in the way the *qadi* acquired broader authority in the neighboring Muslim community in the period of the decline of the caliphate.

And yet, the decline of exilarchal and negidic power could not help but prepare everywhere the ground for a more self-governing local Jewish community. This is evident from the fact that in Spain, where negidim appeared only sporadically and in specific territories, powerful communal organizations began to emerge as early as the tenth century, whose judiciary could punish culprits even with the death penalty. In countries where the death penalty was not within the competence of the local Jewish judiciary, the community could still enforce its regulations by excommunication or expulsion. The authority of the local community was further enhanced by the fact that in most cases its leaders were the scholars rather than the wealthy and the mighty.

Chapter 5

The Cultural Scene

The Growth of Culture

At the time of the great Muslim conquests, Jewish cultural life was everywhere in a state of decline. In Babylonia, the center of Jewish culture, the period of the Saboraim (cf. Vol. I, Sec. IX, Chap. 2), with all its importance, was a rather pale reflection of the former cultural heydays. In the Byzantine empire Jewish cultural life was generally depressed, and in the western parts of the former Roman empire Jewish culture still remained for a long time in a state of infancy.

Soon, however, the cultural situation of the Jews in the orbit of Islam began visibly to improve. The solidification of the empire and Jewish participation in the new prosperity prepared the ground not only for a revival of Jewish culture but also for its expansion. The fact that as a religion Islam was much closer to Judaism than to any other faith, and that the Muslim law so strikingly resembled the Halakhah, greatly helped to create an atmosphere in which a cultural symbiosis became a possibility. Except for attire, little distinguished a Jew from his Muslim neighbor in everyday life, and this was further conducive to the creation of a cultural partnership. Thus, the Jews became more and more acculturated to Arab civilization.

Nothing proves this better than the cultural character of Sicilian Jewry in the Middle Ages. Although Muslim rule in Sicily was of much shorter duration than in Spain, Sicilian Jewry's entire religio-cultural orientation remained tied to North African Jewry for hundreds of years after the restoration of Christian rule on the island. The Judeo-Arabic cultural symbiosis was so natural that Jewish thinkers used the style of Islamic theology in their exposition of the tenets of the Jewish religion. It is even more striking that Jewish jurists employed Muslim legal terms in halakhic discussions.

The flourishing of Jewish culture was so natural to the orbit of Islam that often it seemed to have sprung up quite spontaneously. The revival of talmudic learning in Babylonia-Iraq could draw on the preceding magnificent centuries of the Amoraim. But it is still something of an enigma how Saadiah Gaon could acquire his enormous Jewish learning in his native Egypt, where little is known of a Jewish cultural life for centuries prior to his times. The same is true of Spain, where Hebrew poetry, great enough to give its time the character of a golden age, came into being without having been preceded by any local Jewish poetic tradition.

It was in the first place the general intellectual climate in the caliphate, and later in the breakaway states, which made Jewish cultural growth possible. The cultural interests of the Jews were varied. Those who could afford it cultivated the art of music and had their books illuminated by talented artists. Poetic expression, as will be seen, was incomparably more widespread than music and the visual arts. But it was mainly the experience of learning which captivated the heart and mind of the Jew in the Muslim world. Whether it was Torah learning, or the hitherto unknown discipline of philosophy, their study was more universal among Jews than even Hebrew poetry.

Characteristic of this was a great diversification of the disciplines cultivated among these Jews, coupled with a progressive professionalization of learning. Support of scholars and poets by the wealthy was common and, as later in Renaissance Italy, literary activity and dependence on the good will of the magnanimous went hand in hand. Hisdai ibn Shaprut in the tenth century, and other Andalusian Jewish plutocrats in the eleventh, established a basis for the furtherance of learning and poetry by employing scholars and poets as writers of their correspondence and by showering them with gifts and flattery.

No less an act of encouragement was the uninterrupted flow of financial support to the Babylonian academies which came from Jews in all corners of the Muslim world. Economically less fortunate areas, such as Sicily, were not forgotten by a man like Samuel ibn Nagrela at a time when he distributed his funds designed for the support of culture. Curiously, little is known of anything resembling a Jewish public school system in these countries in the period of the Early Middle Ages. At most, communal care was given to the education of the poor, as was, for example, the case in Egypt in the first half of the thirteenth century. Obviously, private instruction seems to have been considered sufficient.

Linguistic Conditions

At the time the Arab empire was established, the Jews living in its various regions spoke different languages. In the eastern part of the former Persian empire they spoke Persian, or a Judeo-Persian dialect. In the more western areas, and especially in Babylonia, the language of the Jews was Aramaic. In the Holy Land, too, Aramaic was the daily language of most Jews, while some spoke either Greek or Latin. (The Aramaic spoken in the Holy Land was permeated with a host of Greek and Latin words.) In the eastern regions of North Africa the Jews spoke Greek, while in its western parts, as well as in Spain, they spoke either Latin or the various vernaculars which began to emerge out of the classical Latin language.

With the solidification of Arab rule in these countries, the Jews increasingly began to abandon the languages in use among them in favor of Arabic. The process of Jewish linguistic acculturation did not proceed with the same rapidity and intensity in all corners of the Muslim world. While in Spain and North Africa the process was rapid and thorough, it was rather insignificant in Persia, where the Judeo-Persian dialect continued to be used. In Babylonia, too, Aramaic continued to live on temporarily as a spoken language among the Jews even at the time when this region became the center of the Arab empire. All the time, however, Arabic was gaining ground, and by the middle of the tenth century it had become the spoken language of the overwhelming majority of the Jews. The acculturation of the Jews also found expression in the widespread use of Arabic proper names in everyday life. Characteristically, although Hebrew played an important role in Jewish international trade, Jewish merchants also used Arabic as a major language of correspondence. The degree to which Arabization became universal among the Jews in the orbit of Islam is amply demonstrated, as we have seen, by the cultural character assumed by Sicilian Jewry. Its acculturation was total with regard to such everyday phenomena as language, names, and customs.

Jewish linguistic otherness survived in the areas of religion, scholarship, and literature. Hebrew continued to be the language of worship. Aramaic too, being the language of the Talmud, the main subject of Jewish studies, continued to be used in writing, and even in speech to a certain degree as late as the tenth century. In the literature the phenomenon of bilingualism developed, for which no full explanation has been found. Poetry, liturgical as well as secular, was written exclusively in Hebrew, while many of the works in prose were composed in Arabic. Ture, here and there dissatisfaction was expressed at the tendency to eliminate the use of Hebrew in Jewish prosaic literature, but most writers were sincerely convinced that Arabic was a more suitable vehicle for philosophical and scientific expression than Hebrew. Thus the use of Arabic in prose penetrated even the field of the Halakhah.

Isaac Alfasi, Spain's greatest halakhic authority, wrote most of his responsa in Arabic. If we are to believe Judah ibn Tibbon (1120–90), most of the Jewish legal literature in the Muslim lands was composed in Arabic. Even more striking is the fact that most works then written on the grammar of the Hebrew language were composed in Arabic. The sincere admiration Jews had for Arabic is expressed in the enthusiastic statement of as great a Hebrew poet as Moses ibn Ezra that Arabic had wonderful qualities, because it developed in the favorable climate of the Arabian peninsula. Of course, as in their other adopted languages, the Jews used the Hebrew alphabet in their Arabic writings. An exception seems to have been Saadiah Gaon, who wrote often in Arabic characters.

Characteristically, at the time when Jewish scholars and poets sang the praise of the Arabic language, a great interest arose to uncover and describe the grammatical fundamentals of the Hebrew language and to write Hebrew in strict adherence to its grammatical rules. As in many other fields of Jewish knowledge, here too Saadiah Gaon was the first to lay the foundations of Hebrew grammar. In the Introduction to a guide to the art of Hebrew versification, which he called *Egron (Collection)*, he provided a history of the Hebrew language and an exposition of the fundamentals of its grammar. Saadiah kept on returning to grammatical and lexicographical studies throughout his entire literary career. He wrote what may be termed a systematic grammar of Hebrew (of which only fragments have survived), and addressed himself to various grammatical issues in all his writings, including his polemical works against Karaism. But it was not until late in the tenth century and in the first half of the eleventh century in Spain that Hebrew grammar became a field which attracted illustrious scholars. The research of Menahem ibn Saruq (c. 910–c. 70), Adonim (Dunash) ibn Labrat (c. 920–c. 90), Judah ibn Hayyuj (c. 945–c. 1000), and Jonah ibn Janah (985–1040) created what may be safely called the discipline of Hebrew grammar. The research of these scholars and of many others was among the decisive factors that forged the immense poetical explosion in Spain which became known as the Golden Age of Hebrew poetry.

The Academies and the Geonim

Babylonia-Iraq, with its large Jewish community, was the main center of Jewish cultural life during the period of the expansion of the caliphate. With the coming of the Muslims the difficulties encountered by the Jewish scholarly institutions under the latter Sassanians became a matter of the past, and Jewish cultural activity could again be conducted in a climate of freedom. The situation further improved greatly when Iraq became the center of the caliphate in the middle of the eighth century. The two old academies of Pumbedita and Sura entered a new period of prominence with increased prestige and larger numbers of students. In fact, at times they even enjoyed more prestige than in the period of the Amoraim.

The two schools now also had a stronger and more effective administrative leadership in the persons of their heads, now called geonim. To be sure, the office of the gaon, meaning eminence or the pride (of the Jewish people), possibly came into being in both schools several decades prior to the Muslim conquest: in Pumbedita in 589 and in Sura in 591. But only with the expansion of the Muslim empire, and the inclusion of a majority of the Jewish people within its confines, could the geonim attain the high authority wielded by them during their heyday, between the eighth and the middle of the tenth century.

The character and organizational structure of the two leading Babylonian schools under the geonim were not basically different from that in the period of the Amoraim. Now too each school was headed by a president, the gaon, and a vice-president, the *av-beth-din*. Each school had a few score members-scholars and a multitude of younger students. But the democratic nature of the leadership characteristic of the amoraic period (cf. Vol. I, Sec. IX, Chap. 2) was gone. Now the members-scholars were recruited from a limited number of families, and *geonim* from an even smaller circle of privileged clans. The sole exception was Saadiah, a native of Egypt, who was appointed gaon of Sura in 928 due to his immense learning and the special circumstances that prevailed at that time.

Simultaneously with serving as institutions of higher studies, the schools of Sura and Pumbedita became under the geonim centers of religious guidance for the Jewry of the caliphate. This was done in a dual way. The geonim, like the Tannaim and Amoraim earlier, issued a variety of ordinances (*taqqanoth*) for the regulation of religious and social matters in the life of the Jewish communities. In addition, countless inquiries were streaming into the schools from all corners of the caliphate, to which solutions were worked out by the resident members-scholars. In this way the responsa literature came into being, a sort of law by correspondence.

The responsa literature, which has been a widely used genre in Rabbinic writings till our own times, was an innovation introduced by the geonim, and became their main contribution to Rabbinic literature. The books composed in Babylonia by individual scholars during the about four-and-a-half centuries of the geonic period are quite small in number. Again, Saadiah, the immigrant, was the only prolific writer among them. This lack of individual literary ambition may have resulted from the wish of the geonim to emulate the Amoraim and like them leave to posterity a great collective work on Jewish law. The principle of literary collectivism may also have provided a comfortable framework of literary expression to those geonim whose scholarly acumen was not above average, and who were able to ascend to their high position through the oligarchic method of selecting them from a closed circle of families. It is worth noting that in the geonic period the Adar *kallah* assemblies (cf. Vol. I, Sec. IX, Chap. 2) also served as a forum for discussion of incoming inquiries, thus giving the responsa even more the character of a collective literature. The *kallah* continued to function basically unchanged in the geonic period. If anything, it now attracted more participants and was a major semi-annual event in the life of Iraqi Jewry.

The considerable funds necessary for the maintenance of the two schools with their staffs and large student bodies came from various sources. Originally the exilarchal treasury appropriated ample subsidies to the schools. Additional income was derived from donations accompanying incoming inquiries and from charitable sources in the caliphate, the breakaway countries, and the Diaspora living under Christendom. With students now coming to the academies from other countries, such as Byzantium and Italy, the flow of donations from foreign lands increased. Yemenite Jewry, for example, was known for its lavish contributions to the Babylonian schools. The schools possibly also possessed real estate holdings, which provided them with additional income. Of course, all these sources could not provide a stable income to the schools, and the geonim were therefore pressing for partnership in the income flowing from the provinces to the exilarchal treasury. We have seen (cf. above, Chap. 2) that they ultimately succeeded in securing on a permanent basis the income from a number of provinces in Persia and Central Asia. We have also seen how the rivalry for income and influence caused repeated friction between the geonim and the exilarchs and how they ultimately came to influence each other's election.

The schools were known as the Academy of Sura and the Academy of Pumbedita because of the localities in which they were founded. And even though both these towns were located not too far from Baghdad, both *yeshivoth* ultimately moved to the capital city: the academy of Pumbedita in 890 and that of Sura early in the tenth century. By moving to Baghdad, the geonim probably hoped to more directly influence the course of events in the life of the Jewish community. In the early geonic period, the Academy of Sura enjoyed a status of greater prominence than the one of Pumbedita, and also received a larger share of the funds provided by the public. This, of course, evoked much bitterness in Pumbedita, and the two academies were in a state of continuous rivalry. By the end of the first quarter of the tenth century, however, the Academy of Pumbedita attained a status equal to that of her rival. It is worth noting that both academies were accorded some form of caliphal recognition by the Umayyads as well as the Abassids.

Until the second half of the tenth century, the two Babylonian academies and their leaders enjoyed the undisputed loyalty of the Jewry in the orbit of Islam and beyond. They were universally recognized as the center for the study of the Talmud, the great repository of Jewish law and thought, and on this rested their great prestige and popularity. However, late in the tenth century, their prestige began to wane. Various factors contributed to the decline of the gaonate, and not least was its own success. As a result of the educational activity of the geonim, the knowledge of the Babylonian Talmud had spread by then to all countries of Jewish settlement. Local *yeshivoth* and talmudic scholars emerged everywhere, and the outlying areas were no longer as dependent on the geonim and their teachings as before. The shrinkage of the caliphate, too, worked for the decline in the status of all the institutions located within its center. The impoverishment of the Jewry in the eastern parts of the Muslim world made the two academies even more dependent financially on handouts from the ascending Jewish communities in the breakaway countries, which further contributed to the lowering of the gaonate's prestige.

Between 589, when for the first time a man bearing the title of gaon headed the Academy of Pumbedita, and 1038, when Hai, the last gaon of Pumbedita, passed away, 92 geonim presided over the two academies, 42 in Sura and 50 in Pumbedita. Although in practice they all came, as we have seen, from a closed circle of families, the office never became hereditary in the sense that a son would immediately follow his father as gaon. Sons of geonim from time to time did attain the office held by their fathers, but usually only after some time had elapsed. An exception were the Pumbedita geonim Sherira (968–98) and his son Hai (998–1038), who through the 70 years of their combined "reign" provided a memorable conclusion to the geonic period through their outstanding scholarly leadership.

As is the case with institutions which have had a great past, the Babylonian gaonate was reluctant to go out of existence even when the foundations for its continuation had crumbled. And so some later scholars attempted to revive the office by establishing the Academy of Baghdad about 1070. To demonstrate that their school was a direct continuation of the academies of Sura and Pumbedita, the 11 men who headed the Academy of Baghdad between 1070 and the end of the thirteenth century used the title *gaon* to describe their position. One of them, Samuel ben Ali (1164–94), even attained a status of prominence in the Jewish scholarly world. But this all was of passing significance, because there was no longer a need for the gaonate as it had functioned during its heyday.

Saadiah Gaon (882–942)

The most outstanding personality among the geonim was Saadiah ben Joseph. He was born in 882 in the district of Fayyum in central Egypt, and possibly was the son of a laborer. No information is available about his education and teachers, but already as a young man he was an accomplished scholar in Judaic lore as well as in the sciences. He had a number of pupils and had also begun his career as a writer. Otherwise little is known of Saadiah's activities up to the year 915 when he was compelled to leave Egypt, possibly as a result of quarrels with the local Karaites. During the following few years Saadiah visited various countries in the Near East, including the Holy Land, and in 922 settled in Baghdad. Here he was appointed to an important post in the Academy of Pumbedita.

About the same time events took place which brought Saadiah to the attention of the Jewish public. The head of the Academy of Jerusalem, Aaron ben Meir, who like other heads of this academy used the title of gaon (cf. the next chapter), made a controversial calendric decision: Rosh Hashanah of the year 4683, corresponding to 922–23, was to be observed on a Tuesday. Upon learning the details, Saadiah became convinced that the Jerusalem gaon's computation was incorrect, and he then convinced the Baghdad Jewish leadership to reject it in favor of a different day. To be sure, the Jewish communities customarily recognized the authority of the Palestinian leadership in matters of calendation; in fact, the Babylonian Jewish community formally stated its recognition of Jerusalem's calendric authority in 855. But Saadiah's arguments, and Saadiah was an expert par excellence in matters of Jewish calendation, seem to have been so convincing that the Babylonian leadership consented to break with tradition and to reject Aaron ben Meir's announcement. Saadiah first urged the Jerusalem gaon privately to change his mind. But Aaron ben Meir was not to be moved, because he believed in the correctness of his computation and in the inalienable right of the Jerusalem leadership to proclaim the dates of the Jewish holidays. Thus the conflict heated up and in 922 the Jewish world split and observed the holidays on different dates. The exact course of the events is not known. But it seems that the

Jerusalem leadership temporarily lost out in the struggle for the preservation of its exclusive authority in matters of calendation.

The victory over the gaon of Jerusalem added much to Saadiah's prestige. Thus, when the question of appointing a gaon for the Academy of Sura came up, David ben Zakkai, who had held the office of exilarch since 916, began to think of appointing Saadiah to this post. The Academy of Sura was in a state of decline, and Kohen Zedeq, the energetic gaon of Pumbedita began to advocate the merger of both academies under his leadership. But the exilarch did not favor the idea. Possibly he was afraid that Kohen Zedeq might become too strong a rival. He also strove to save the school which had such a glorious past. The man best qualified to return the Academy of Sura to its former glory was Saadiah. As a scholar he was far above all his contemporaries. He also possessed the necessary energy for rebuilding the institution. But, the exilarch was also afraid of Saadiah, who "fears no man and kowtows to no one," as an old scholar told him. Ultimately, however, the exilarch appointed Saadiah as gaon of Sura in 928. The only precaution he took was to make Saadiah swear an oath of allegiance to him.

Upon taking office Saadiah went ahead with much vigor to rebuild the academy. The situation in the school began, indeed, to improve, and the new gaon was also successful in securing financial stability for the institution. Soon, however, the peaceful course of the events was interrupted by a serious conflict which broke out between Saadiah and the exilarch. The available sources do not make it clear what the quarrel was about. All that we know is that Saadiah refused to endorse a judgement issued by the exilarch in a civil case, and failed to state the reason for his refusal.

This seemingly minor issue, however, led to a nasty quarrel in which the entire Jewish community became involved. The exilarch and Saadiah deposed each other, and a counter-gaon and counter-exilarch were respectively appointed by the two warring camps. In the course of the seven years of its duration the conflict assumed more and more ugly forms. Ultimately, in 937, a few men who could still be considered neutral succeeded in bringing Saadiah and David ben Zakkai together and in restoring the peace between them. The prolonged struggle, however, had brought ruin to both opponents. The exilarch died in 940, and Saadiah in 942.

Saadiah's personality as a scholar of major proportions and as a perpetual fighter represents a strange combination. We know too little of Saadiah's early experiences in Egypt to find in these an explanation for his bitterness and eagerness for struggle. Some light could perhaps be shed on the enigma by Saadiah's belief that in every generation Providence chooses one of the sages to lead the Jewish people in the ways of righteousness. It seems that he was convinced that God had elected him to such leadership, and this belief deprived him of the ability to understand attitudes not agreeable to him. The only course open to him seems to have been to fight for his views, and to carry the struggle to the bitter end. From a historical perspective the only consolation to be derived from the years of his struggle with David ben Zakai lay in the fact that he used them for the composition or completion of his literary works.

Like many scholars of the Middle Ages, Saadiah had achieved a degree of expertise in many fields of Judaic lore. We have seen that he was the first to lay the foundations for the exploration and description of the grammar of the Hebrew language. His knowledge of Arabic was thorough, and he used it to compose what became the first Arabic translation of the Bible. By intertwining the translation with exegetic material, he gave it the character of a book designed for the use and enlightenment of the masses. This translation has, indeed, been widely used by Arabic-speaking Jews both in the synagogue and home. Another first provided by Saadiah is his prayer book, in which he included his own liturgical poems, as well as commentaries to the prayers in Arabic. The prayer book too was widely used by Near Eastern Jewry until it was superseded by the hundreds of magnificent *piyyutim* of the great Spanish poets of the Golden Age. The Yemenite Jews still use Saadiah's prayer book in their religious services.

Saadiah's writings on halakhic literature were quite impressive. He contributed to halakhic methodology by writing an introduction to the Talmud and a treatise on the 13 hermeneutical principles, that is, the principles by which laws and religious customs can be established as legitimate. As for the interpretation of the Talmud, ample evidence indicates that he wrote systematic commentaries on all, or at least considerable parts of, the Mishnah and the Talmud. Of course, like the other geonim, he wrote a considerable number of responsa. These writings were mostly lost in the course of time to a much greater degree than his other works.

A new type of literature was created by Saadiah in his polemics against Jewish sectarians. His sharp pen turned, of course, first and foremost against the Karaites, who had seceded from normative Judaism over 100 years before he was born (see further, Chap. 7). Both before him and after him Jewish scholars fought against the Karaite schism. But no one did it as effectively as Saadiah. It may well be said that if the Karaites ultimately lost out in their struggle against normative Judaism and shrank to become a group of relatively insignificant size, it was to a great degree due to the struggle Saadiah waged against them.

Saadiah also made a major and lasting contribution to nascent Jewish philosophy. He felt, as did so keenly Judah Halevi and Maimonides afterwards, that in the sophisticated semi-capitalist Muslim society the main concepts of the Jewish faith needed to be interpreted by way of reasoning. He undertook this task well equipped with a broad knowledge of classical and Arabic philosophy. Saadiah did not create a comprehensive philosophical system of his own, but he succeeded, through the many philosophical excurses interspersed in his writings, and his major Arabic work *Beliefs and Opinions*, to satisfy the quest for a philosophical clarification of the foundations of the Jewish faith.

The name of the work implies the author's desire to present the basic harmony which he thought he had found between *religious belief* and *philosophical opinion.* And so he explains in the ten sections of the work such basic concepts of Judaism as *creatio ex nihilo,* the unity of God, resurrection, redemption, as well as other religious ideas. Although medieval, the book has much appeal to students of the Jewish religion and Jewish thought in modern times. Judah ibn Tibbon translated *Beliefs and Opinions* into Hebrew and so made it accessible to all Jewry in the Middle Ages. It has also been translated into various other languages, including English. Saadiah's remarkable erudition and ramified literary accomplishments made him the outstanding sage among the geonim of Babylonia.

Other Schools and Scholars

The schools of Pumbedita and Sura were the foremost centers of Jewish learning in the Muslim countries during the period of the Early Middle Ages. But they were not the only ones. In fact, other schools of Rabbinic learning existed even in Babylonia-Iraq. In the second half of the twelfth century when the energetic gaon Samuel ben Ali dominated the academic scene in Baghdad, no less than ten talmudic schools existed there. Characteristically, the traveller Pethahiah of Ratisbon, who had come to Baghdad from the Germany of the Tosafists (see further, Sec. XV, Chap. 9), was impressed by the high standards of Torah study in Baghdad.

Great centers of Torah learning existed in the other parts of the caliphate as well. All of these centers, especially after their host countries broke away from the caliphate, demonstrated a clear tendency to make themselves, and the Jewish communities they served, independent of the Babylonian geonim and their schools. These tendencies began to show up as early as the ninth century, when the Babylonian gaonate was at the peak of its influence, and the Jewries of the outlying regions of the caliphate were still generally willing and eager to accept its guidance.

It is not surprising that the first to claim independence from Babylonia was the talmudic academy of the Holy Land. Early in the Muslim period the academy continued to exist in Tiberias, as it had in the late patriarchal times. We will see further that during this period the scholars of Tiberias were mainly occupied with biblical studies. But when the academy was transferred to Jerusalem some time during the ninth century, the focus seems to have been again on halakhic studies. Significantly, the heads of the Jerusalem Academy assumed the title of gaon, thereby demonstrating their independence from the Babylonian geonim. We have seen above how one of the Jerusalem geonim, Aaron ben Meir, attempted to assert his authority in matters of calendation. All in all, 18 or possibly 20 heads of the Jerusalem Academy claimed the right to call themselves geonim between the second half of the ninth and the beginning of the twelfth century. Unlike the Babylonian gaonate, the office of the geonim of the Holy Land was hereditary, and this was responsible for the small number of outstanding personalities among them.

Of course, the Babylonian geonim considered the Jerusalem gaonate an illegitimate institution. Nevertheless, the geonim of the Holy Land were recognized as legitimate in various Jewish communities in the Near East. Their prestige rose even further when the Fatimid rulers of Egypt began to appropriate subsidies for the academy over which they presided. Besides Jerusalem, Ramleh served for a time as a seat of the academy. In 1071, when the Seljuks occupied Palestine, a number of leading scholars of the Academy of the Holy Land fled to Tyre, in today's Lebanon, and re-established it there. But when the crusaders occupied the Lebanese coastal towns by the end of the century, the academy had to move again. It relocated in Syria's capital Damascus, where it existed for several more generations.

Talmudic studies also flourished all over North Africa. True, information about Torah learning in Egypt prior to the Fatimid conquest is rather scarce. But the fact that a scholar of Saadiah's stature could have arisen in Egypt late in the ninth century indicates that schools with teachers of high caliber must have existed there. More information about Torah learning in Egypt is available beginning with the second half of the tenth century, when Shemariah ben Elhanan, an immigrant who possibly came from Babylonia, settled in Fustat. Henceforth the Academy of Fustat became known and prestigious, and some of its heads even claimed for themselves the title of gaon. Fustat's greatest fame as a center of learning was acquired, of course, during the second half of the twelfth century when Moses Maimonides, the "Great Eagle," settled there.

Further west, Kairuwan in Tunisia and Fez in Morrocco became the most outstanding centers of Torah learning. Kairuwan already had a yeshivah in the first half of the tenth century. But the climate of Torah learning was here too greatly enhanced by the arrival, late in the century, of an immigrant scholar Rabbi Hushiel, who came either from Italy or Babylonia. The results of Hushiel's teaching activity would be fully realized in the generation after him, when both his son Hananel (c. 980–1053) and his pupil Nissim ben Jacob (c. 990–1062) taught in the schools of Kairuwan. They both count among the greatest talmudic scholars of all times. It is noteworthy that Hushiel and Hananel energetically promoted the study of the Jerusalem Talmud, which was an academic innovation and an act of "liberation" from Babylonian geonic influence. Unlike Egypt and Tunisia, Morocco attained its fame as a center of Torah learning through a native North African sage.

Isaac ben Jacob, later known as Alfasi because of his sojourn in the city of Fez, was born in Algeria in 1013. It seems that he studied in the schools in Kairuwan, before going to Fez. Here he taught for about half a century, establishing the city as the major center of Jewish studies in Morocco. In 1088, due to political unrest, he was compelled to flee to Spain. His departure, however, did not spell the end of Morocco's great age of Jewish learning. Fez continued to rank high as a Jewish cultural center. Other Moroccan towns had their yeshivoth as well. Significantly, talmudical schools existed even in remote localities in the Atlas mountains. As for Rabbi Isaac Alfasi, although he arrived in Spain at the age of 75, he still helped to write a golden page in the history of Torah learning in his new home, before he died in 1103.

Spanish Jewry's interest in talmudic studies is demonstrated by its request to Paltoi, who was gaon of Pumbedita between 842 and 858, to send to Spain a copy of the entire Talmud. In those times of scarcity of books this was no mean cultural event. But here too the flourishing of talmudic studies followed the arrival of a great scholar from abroad. Moses ben Hanokh, possibly a native of southern Italy, arrived in Cordova in the 950s, after what seems to have been a troublesome and tragic sea voyage. His greatness as a talmudic sage was soon recognized, and the local scholars readily accepted him as their leader. During the years of his leadership he succeeded in developing a local class of scholars, whose learning made it possible for Spanish Jewry to effectively detach itself from Babylonian tutelage. Constant progress could be observed during the entire eleventh century. Thus, when Isaac Alfasi arrived in 1088, he found in Spain a climate as favorable for the study of Torah as the one he had known in Fez. The school which he headed in Lucena had become a leading academy among many others. Some of the great scholars of the following generation, including the poet-philosopher Judah Halevi, were among his disciples. Spanish Jewry's interest in philosophy and poetry probably limited to a certain degree the scope of talmudic studies. This is indicated by the popularity of Alfasi's *Sepher hahalakhoth, Book of Laws*, which is basically a sort of abridgment of the Talmud. Nonetheless, during the entire period of the Early Middle Ages Spain could boast of a galaxy of brilliant talmudic scholars and authors. One modern Jewish literary historian even expressed the view that the Spanish yeshivoth of this period not only rivaled, but even surpassed in importance those of Babylonia.

Rabbinic Literature

The spread of Torah learning in the Jewish communities in the orbit of Islam was accompanied by the emergence of a Rabbinic literature vastly different from that of the preceding talmudic period. We have seen that the Babylonian geonim forged a new literary genre in the form of the responsa. And, like the responsa, the new *pesaqim* and *halakhoth* literature was designed to fill the need for books of religious guidance more easily usable than the Talmud proper. A book of *pesaqim* usually contains a set of concisely formulated laws derived from the Talmud. A book of *halakhoth* has a wider scope, and offers a set of talmudic laws preceded by the Amoraic discussions about them, as recorded in the Talmud. The need for such compendia appeared in the caliphate and the breakaway countries as a result of the Jewish involvement in the new semi-capitalist economy and its variegated forms of culture. The new lifestyle left some segments of the Jewish population little time for immersion in the vast sea of the Talmud. The struggle against the Karaite schism also may have necessitated the preparation of more concise and clear-cut formulations of the Jewish law.

Be this as it may, as early a work as *Sheeltoth, Questions*, (or, *Discussions*) of Ahai of Shabha (about the middle of the eighth century) clearly possesses a code-like character. The same holds true of *Halakhoth pesuqoth, Concise Rules*, by Ahai's contemporary Yehudai Gaon, the head of the Sura Academy. A much more elaborate code is the compendium *Halakhoth gedoloth, Major Laws* by Simon Qayyara, of Basra (Iraq), composed about 825. The most important work in this field, however, was Isaac Alfasi's *Sepher hahalakhoth, The Book of Laws*. Responding to the need of the times, Alfasi provided in his work both an excellent compendium of the Jewish law suitable for ready reference, and a summary of talmudic passages from which the laws derived. This latter part of the work is in fact a digest of the Talmud. Later generations justifiably called it *Talmud qatan,* that is, *The Little Talmud.* Characteristically, when the Church authorities outlawed the printing of the Talmud in Italy in the sixteenth century, Alfasi's *Sepher hahalakhoth* became its natural substitute as a textbook in use in the talmudic schools. How much Alfasi's work filled a contemporary need in the Muslim countries is indicated by the fact that Moses Maimonides taught it himself and recommended its use to other teachers.

Another genre of literature designed to fill the need for legal manuals was the monograph discussing specific issues or areas of the Jewish law, which began to appear during the tenth century. Some attention was also given to exegesis of the Talmud not directly related to the practical needs of administering the Jewish law. Examples of such literature are sporadically interspersed in the geonic responsa. Some scholars even undertook the writing of systematic running commentaries to larger or smaller portions of the Talmud.

A review of Rabbinic literature written in the Muslim countries in this period reveals that it developed along patterns set by the geonim of Babylonia. This is evident in the commentary-compendium of Rabbi Hananel of Kairuwan, as well as in Isaac Alfasi's responsa. True, some of the works written outside of Babylonia surpassed in scope and depth the writings of geonim other than Saadiah. But their basically geonic character as far as content, form, and style are concerned is unmistakable.

The period of the Early Middle Ages also produced a sizable body of midrashic literature in the Muslim countries. But these late midrashic writings are quite different from the classical *midrashim* of the tannaitic and amoraic times. They are written in what may be termed medieval Hebrew, and for obvious reasons are devoid of Greek and Latin linguistic elements. They are mostly short treatises, mainly of homiletical rather than exegetical nature. As may be expected, Muslim influences are not lacking in them. Much, much larger than the other medieval midrashim is the *Midrash hagadol, The Great Midrash,* compiled or translated in Yemen in the thirteenth century by David ben

Amram al-Adeni from an Arabic work of Abraham Maimuni. This compilation, which is a restatement of much midrashic material of earlier times, effectively concluded the Jewish midrashic literature.

Moses Maimonides (1135–1204)

The greatest Jewish sage in the Muslim world in this period was Moses ben Maimon, known in modern times by the name of Maimonides. Maimonides is considered the greatest Jewish scholar and thinker in post-talmudic times, towering above contemporary and later scholars. He was equally great as halakhist and philosopher, and in both these capacities exerted a deep and lasting impact down to our own times.

Moses was born in Cordova in 1135, the son of the local rabbinic judge Maimon. Almost nothing is known of his early youth and studies. In the thirteenth year of Moses' life his home town was occupied by the Almohades (see above, Chap. 3) and the family had to leave. It seems that during the next 12 years the family wandered all over Spain, both Muslim and Christian, probably in search of a place where it could openly profess the Jewish religion. Some modern historians believe a tradition recorded by medieval Muslim sources that the Maimon family did acknowledge Mohammed as a true messenger of God. Be this as it may, in 1160 the family settled in Fez, Morocco, where it had been permissible since 1159 to openly profess Judaism, although the country was ruled by the Almohades. All through the years of his peregrinations young Maimonides was able to continue his studies, and it was during this time that he acquired a large portion of his enormous erudition, if not most of it. It was also then that he composed one of his early treatises, *The Epistle on Conversion*, also known as *The Discourse on the Sanctification of the Name of God*. In this treatise he came out vigorously against a certain rabbi who had stated that Jews who accepted Islam under Almohade pressure were condemned forever, even though they returned to Judaism later in their life. Young Maimonides himself experienced in one way or another the anguish of these hapless Jews. He, therefore, refrained from condemning them, but rather attempted to encourage them to leave the areas of oppression, as his own family had done, and to settle in places where they could serve their God openly.

The Maimon family lived in Fez for about five years. During this period Moses seems to have devoted much time to medical studies. He received some of his knowledge in medicine from his father, but most of it came from the study of medical works. In 1165 the Maimon family left Fez for reasons not fully clear. The political climate there seems to have changed, and it was again impossible to profess Judaism openly. This time the family went to the Holy Land and settled in Acre, in the territory of the Christian kingdom established by the Crusaders. But here too the family stayed only a few short years. From the Holy Land the family emigrated to Egypt, and made Cairo its permanent residence. The old Rabbi Maimon was no longer alive, having died either in the Holy Land, or shortly after arriving in Egypt.

At first Moses could devote all his time to his studies, since his brother David, a dealer in precious stones, cared for the maintenance of the entire family. However, in 1169 disaster struck, and David drowned on a voyage to India. The burden of supporting the family now fell on Moses, and like many other medieval Jewish scholars, he took up the practice of medicine. In 1185 Moses Maimonides became a court physician. He held this position with great distinction till his death. And although his duties in the palace took up most of his day, and in his later years his strength was sapped, he still advised and treated throngs of patients, Jews and Gentiles, who daily sought his advice. In addition, as we have seen (cf. above, Chap. 4), he also devoted much of his time to the communal and religious leadership of Egypt's Jewry. Maimonides died late in 1204 and was buried in Tiberias, in the Holy Land. There is no evidence that the widely known portrait of Moses Maimonides is authentic.

Despite his perpetual wanderings during the prime years of his life and his preoccupation with the practice of medicine and with communal affairs in his later years, Moses Maimonides was one of the most prolific writers the Jewish people ever had. But more than the quantity of his writings, the supreme quality of most of his books gave his literary work its monumental significance.

The most important aspect of Maimonides' literary work was its responsiveness to the needs of the Jewish people in his generation. He realized that in the climate of the semi-capitalist system prevalent in the caliphate and the breakaway states, tools were needed to readily administer the Jewish law and to strengthen the Jewish convictions of those in whose hearts religious doubts were budding under the impact of the contemporary rationalistic philosophies. Although there is a likelihood that early in his life Maimonides wrote commentaries to certain tractates of the Talmud, he later realized that in the immediate future the study of the Talmud proper, which is a voluminous, deliberative work, had no real prospects. He therefore discontinued working on the Talmud commentary and concentrated on interpreting the Mishnah, which is a much shorter and more code-like work. He wrote this commentary in Arabic, possibly because of his wish to make it accessible for widespread use.

The most important step, however, that he undertook in this direction was the composition of the code of laws, which he called *Mishneh Torah*. Some scholars believe that the title means "Second to the Torah," or "Repetition of the Torah," while others believe that "The Second Torah" would be the proper translation. In any case, Maimonides made it clear in the Introduction to the work that with its help the Jewish religious law could be taught with the concomitant study of the Holy Scriptures. The tacit implication, of course, was that due to "the hardships of the times" one was permitted to bypass the Talmud and still expect to be able to fulfill one's religious duties.

Mishneh Torah was thus composed as the first genuine code of the Jewish law, almost strictly arranged according to subject matter. The affinity between the *Mishneh Torah* and the Mishnah may further be indicated by the fact that, like the latter, Maimonides' code was composed in Hebrew. Although the influence of Arabic is noticeable, the beautiful style of *Mishneh Torah* clearly resembles the specific style in which the Mishnah was composed about 1,000 years earlier. The work is divided into 14 parts, and since the Hebrew word *yad* (meaning "hand") is the numerical equivalent of 14, the work also came to be called *Yad hahazaqah, The Strong Hand.* In Rabbinic literature the work is mostly quoted as "The Rambam," which is an abbreviation of the

author's name Rabbenu Mosheh ben Maimon. Although composed later, the *Book of Precepts*, written in Arabic, was possibly
conceived as an introduction to *Mishneh Torah* for the purpose of
describing the 613 commandments recorded in the Bible.

A literary work sui generis is the *Epistle to Yemen*, which
Maimonides composed in 1172. It was written to give succor
and guidance to Yemenite Jewry, which was experiencing trying
times. We have seen (cf. above, Chap. 3) how in 1165 the ruler of
Yemen had decreed the forced conversion to Islam of his Jewish
subjects. It seems that at this time a Jew turned Muslim was
preaching to his former co-religionists in an attempt to prove
from the Bible that Mohammed was indeed God's true messenger. To increase the confusion, a man appeared, as often hap-
pens in times of stress, and claimed to be the true Messiah. In
their predicament the leaders of Yemenite Jewry turned to
Maimonides for guidance. The *Epistle to Yemen* was
Maimonides' reply. The anguish experienced by Maimonides in
view of the critical situation in Yemen is reflected in the style of
the *Epistle*. It lacks the sober and detached tone of the Code and of
the philosophical works. It much more resembles the emotional,
and even passionate *Epistle on Conversion*. It eloquently dis-
proves from the Bible the nonsensical claims of the apostate, and
strengthens the belief of the Yemenite Jews in the coming of the
true Messiah. This is accompanied by a popular description of the
nature of the true Messiah and of the deeds expected of him. The
Epistle, written in Arabic, contains derogatory remarks about
Mohammed. Although worried about the possible consequences,
Maimonides did not hesitate to request that it should be read
publicly in all the Jewish communities in Yemen.

Maimonides' great philosophical work, *The Guide of the
Perplexed*, also was written in response to an acute need.
Maimonides was aware that many Jewish intellectuals, who like
himself and Saadiah Gaon before him, had engaged in the study of
philosophy, were in need of reinforcement in their religious beliefs by philosophical speculation. In fact, much confusion had
arisen in this elite group with regard to the anthropomorphic
descriptions of God and His actions in the Bible. These circles
were very dear to Maimonides, himself deeply steeped in philosophical speculation and the most prominent Aristotelian among

the Jews. He was so much of a philosopher that he included philosophical discussions in his writings designed for the use of the broad masses. Thus, curious as it may be, the first book of *Mishneh Torah*, which he named "The Book of Knowledge," is in reality a treatise on metaphysics. It is therefore not surprising that he saw the need to write a full-fledged, systematic exposition of his philosophical views for the purpose of solving the perplexities common among the intellectuals, and of enabling them to harmonize their religious beliefs with the current philosophical thought.

To indicate his intention, Maimonides dedicated the *Guide* to Joseph ibn Shamun, who among his pupils was closest to him. In the first of the three parts of the book Maimonides discusses various nouns and verbs used in the Bible to describe the attributes of God and His actions, and clarifies them with a view to eliminating the idea of the corporeality of God seemingly implied by them. This section of the work is therefore sometimes referred to as the lexicographical part of the *Guide*. Maimonides further discusses in the *Guide* some of the basic concepts of the Jewish religion, such as creation, prophecy, evil, and Divine providence. Much space is also given to a rational explanation of the precepts. Maimonides believed that the source of all commandments is God's immense wisdom, and they should therefore be intelligible by means of reason. He even believed that the small number of religious precepts for which the Rabbis failed to find a reasonable explanation (*huqim*) are not totally beyond intelligibility. In general, he promoted the idea that the precepts were designed to further the physical and mental well-being of man. The ultimate goal, of course, is to reinforce man's well-being to a degree which would enable him to attain the knowledge of God. To be sure, Maimonides is aware of the great difficulties in attaining this lofty goal under the conditions of suffering and misery prevalent in the world. He therefore hopes that in the Messianic times man will be free of worry and sickness, and thus be able to attain the true knowledge of his God.

Maimonides was aware that philosophical speculation and esoteric ideas, if not properly understood, may cause more confusion than enlightenment. He also knew that many rabbis looked askance at people who devoted their time to the study of metaphysics and esoteric issues. He therefore wrote the work with the clear intention of keeping it away from the ordinary man. He achieved this goal by using cryptic methods of argumentation and by composing the work in a generally enigmatic style.

When Maimonides completed the *Guide* in 1195, it became apparent that it was the greatest philosophical work ever written by a Jewish thinker. The work retained this distinction for another half a millenium, down to the times of Baruch Spinoza. It greatly influenced subsequent Jewish and Gentile thinkers, including Thomas Aquinas, Spinoza, Leibnitz, and Moses Mendelssohn. Maimonides' writings were especially cherished by the *maskilim* of the eighteenth and nineteenth centuries, who believed they had found in them the justification for their own rationalistic tendencies. The sole exception was the great Italian Jewish scholar Samuel David Luzzatto, who adhered to the ideal of a Judaism emanating from the heart rather than from the mind.

Tradition has it that upon completing the *Guide* Maimonides felt the desire to translate it, as well as his other Arabic writings, into Hebrew. But he already was too old to undertake this task. He had, however, the satisfaction of knowing that Samuel ibn Tibbon, of the famed family of translators in Provence, was working on such a translation. Samuel even wanted to come to Cairo to consult with Maimonides on some problems in the work of translation, but the aging sage, still a busy physician in 1199, did not believe that the long and dangerous voyage from southern France to Egypt was justified. Samuel's translation, completed only two weeks before Maimonides' death, turned out to be rather literal and rigid, like the other translations from Arabic into Hebrew made by members of his family. A more free and less precise translation of the *Guide* into Hebrew was made somewhat later by the poet Judah al-Harizi. From this translation the *Guide* was translated into Latin, and thus became known in the Christian world in the al-Harizi version.

In addition to the *Guide* and the first part of the *Code*, Maimonides also used the *Commentary on the Mishnah* to express his views on man and Jew. He did it in the form of lengthy introductions to the *Sayings of the Fathers* and to the tenth chapter of tractate Sanhedrin. The introduction to *Sayings of the Fathers* is composed of eight chapters, and became an independent treatise known as *The Eight Chapters of Maimonides.* It may be said that in this treatise Maimonides presented his views on human psychology and on the way man can attain high moral goals. It represents simultaneously an attempt to harmonize Aristotelian ideas with the moral principles of Judaism. In the introduction to the tenth chapter of tractate Sanhedrin (known as the *Introduction to Pereq heleq*), Maimonides uses the fact that the chapter begins with the statement that all Jews have a part in *olam haba,* the wondrous world of the hereafter, to describe who is the ideal Jew. The ideal Jew is the one who believes in 13 principles which, according to Maimonides, are the basic tenets of the Jewish faith. The detailed description of these 13 principles, whose believers are the ideal Jews, is followed by a vigorous condemnation of those who reject them. An unknown author at a later time used this lofty description of the ideal Jew to formulate the set of 13 articles of the Jewish faith, popularly ascribed to Maimonides himself.

In addition to his major works, Maimonides also wrote a number of minor treatises on various philosophical and religious themes. And great rabbi that he was, he wrote responsa to inquiries which arrived from Jewish communities between the Persian gulf and the Atlantic ocean. It is worth noting that Maimonides' responsa were usually written in the language in which the inquiries were submitted. He was also the author of ten medical works which he composed in Arabic.

In the long history of Jewish cultural life, few men, if any, were accorded the admiration which the Jewish people gave to the "Great Eagle," Moses ben Maimon, in his lifetime as well as in subsequent generations, down to our own times. But Maimonides also had opponents. His enormous learning, the towering excellence of his works, and his daring in introducing innovations aroused fear and envy as well as admiration. A state of perpetual tension developed between him and Samuel ben Ali, the head of the Baghdad Academy. Samuel, as we have seen, dreamed of reviving the grandeur of the gaonate and insisted on imposing the authority of his academy on all the Jews living in the orbit of Islam. The presence of a spiritual giant of Maimonides' caliber in nearby Egypt ran counter to Samuel's ambitions. Samuel and his circle therefore looked with critical eyes at whatever Maimonides was doing. From these circles the partly justified argument emerged that Maimonides did not sufficiently emphasize in the *Code* the belief in bodily resurrection. Upon learning of this, Maimonides wrote in 1191 the *Treatise on Resurrection*, in which he described the Jewish belief in the immortality of the soul and in resurrection in a much broader and more affirmative manner.

Opposition to the *Code* also developed in Western Europe, and especially in the Provence. Here the prominent talmudist Abraham ben David of Posquieres (c. 1125–98) developed a whole system of criticism of the *Code*, the starting point of which was the accusation that by failing to list his sources, Maimonides was depriving the student of Jewish law of the opportunity to arrive independently at halakhic decisions. Abraham's aversion to Aristotelianism could only aggravate his displeasure with *Mishneh Torah*. But Maimonides and his *Code* also had many admirers in southern France. At that time the city of Lunel was a great center of Jewish learning. Its talmudical academy had among its scholars both admirers and opponents of the *Code*. They therefore addressed an inquiry to Maimonides, in which they pointed out the difficulties caused by the terse style of the *Code*. Maimonides responded somewhat apologetically and expressed the hope that he might be able to reorganize the *Code* by indicating the sources of his legal decisions.

Much more disastrous was the attack launched in southern France on the *Guide*. Traditionalist rabbis had been deeply concerned by a tendency prevalent there to interpret the Bible by way of allegory. These circles became terrified by the appearance in 1204 of Samuel ibn Tibbon's Hebrew translation of the *Guide*. They first sought the assistance of rabbis in northern France, and these responded with a ban on the study of the great philosophical work. The pro-*Guide* circles reacted with a counterattack, and reconciliation was not in sight. All this happened at a time when the Catholic Church was fiercely eradicating the Albigensian heresy, and had entrusted the order of the Dominican monks with inquisitorial powers to facilitate its campaign. Some hotheads among the opponents of the *Guide* then took a perilous step and denounced the work to the Dominicans. The latter condemned the work, and it was publicly burned in 1233. Jewish society was horrified by this tragic happening, and ascribed to its Jewish perpetrators the guilt for the burning of the Talmud in Paris about ten years later. Some of Maimonides' opponents reportedly regretted their action when learning of the tragedy which took place in Paris.

And yet, late in the thirteenth century the conflict broke out again, this time both in the Near East and the West. A certain scholar in Acre by the name of Solomon, an immigrant from France, renewed the propaganda against the writings of Maimonides. But this time the pro-Maimonides forces struck back with vigor, and under the leadership of Maimonides' grandson David, the nagid of Egypt, a number of rabbis in the Near East excommunicated the agitator. In southern France the issue heated up again as part of the old struggle against the allegorical interpretation of the Bible. Some scholars, among whom was Menahem Meiri, author of an excellent commentary to the Talmud, tried to present a conciliatory attitude. Ultimately, however, a ban was issued by a group of more than 30 rabbis, led by Spain's most distinguished talmudist Solomon ibn Adret, prohibiting the study of philosophy and of most of the sciences by men under the age of 30, who had not yet acquired a high degree of Jewish learning.

As for *Mishneh Torah*, the fears of its opponents turned out to be unfounded. Almost immediately after its completion it was accepted enthusiastically by most Jewish communities, including Babylonia. Some Jewish communities even passed formal resolutions recognizing it as binding upon themselves. No other work besides the Bible and the Talmud attracted the interest of the scholars like *Mishneh Torah*. By now, about 800 years after its completion, well over 200 commentaries have been written on it. Not only did it not render the Babylonian Talmud obsolete but, on the contrary, it added new vistas to its study, and immensely fructified all Rabbinic literature down to our own times. It is, indeed, the immortal work of the greatest Jewish mind of the Middle Ages.

The Other Philosophers

Saadiah and Maimonides were not the only philosophers among the Jews in the Muslim world in this period. The general cultural climate and the availability of the works of the great Greek philosophers in Arabic translations could not help but awaken interest in philosophical speculation among the Jewish intellectuals. Thus, Jewish philosophical writings began to appear about the year 900. Isaac Israeli, a native of Egypt, may be considered the first Jewish author who wrote philosophical works. In fact, young Saadiah had an opportunity to meet and consult Isaac on philosophical issues prior to his departure for Syria and Babylonia.

A review of the Jewish philosophical literature composed in Arabic during the subsequent three centuries reveals that it discussed general philosophical issues to a rather limited degree, and that it devoted its main attention to an attempt at resolving possible conflicts between rational speculation and the revealed Jewish religion. This imbalance is due to the fact that Jews in the Muslim world who were interested in philosophy could easily satisfy their interest in general philosophical issues by reading works of Arabic thinkers. The Jewish philosophers were greatly influenced by ancient Greek and contemporary Muslim philosophy. It is remarkable how few were the Jewish thinkers quoted by Maimonides in the *Guide* in comparison with the many non-Jewish philosophers whom he mentioned. The Jewish philosophers of the tenth and eleventh centuries, such as Isaac Israeli, Saadiah, and Solomon ibn Gabirol, were largely influenced by Platonic and Neo-Platonic thought. Neo-Platonic leanings are evident even in Ibn Gabirol's poems. Only at a later time did Aristotelianism begin to take roots within Jewish philosophy; it achieved its greatest triumph in the writings of Maimonides.

Practically all Jewish works in philosophy were composed in Arabic, which is less surprising than the fact that such a typical "inner-Jewish" book as Maimonides' *Commentary to the Mishnah* was written in this language. After all, Jewish philosophical literature could be of great interest also to the non-Jewish world. This is amply illustrated by the appearance of translations into various western languages of such works as the *Guide of the*

Perplexed and Judah Halevi's *Kuzari.* Most curious, however, in this respect was the fate of Solomon ibn Gabirol's philosophical work *Fountain of Life,* composed in the form of a dialogue between a master and his pupil. Written in Arabic in a way not fully demonstrating its Jewish character, the book "lost" its author for many centuries and instead was ascribed in a Latin version, *Fons Vitae,* to a Christian or Muslim named Avicebrol (or Avencebrol), an obvious distortion of the name Ibn Gabirol, until modern research returned it to its rightful author.

While Saadiah's *Beliefs and Opinions,* Maimonides' *Guide of the Perplexed,* and Ibn Gabirol's *Fountain of Life* were written in an objective and detached manner, Bahya ibn Paquda's *The Duties of the Hearts* and Judah Halevi's *Kuzari* were written in an impassioned and emotional style. These two works belong to the pietistic genre in Jewish philosophical literature. *The Duties of the Hearts,* written toward the end of the eleventh century is a devotional and moralistic work clearly designed for the purpose of helping the reader to fulfill his duties to God in a meaningful way. Bahya's main sources are Jewish, but he also drew his material from a variety of Greek philosophical writings, as well as from works of Muslim mystical and ascetical circles. Although Bahya used many Arabic philosophical terms, his work has demonstrated an unusual power of attraction on Jews through the centuries. Its ten "gates" (i.e., chapters) discuss such concepts as the unity of God, worship, humility, penitence, asceticism, and love of God. Judah ibn Tibbon translated *The Duties of the Hearts* into Hebrew in 1161. Among the many other translations there is one in the Yiddish language.

With even greater zeal and emotion, Judah Halevi wrote his *Kitab al Khazari, The Book of Kuzari.* The author describes his work as "a book of argument and proof in defense of the despised faith." It is written in the form of an imaginary dialogue between the king of the Khazars, who in the eighth century converted to "the religion of Abraham" (cf. further, Sec. XIV, Chap. 2), a philosopher, and representatives of the three monotheistic religions. The views expressed by the rabbi are, of course, the views of the author. They contain an ardent and enthusiastic glorification of the Jewish people, its religion, and the holy tongue. In it the famous statement is found that Israel among the nations is like the heart among the organs of the human body: the most vulnerable, but also the strongest. Thus, the uniqueness of the Jewish people and of its religion is defended against the attacks coming from Aristotelians, Muslims, and Christians. During the 20 years the great poet worked on this book he did not create a comprehensive philosophical system. He rather brought up from the depth of his soul his own unique concept of Judaism, which is by no means overshadowed by the Greek structure and Islamic style of the work. The book was completed just before Judah Halevi set out on his journey to the Holy Land, and a few years later Judah ibn Tibbon translated it into Hebrew. It enjoyed, and still enjoys, immense popularity among Jews. Translations into most of the western languages made the work accessible to the Gentile world as well. A new excellent Hebrew translation by Yehudah Even Shemuel appeared in 1972.

Sherira's Epistle

Compared to the widespread interest in philosophy, the interest in history seems to have been quite limited. The *Epistle of Sherira Gaon,* written in Babylonia in 987, is the only major work produced in the Muslim world in this field during the entire period of the Early Middle Ages. Characteristically, the *Epistle* seems to have been written for the purpose of countering Karaite attacks on the validity of the Rabbinic tradition. Sherira wrote his *Epistle* in Aramaic in reply to a request from scholars in Kairuwan. It is thus in fact a geonic responsum describing the chain of Rabbinic tradition, and not a chronicle to be read by ordinary people for the purpose of learning the past. But the fact that Sherira composed it on the basis of records in the archives of the Academy of Pumbedita made the *Epistle* a valuable historical document.

The paucity of Jewish historical literature mostly resulted from the largely tranquil course of Jewish life in the caliphate and the breakaway states. Thus, no need arose to record deeds of martyrs for the faith in the way Ashkenazic Jewry portrayed Jewish martyrdom in the time of the Crusades (cf. further, Sec. XV, Chap. 9). Maimonides' lack of interest in, and even rejection of, the contemporary Arab historiography also contributed its share to the absence of a meaningful Jewish historical literature in the orbit of Islam. Abraham ibn Daud, though a native of Muslim southern Spain, wrote his historical work *Sepher haqabbalah* after emigrating to Christian Spain. Significantly, *Sepher haqabbalah* is also mostly a description of the chain of tradition, and likewise was composed for the purpose of refuting Karaite challenges.

Exegesis of the Bible

As was the case for philosophy, the general climate was also favorable, and even encouraging, for important developments in the field of biblical exegesis. The emergence of the Karaite schism with its emphasis on the study of the Bible (cf. further, Chap. 7) called for parallel efforts in the Rabbanite camp. The gradual decline in the use of Aramaic as a Jewish vernacular rendered the Aramaic translations of the Bible almost obsolete as a means by which ordinary men could study the Bible, and accentuated the need for new commentaries on the Book of Books. Indicative of the situation is the fact that practically the entire contemporary literature in the Judeo-Persian dialect consisted either of translations of, or commentaries to, various books of the Bible. The need for exegetical literature is also illustrated by Saadiah's Arabic translation of the Bible (see above in this chapter), which abounds in exegetical material. An additional favorable factor appeared in Spain. The concentration of the greatest Hebrew grammarians in this country in the tenth and eleventh centuries placed the Hebrew Bible, the main source for Hebrew grammatical studies, in the center of scholarly attention.

To be sure, the contribution of the Babylonian geonim to biblical exegesis, except for Saadiah, was not very conspicuous. In fact, it was limited to occasional commentaries on biblical passages interspersed in the responsa. Geonic activity limited itself to assembling and editing commentaries of former generations. In the same period between the sixth and tenth centuries, "exegetical" work of major importance was done in the Holy Land. Here, and mainly in the circles of the academicians of Tiberias, the *masorah* was developed, consisting of a standardized system of recitation and vowelization of the consonantal text of the Pentateuch. Simultaneously, a new efficient system of *niqqud*, punctuation, was developed and became universally accepted and used down to our own times.

The commentaries on the Bible or on some of its parts then written took on various forms. Some commentators followed the *midrashim*, some, to the great dismay of the traditionalists, employed the allegorical method, others included in their commentaries discussions on unrelated topics, and still others presented interpretations which totally disregarded Rabbinic tradition. First and foremost among the latter was Moses Chiquatilla, who in the eleventh century wrote in Arabic a commentary to most of the biblical books. Although only fragments of his commentary have survived, these leave no doubt that it was full of original and unorthodox interpretations. As he was the first commentator to suggest that chapters 40–66 of the Book of Isaiah belong to a prophet other than Isaiah, Moses Chiquatilla is sometimes referred to as one of the earliest Bible critics. Others, such as Shemariah ben Elhanan in his commentary on the Song of Songs, or Joseph ibn Abitur in his commentary on the Psalms, are much closer to the path of traditional exegesis. What became a commentary to the Bible, towering high above all other exegetical works, was written by Abraham ibn Ezra after he left Spain, and will therefore be discussed in a later chapter describing Jewish culture under Western Christendom.

The Golden Age

The Judeo-Arabic cultural symbiosis attained its highest fruition in the area of Hebrew poetry and belles-lettres. Hebrew poetry, especially in Muslim Spain, reached such heights that it became customary to designate this era as the Golden Age of Hebrew poetry. The explosion of Jewish literary activity was made possible by the fact that Islamic culture in Spain, more than in the other parts of the Muslim world, was pure and new. Here, under Visigothic rule, no heavy residue of former cultures, as in

Byzantium and Persia, had remained, and the way was open to original creativity and innovation.

In the same spirit of innovation, a magnificent secular Hebrew poetry came into being. All the great developments to be described here were closely linked to the political and general situation of the Jews. In those times, before the invention of the art of printing, literature could not become a medium of mass circulation, and was largely addressed to the intellectuals and the aristocracy. It was, in fact, the presence of a high Jewish governmental officialdom which made the Golden Age possible.

The beginning of the Golden Age must be placed in the times of Hisdai ibn Shaprut. Its end, for all practical purposes, occurred about the middle of the thirteenth century, with the virtual conclusion of the *Reconquista*. True, in Christian Spain Jews rose to high office, too. But the creeping Christian religious intolerance put a damper on the free spirit of the Golden Age. The Hebrew poetry of Christian Spain, as we shall see later, bore only a pale resemblance to its southern counterpart.

Originally, all literary creativity was centered in the city of Cordova. With the dissolution of the Umayyad state and the emergence of the many little states with their capitals, a decentralization of Jewish literary activity took place. Seville (called by Moses ibn Ezra "the town of poetry"), Granada, Lucena, and Saragossa were able to write their own pages in the history of the Golden Age. Characteristically, Granada was a hospitable home to Moses ibn Ezra and to the new arrival from the North, Judah Halevi, about 20 years after the massacre of its Jewish community in the riots of 1066. Even the rule of the Almohades did not completely wipe out all traces of the Golden Age in the cities of Andalusia. The symbiosis with Arabic culture put its imprint on many aspects of the literature of the Golden Age. There were translations from Arabic literature, and many Arabic literary forms were harmoniously adopted by the Hebrew poets. Even the rather inexplicable phenomenon of the bilingualism of the literature of the Golden Age, mentioned above, to a degree had its counterpart in Arabic literature. While the population of Andalusia spoke in a distinctly local Arabic idiom, the contemporary Arabic poetry was written in a pure quranic style.

The magnanimity of the Jewish aristocrats which made the Golden Age possible, was also responsible for a decisively unsavory aspect it had. The dependence of the poets on the good will of the maecenases drove the former to often uncontrolled flattery and rivalry. The fact that Judah Halevi, although a physician, was forced to rely on the gifts of the plutocrats, demonstrates the plight of the poets. In light of this, it is not surprising that the poets often resorted to intrigues and plagiarism. It was probably the fear of being plagiarized which prompted so many to include their names in their poems in the form of an acrostic. How commonplace the vying for the favors of the rich was, and, how deep the accompanying frustration, is demonstrated in a cynical verse of one of the giants of the Golden Age, Judah al-Harizi: "I wrap my friends in a cloak of glory, but clothe my enemies with a garment of terror."

Compared with its poetry, the prose of the Golden Age appears rather insignificant. It was simply a victim of the period's Jewish literary bilingualism. Even as passionate a lover of Hebrew as Judah Halevi had no qualms about writing his major philosophical work in Arabic. No doubt the Jews of the Golden Age satisfied their need for entertainment by reading fiction in Arabic. Even the original Jewish collection of short stories composed by the talmudic scholar Nissim ben Jacob of Kairuwan was written in Arabic, and then translated into Hebrew. This widely read translation is known under the name *Sepher hamaasiyoth, The Book of Tales,* or *Hibur yapheh me-ha-yeshuah, The Beautiful Book of Comfort.* Among its 34 stories we find many genres, including romantic narratives, as well as descriptions of pious and charitable acts. While the author's main objective may have been to provide the Jewish reader with edifying and instructive material, he clearly also tried to make his collection cheerful and entertaining. Curiously, the style of the book resembles the language of the philosophers.

Other writers also manifested a preference for the short story by including it in larger works of a nonfictional nature. A classic example of this is Bahya's *Duties of the Hearts.* Often authors used biblical and talmudic motifs to weave fictional narratives, fables, and anecdotes. Nissim's narratives embodied all the elements characteristic of the medieval story, such as witches, evil powers, and evil people. Most of the time, however, the noble and good ultimately had the upper hand. Often, too, the story had a happy ending. A fully developed fictional narrative of the ten "lost" tribes was supplied in the ninth century by an author who posed as one of those lost Jews, Eldad "the Danite." Against this rather modest showing of belles lettres, the nonfictional prose towers high in the various areas of religious literature, as we shall see in the next chapter.

The poetry of the Golden Age was of a dual nature. Its liturgical part, although by far surpassing in quantity and beauty the liturgical poetry of former generations, was basically no different in style and content from the latter. Its secular part, however, was a total innovation, both in its themes and style. More than anything this poetry expressed the cultural symbiosis of the Jews and their Arab contemporaries. And yet it was written exclusively in Hebrew. It was much easier for Jewish poets to express their feelings in the language of the Bible, so well known to them and so dear to them, than to imitate the intricate, and in Spain uncommon, quranic Arabic style.

Simultaneously, when writing secular poetry they consciously moved away from the familiar style of the liturgical poem to a language of biblical purism. Already in the tenth century the poet and grammarian Dunash ibn Labrat demonstrated how the poetic meter employed in contemporary Arabic poetry could be applied to Hebrew verses, and by this charted a road for the giants of the Golden Age. The exquisite beauty of the verses written by Solomon ibn Gabirol and Judah Halevi shows how harmonious and natural the fusion of the Arabic meter and biblical Hebrew had become. Not in vain did Moses ibn Ezra attempt to show in his Arabic work on Hebrew poetry that there was a basic unity between the new Arabic literary forms and the old Hebrew biblical literary heritage.

The basic economic dependence of the poet on the Jewish plutocracy put the imprint of the aristocratic court on his secular poems. Their themes were the beauty of nature and of women, the sweetness of wine, and the delight one finds in true friendship. The court setting also imposed an idealized rather than realistic coloration upon the main themes of the poems. The poets were also keenly aware of the entertainment element which could not be omitted in their poems. They knew that their poems had to compete for attention with the widespread love of music and wit. Only a totally disgruntled Solomon ibn Gabirol, ill and unhappy, who no longer had much hope for social acceptance, could permit himself to pour out his wrath and scorn at the world in some of the most beautiful verses ever written in Hebrew (cf. his poem "My throat became dry from crying").

A poet could expect to be admired when he appeared in the garden among the glittering aristocratic crowd ready to recite a new poem in one of the frequent promotional contests. He was even more admired if he was able to improvise exciting verses on the spot. It is this which explains the inflated number of occasional poems written by the giants of the Golden Age. Naturally, the poetry of the Golden Age was highly personal and very often recounted the experiences of the poet. And as many of them seem to have been perpetually on the move, wandering from place to place and from patron to patron, their poems are like a mirror reflecting conditions, events, and the men and women of the epoch. The first poet of note in this period, Samuel ibn Nagrela, even told in his poems of his experiences while in the field with the forces of the kingdom of Granada.

Under these circumstances writing poetry became a preferred pastime for many. Already in the ninth century Saadiah Gaon felt the need to compose a collection of words suitable for use in versification. It is impossible to say to what degree this manual called *Egron, Collection,* was actually used by people who aspired to write verses. But that there was a need for guides to poetry can be seen from the work of Moses ibn Ezra *The Book of Discussions and Observations* (on Hebrew poetry), which he wrote late in his life. Between the poet-scholar-statesman Samuel ibn Nagrela (Samuel Hanagid) in the middle of the eleventh century, and the end of the period 200 years later, many tried their hand at writing poetry. Moses ibn Ezra, in the middle of the twelfth century, was able to present in the fifth chapter of the above guide to poetry a "history" of Hebrew poetry before his times, with names of poets later almost forgotten. This multitude of poets included, of course, only a limited number of men who had some part in the greatness of the Golden Age. But those who gave it its immortal glamour were mainly Samuel ibn Nagrela, Solomon ibn Gabirol, Moses ibn Ezra, and Judah Halevi. Their poetry signifies the peak of the Golden Age not only by its quality but also by the time of its appearance.

Samuel ibn Nagrela began to write poetry about three quarters of a century after the time considered the chronological beginning of the Golden Age. Judah Halevi disappeared in 1141 and probably died at that time, about 100 years before the date usually considered the chronological termination of the Golden Age. Thus, the poetry of the giants was not an incidental phenomenon but rather a product of a great development that began to peak with Samuel ibn Nagrela. Abraham ibn Daud, a later historian, had a proper perspective of the Golden Age, when he remarked in his work *Sepher haqabalah, Book of Tradition*: "in the times of the *nasi* Rabbi Hisdai (ibn Shaprut), the poets began to chirp, and in the times of the *nagid* Rabbi Samuel (ibn Nagrela) they burst into a loud song."

Solomon ibn Gabirol was born in 1021, probably in Malaga, on the southern tip of the Spanish peninsula. Having lost his parents while still a youngster, he seems to have come soon afterwards to Saragossa, where he spent a considerable part of his life. He was a very studious young man, and devoted all his time and energy to the study of philosophy and of other areas of contemporary knowledge. His great achievements in learning were only matched by his superb poetic talent, which began to reveal itself quite early in his life. He was very poor and thus dependent on handouts from rich patrons. His situation became critical when, due to political intrigues, his main patron was assassinated in 1039. But what really brought undescribable suffering to his short life was a chronic (skin?) disease, which plagued him until his death and virtually isolated him from the rest of the world. Small wonder that his surviving secular poems are full of bitterness and frustration. They belong nevertheless to the most remarkable products of the Golden Age by virtue of their exquisite style and elegant rhyme. As for the themes, they are not much different from those found in contemporary Arab poetry and later Hebrew poetry: nature, love, wine, and friendship. One would assume, however, that in Ibn Gabirol's case these may rather be a response to what was generally expected of a poet than a reflection of his personal experiences. Solomon died in Valencia sometime after 1053.

Moses ibn Ezra was also born in the south of the peninsula, in Granada. The year of his birth is placed between 1055 and 1070. His wealthy parents gave him a thorough Jewish and general education. Until about 1090, when the Almoravids occupied Granada, his was a happy life of a wealthy poet and scholar, admired by many friends, among whom was Judah Halevi. After 1090 Moses' fortunes took a decisive turn for the worse. He had to leave his native city for the life of a wanderer till his death some time before 1140. As was the case with the other great poets, Moses' secular poetry survived to a lesser degree than his religious poems. But what survived attests to his exceptional ability to employ a multifaceted technique of versification. In fact, he was so deeply involved in the art of versification that his lines sometimes sound artificial. All the themes which appeared in the secular poetry of the Golden Age, such as nature, love, friendship, suffering, and death, are represented in Moses' poems too. A sort of mirror of his secular poetry is his work *Anaq, Necklace,* in which he included epigrams and poems on various themes. The work, in which the homonym is the preferred instrument of rhyming is composed of 1,210 verses, and therefore also called *Tarshish,* the Hebrew numerical equivalent of 1,210. The opinion was voiced that Moses' poetry is reminiscent of the verses of his contemporary, Omar Khayyam, the great Persian poet. Moses' work *Discussions and Observations,* mentioned above, made him the first literary critic and theoretician among Jews. In addition to the historical sketch of Hebrew poetry, in this work he discusses rhyme and meter as they appear in the Bible and in Arabic poetry, as well as other aspects of the art of versification. In its totality the book served as a guide to the writing and appreciation of poetry. The work, like most prosaic writings of the Golden Age, was composed in Arabic. It has been translated twice into Hebrew in recent times.

Moses' contemporary, Judah Halevi, was born in Toledo or Tudela, in the center of the peninsula. The date of his birth is a matter of debate and usually given as between 1075 and 1086. However, a review of his biography suggests that he must have been born much earlier, and closer to the year 1060. In his home town he received a thorough Jewish education, and began to show overwhelming poetic talent as a very young man. At what time he received training in the art of medicine is hard to determine. His talent and early fame opened for him the doors of the Ibn Ezra family in Granada. Moses ibn Ezra, then the leading Hebrew poet in Spain, became his close friend and mentor. After spending a few enjoyable years in Granada and its vicinity, Judah went northward, probably compelled to do so by the Almoravid conquest of Granada. He settled in Toledo, then already under Christian control. Here his fame as poet began to surpass that of his mentor. His renown as physician resulted in a call to serve as the king's doctor. He lived in Toledo quite a number of years, but then returned to Muslim Spain to live in Cordova, whose glamor as the cultural capital of Muslim Spain and of its Jews had not yet waned.

About the year 1140 another great change took place in his life. It seems that the general deterioration in the situation of the Jewish people both under Christians and Muslims convinced him that the Jew basically was an alien everywhere. He seems then to have decided that a solution to the Jewish situation lay in emigration to the Holy Land. This was the period when the Muslims began to counterattack the Christian crusaders who had established their rule over Palestine and parts of Syria. Jewish messianic hopes often resurged when *Edom*, that is, the Christians, and *Ishmael*, that is, the Arabs, fought for the possession of the Holy Land. It is therefore not improbable that Judah Halevi believed that the great moment of redemption was arriving. True, at an earlier date he stated his belief that the Messiah would appear in 1130, and experienced the painful disappointment of realizing that his messianic "computation" was wrong. But the author of the *Zionides* continued to cling to his hope of imminent redemption and thought it his personal duty to proceed to the Holy Land.

Be this as it may, in 1140 Judah Halevi left Spain and reached Egypt in the same year. What happened later is not fully clear. After visiting Alexandria and Cairo where he was received with much enthusiasm, he possibly went to Syria. Whether he ever entered the Holy Land cannot be determined. In all likelihood he died in Egypt in 1141. But, the possibility should not be dismissed that there is truth in the widespread legend that the great poet did reach the Holy Land and was killed by an Arab (or, possibly crusader knight) when he prostrated himself to kiss the holy soil, as Jews arriving in the Holy Land used to do.

Due to his enormous poetic talent, his penetration of the depths of the holy tongue, and his ability to express the deepest feelings of the Jewish people, Judah Halevi was considered by his contemporaries, and is still considered today, the greatest Hebrew poet after the biblical writers. As a result, more of his writings came down to us than of any other poet of the Golden Age. This is true of his liturgical as well as of his secular poems. Most of the secular poems are of the type of friendship poems. Evidently, his devotion to personal friends was as deep and sincere as his emotional involvement with the sufferings and hopes of his people. One cluster of his poems is on a theme unique to him. He describes in them a stormy voyage on the high seas in a manner which placed them at the top of the "nature poetry" of the Golden Age. It is generally assumed that these reflect his actual experiences during the voyage to the Near East in 1140. But a perusal of some of the sea poems may also lead to the assumption that Judah perceived his stormy life as sailing on a rough sea. The sea poems could thus be considered a poetic autobiography of "the sweet singer in Israel."

Although Judah Halevi's song signifies the peak of the Golden Age, great talent continued to appear down to the end of the period in the middle of the thirteenth century. Two poets of this time attract our special attention, Abraham ibn Ezra and Judah al-Harizi. Unlike their earlier colleagues they both wrote only in Hebrew and not in Arabic, each for a different reason. Abraham ibn Ezra was born in 1092, probably in Toledo. His fame rests mainly on his commentary to the Bible, one of the major works of all times in this field, and on his prolific writings in various areas of the sciences. But, since he wrote most of these works after leaving Spain, their description will be given later, against the backdrop of Jewish cultural life under Western Christendom. Writing his works in prose in countries outside of the orbit of Arabic culture, he composed them in Hebrew. As for his poetry, it was, of course, written in Hebrew, and mostly composed in Spain. His main contribution as a poet was likewise in the area of liturgy. But he also wrote quite a number of secular poems. Unlike the secular poems of the three giants, his poems contain humor, satire, puns, and linguistic riddles.

A true master of satire and humor was Judah al-Harizi. He was born c. 1168 in Toledo. His mastery of Hebrew and Arabic was unequaled and it was therefore natural that he became a translator par excellence from Arabic into Hebrew of writings by both Jewish and Arab authors. He became aware of the need for such translations when he left Spain to visit southern France, where few Jews could read Arabic works. His poetic soul did not permit him to make literal, painstakingly accurate translations in the way the members of the Tibbon family translated the great works of Sephardic Jewish philosophers. But then, his translation of Maimonides' *Guide of the Perplexed* by far surpasses that of Samuel ibn Tibbon in beauty of style. He also ventured something hitherto untried when he translated into Hebrew a great and popular work of the Arab poet al-Hariri (1054–1122), a native of Iraq. Al-Hariri's fame rests mainly on his *maqamas*. *Maqama* is a literary form developed by the Arabs in which the poet offers a collection of stories and discussions in rhymed prose with metrically designed poems interspersed within the text. Hariri's work is precisely such a collection of *maqamas*. About the time al-Harizi translated Hariri's work he set out on a journey to the Near East, from where he possibly never returned to his native Spain.

During a period of over 20 years he traveled widely in Egypt, the Holy Land, Syria, and Iraq. He, it seems, more than any other of the poets of the Golden Age was dependent on handouts from wealthy patrons, and therefore was perpetually on the move. During these peregrinations he accumulated a wealth of observations, experiences, and impressions. He then recorded all these in the greatest Hebrew work of rhymed prose, which he called *Tahkemoni* (cf. II Samuel 23:8), *Book of Wisdom*, or *Poetic Miscellany*. He clearly modeled *Tahkemoni* after Hariri's work, and likewise arranged it in 50 *maqamas* ("gates"). The Hebrew term *mahbaroth* for *maqamas* was probably coined by him. *Tahkemoni* is a magnificent literary work, overflowing with humor and satire and descriptions of nature, much more realistic than those found in the writings of the other poets of the Golden Age. It possesses a unique vitality with its vivid descriptions of real people and real happenings. Its style endows the work with unique dynamic dimensions. True, the style of *Tahkemoni* never rises to the noble heights of the poems of Judah Halevi. But no one of al-Harizi's predecessors had wrought such magic with the Hebrew language as he did in *Tahkemoni*.

In the almost 300 years since the magnanimity of Hisdai ibn Shaprut launched the great adventure of the Golden Age until the completion of *Tahkemoni* close to the middle of the thirteenth century, a great literature in Hebrew and Arabic came into being in the orbit of Islam, which left an indelible mark on Jewish culture. The religious poetry, as we shall see in the next chapter, gave expression to the deepest feelings of the Jewish people. But it was the laughing, satirical, and often arrogant secular poetry that was the greatest innovation of the Golden Age. True, in the increasingly tense religious atmosphere of the Middle Ages some of the poets, including Moses ibn Ezra and Judah Halevi, are said to have regretted late in their lives having given their talent and time to poems praising wine and women. But the secular poetry was an inevitable phenomenon of the Golden Age, without which much of its glamour would have been lost.

The Sciences

The general climate in the Muslim world was as conducive to science as it was to poetry. The encounter with Greek and Roman culture and the semi-capitalist economic system made scientific inquiry both possible and desirable. The rich scientific Greco-Roman heritage which the Arabs found in the areas conquered from Byzantium and in North Africa beckoned to be translated into Arabic, and so was made an integral part of the new culture of the caliphate and its successor states.

It is not surprising that the mind of the Jew, trained in the dialectics and logic of the Talmud, was receptive to the treasures of science made available to it. Under the new circumstances some of the traditional opposition to "Greek wisdom" may have lost at least some of its strength. Thus we find a Jewish mathematician in the eighth century participating in the drawing up of the plan for the new capital of the Abassid caliphs, Baghdad.

About the same time a Jewish mathematician-astronomer in Egypt made some significant contributions to mathematics. There may also be truth in the theory that the Radhaniya, the Jewish traveler-merchants (cf. above, Chap. 3), or some other Jews, played an important role in transmitting Indian mathematical knowledge to the Arabs. As in the field of philosophy, the first half of the tenth century was the period when the study of the sciences became a visible part of Jewish scholarly endeavor. But only in the eleventh and twelfth centuries did the scientific movement among the Jews of the Muslim world come to its full fruition. Jewish interest manifested itself in most of the sciences. But a real Jewish concentration could be found in mathematics, astronomy, and medicine.

Jewish interest in astronomy was genuine already in the late Antiquity due to the introduction of the pre-calculated calendar. Small wonder that the chapter on the sanctification of the New Moon in Maimonides' *Code of Laws* (Pt. III, Chap. 8) is actually an elaborate treatise on astronomical issues. The more than average interest in astronomy is further indicated by the fact that in the *Epistle to Yemen* too Maimonides describes in detail the world of the planets. More than 100 years before him, Solomon ibn Gabirol provided in his magnificent poem *The Royal Crown* (cf. the next chapter) an elaborate description of the planets and their sizes. True, he had more justification for doing so, since the *Royal Crown* is a prayer of confession, and a description of the planets could demonstrate God's greatness as Creator. But it was primarily Jewish preoccupation with astronomy that made out of the first half of this poem almost a systematic course in astronomy. Perhaps Jewish achievement in mathematics and astronomy could best be illustrated by the penetrating knowledge of these two disciplines possessed by the poet-scientist Abraham ibn Ezra. A description of his works in mathematics and astronomy must, however, be deferred to a later chapter (Sec. XV, Chap. 9), since he wrote them after emigrating to the Christian lands.

Much more substantial was the role played by Jews in the field of medicine. Of great importance was the fact that unlike the rulers of the Christian countries and the Church, medieval Muslim states never prohibited their subjects from patronizing Jewish physicians. Many Jews therefore availed themselves of the opportunity to practice medicine. It is due also to this that rabbis in the Near East and the Mediterranean, more than their colleagues in the northern countries, could afford the luxury of teaching Torah without remuneration, and derive their livelihood from the practice of medicine.

Ample sources of medical knowledge were available to the Jewish scientists. Medical works translated into Arabic from Greek and Persian were available to Jewish students in the same measure as to their non-Jewish colleagues. In addition, there was in the Near East a body of Jewish medical knowledge going back to a great Jewish teacher in medicine, Asaph, who lived and taught either in Galilee, Syria, or Babylonia, some time prior to the Arab conquest. His teachings in the art of medicine and in medical ethics were widely studied from a work compiled in Hebrew by his disciples and known as *Sepher Asaph haropheh, The Book of Asaph the Physician.* The influence of this work on Jewish medicine can be estimated from the fact that many terms used in it became part and parcel of the standard Jewish medieval medical terminology. Of course, as in the other sciences, Jews played a non-negligible role in rendering into Arabic ancient medical works from Syriac and Greek.

The Jewish doctors in the Muslim countries received their training by serving as apprentices to other physicians and from medical books. Moses Maimonides, for example, studied medicine with his father Rabbi Maimon, and in turn taught the art to his son Abraham and to a number of disciples. But there is no doubt that the "Great Eagle" received most of his knowledge by studying medical books. Since the terminology he used in his own medical writings was mostly Arabic, Spanish, and Berber, we may assume that in his studies he perused medical works available in these three languages. There must have been a multitude of Jewish physicians in the Muslim countries, and some were called to serve in the courts and palaces. Such was the case with Hisdai ibn Shaprut, Maimonides, and some lesser figures. Of Maimonides we know that he was a very popular physician. His antechambers were always full of patients: "Gentiles and Jews, important and unimportant men, judges and officers, friends and opponents, a mixed multitude." How much Jewish physicians viewed their occupation as a noble vocation is clearly shown by

Maimonides' attitude to the multitude of his patients. Even when he was aging and his vigor waning, he still attended to them after spending most of the day in the sultan's palace. He listened to them, advised them, and wrote them prescriptions while lying on his back from sheer fatigue.

Jewish medical literature, while quantitatively much smaller than that produced by Muslim scientists, was by no means negligible. Original works in medicine were written by Jewish doctors as early as the eighth century. The ninth century produced the first Jewish medical writer of note in the person of Isaac Israeli, who was, as we have seen, equally great as a philosopher. His works were translated into Latin in the eleventh century, and were widely used. They became popular textbooks in use at the famous medical school in Salerno, Italy. In the tenth century, Hisdai ibn Shaprut, the physician-diplomat of Cordova, made himself a name by translating into Arabic, in cooperation with a monk, an important Greek medical work. A first in medical literature was a multilingual pharmaceutical dictionary authored by a Jewish scientist in Saragossa about the year 1080.

As in many other areas, however, it was Moses Maimonides who made the greatest Jewish contribution to the medical literature of the Middle Ages. Significantly, he wrote his medical works during the last 15 years of his life, about the same time he worked on *The Guide of the Perplexed*. Like the *Guide*, his ten works in medicine were composed in Arabic and, like the *Guide*, most of them were translated into Hebrew and Latin. They attained great popularity in the Gentile scientific community, probably more than any other Jewish medical work. Although typical medieval works, they contain many a modern element. Maimonides the physician insisted on careful observation of the patient and his lifestyle in arriving at a diagnosis. He also encouraged the physicians to engage in experimentation, a quite modern attitude. And it is certainly not surprising that the man who as a philosopher insisted on the use of reason in theological thinking, decisively rejected as a physician the use of amulets, incantations, and charms as medical remedies. The daily prayer of a physician, popularly known as the oath of Maimonides, is not authentic, and was possibly written by a doctor as late as the second half of the eighteenth century.

Chapter 6

The Religious Life

Religious Leadership

The religious life of the Jews in the Muslim world during the period of the Early Middle Ages was as vibrant as their culture. The protection promised the *dhimmis* was with few exceptions an effective safeguard for their religious practice. The quest of some intellectuals for a rational justification of the beliefs and practices of the Jewish religion seems to have been satisfactorily answered by Saadiah, Maimonides, and the other religious thinkers. Characteristically, despite the controversies that had arisen around Maimonides' ideas, Jews in the orbit of Islam seem to have had no doubts about his orthodoxy. Such doubts were effectively allayed by his statement in the commentary to the Mishnah (Introduction to Chapter Heleq) that ". . . if a man gives up any one of these fundamental principles [i.e., the 13 articles of faith], he has removed himself from the Jewish community. He is an atheist, a heretic, an unbeliever, who 'cuts among the plantings.' We are commanded to hate him and to destroy him. . . ." Mystic speculation, although not unknown among the academicians of Sura and Pumbedita as well as among other sages, was not taught publicly and did not arouse any controversy.

The area in which controversy was the order of the day was the issue of the legitimacy of the Jewish religious leadership. At the time the Muslim empire emerged, two centers of Jewish religious leadership were in existence. The center of Torah learning in Tiberias (cf. Vol. I, Sec. VIII, Chaps. 5 and 6) continued to wield a high degree of religious authority despite the diminished size of Palestine's Jewish community. Of similar importance was the center of religious authority in Babylonia (Iraq), where the gaonate, as we have seen, had become an established institution on the eve of the Muslim conquest. But it was inevitable that the geonim would soon gain the upper hand in their quest for controlling the religious life of the Jews. To begin with, their authority rested on their being direct continuators of the creators of the Babylonian Talmud, a work which clearly was more suitable as a guide to Jewish religious life than its Palestinian counterpart, the Jerusalem Talmud. The enormous size of Iraq's Jewish population in comparison with Palestine's tiny Jewish community further enhanced the authority of the Babylonian geonim. Their authority, of course, began to reach its peak when the Abassids made Iraq the center of their empire.

The main goal of the geonim was to impose upon the entire Jewish people the Halakhah as presented in the Babylonian Talmud. They did it by deciding which laws of the Talmud were applicable to the contemporary scene. Simultaneously, they attempted to combat, though with only partial success, the proliferation of divergent *minhagim*, that is, customs and usages, resulting from the continuous geographic expansion of the Diaspora. A ninth-century Babylonian scholar, Pirqoi ben Baboi, in his ardor to promote the Babylonian Talmud went so far as to oppose the Jerusalem Talmud and to denounce the religious practice of the Jews of the Holy Land. Whenever necessary the geonim felt authorized to complement the talmudic law by their own ordinances, since they considered the academies of Sura and Pumbedita to be "contemporary Sanhedrins." The technical instrument of their guidance was, as we have seen, the responsum, especially devised by them for this purpose. The leadership bid of the geonim met with full success as long as the caliphate remained a strong and well-knit state. The caliphs accorded recognition to the two-fold law represented by the Talmud. The overwhelming majority of the Jews lived, as we have seen, within the confines of the caliphate. As Baghdad was the political center of the empire, the geonic academies were by nature the religious center of the Jews of the caliphate.

But it was also inevitable that in the Holy Land the leadership of the Babylonian geonim should be followed only grudgingly and even with opposition. This happened especially when, under Muslim rule, Palestine's Jewish community began to grow in number and Jerusalem again became the seat of a sizable Jewish population and an academy. The claim of the heads of the Jerusalem Academy to a status of equality with their Babylonian counterparts was clearly demonstrated by the fact that they assumed the title of gaon. We have seen (cf. above, Chap. 5) how a Jerusalem gaon made the issue of Jewish calendation a test case in his rivalry with the Babylonian geonim. To what degree the Jerusalem geonim succeeded in asserting their authority in religious matters other than the calendar is impossible to say. In the matter of the calendar, however, the old tradition prevailed. Saadiah's victory over the Jerusalem gaon Aaron ben Meir turned out to be of a temporary nature, and Jerusalem again became the authoritative source for Jewish calendric regulation.

With the progressive dissolution of the caliphate, the authority of the geonim of Sura and Pumbedita as the sole religious leaders of the Jewish people began weakening. The many local Rabbinical academies which sprang up in the breakaway countries produced a class of scholars who felt adequate to direct the religious life of their communities. They, therefore, did not see the need, and probably were unwilling, to contact the far-off sages in Iraq.

Reliable evidence shows that in Spain and the neighboring countries the responsa of Moses ben Hanokh of Cordova were accorded validity similar to those of the Babylonian geonim. It was incomparably easier to secure an opinion from a local religious authority than to wait many months, or even years, for a reply from Babylonia. The statement of the historian Abraham ibn Daud that the ruler of Cordova was pleased with the great religious authority enjoyed by Moses ben Hanokh because "the Jews of his kingdom no longer needed the men of Babylon," is probably based on solid historical tradition. A similar motivation may also have prompted a certain Fatimid ruler of Egypt to extend financial support to the Academy of Jerusalem, then within the confines of his realm. It was quite natural that when Palestine and Syria were annexed by the Fatimids late in the tenth century, all Jews of the Fatimid empire looked to Jerusalem for religious guidance. Characteristic of the religious independence of the Jews in the breakaway countries was the title *gaon* by which the sages of Kairuwan were often addressed and which some of the heads of the Cairo academy assumed.

Religious Practice and Prayer

On the local level, the religious life was guided and supervised by a *dayyan*, the Jewish communal judge, who often was an appointee of the head of the country's central talmudic academy. Early in the period the religious behavior of communities and individuals was in a state of variation and fluctuation. In Palestine, for example, it was customary to read the Torah in a triennial cycle. The above-mentioned Eldad, who allegedly belonged to the lost tribe of Dan, brought along, from wherever he came, a set of laws pertaining to ritual slaughter quite different from those usually followed. But in later times more unity appeared. Characteristic of this is the fact that Maimonides' ritualistic decisions differed from those of Isaac Alfasi only in a very limited number of cases. Obviously, toward the end of the Early Middle Ages the Jewry in the orbit of Islam had arrived at more unified forms of its daily religious life. In a sense, Maimonides' *Code* may be considered as the culmination of the endeavor to organize and to formulate a systematic body of Jewish law and ritual. Even the Jews of the Holy Land, who had time-honored practices of their own, gave up some of them. The triennial cycle of the reading of the Torah was abandoned at the beginning of the thirteenth century in favor of the generally followed annual cycle. Under the impact of immigrants from Western Europe they also began to celebrate in the Holy Land the New Year as a two-day festival.

Even greater in the beginning was the lack of uniformity in the orders of prayer followed in the synagogues. Medieval Jewry inherited from Antiquity two different orders of prayer, the Palestinian and the Babylonian. It is worth noting that even as important a prayer as the *amidah* had different texts in the two orders of prayer. Nonetheless, synagogue worship made great strides in this period toward standardization. The reluctance of the talmudic times to have prayers written down was gone, and the Hebrew designation for the prayerbook *Seder tephilah* or *Siddur tephilah*, came into use early in the geonic period.

Three of the Babylonian geonim made an effort to standardize the prayer book, but were only partly successful. First Amram, gaon of Sura in the middle of the ninth century, arranged a prayer book in response to a request from Spain. More than half a century later, Saadiah too arranged an order of prayers. About 100 years later Hai, the last of the geonim of Pumbedita, made a third effort at standardizing the prayer book. Hai's *siddur* has not come down to us, but we may assume that his prayer book, like that of Amram Gaon, represented the Babylonian order of prayer. As for Saadiah's *siddur*, which he began to arrange in 910 while still in Egypt, we may assume that at least in part it reflected local Egyptian worship usages. The scholars are divided in their opinions as to the acceptance of Amram's and Saadiah's prayerbooks by the various Jewish communities. While it is certain that Yemenite Jewry accepted Saadiah's *siddur*, it is debatable to what degree Spanish Jewry followed Amram's order of prayer. Some scholars believe that the Spanish (Sephardic) rite, which assumed its standard form at the end of the Early Middle Ages, originated directly in the Babylonian order of prayer. Others believe to have discovered in the Sephardic rite the old Palestinian order of prayer tinged by influences from Amram's responsum-*siddur*. Be this all as it may, by the end of the Early Middle Ages, the Jewish communities in the orbit of Islam had well-organized orders of synagogue ritual.

In addition to its standardization, the prayer book underwent in this period a process of expansion by absorbing a great multitude of *piyyutim*, that is, liturgical poems. Originally the prayer book consisted of selections from the Bible, especially the Psalms, and a limited number of prayers written during the period of the Second Commonwealth and in the late Antiquity. The custom of writing special poems for the enhancement of holiday worship probably first developed in the Byzantine empire. The presence of many religious hymns in Byzantium's Christian literature may have had some influence on the emergence of the *piyyut*. This is, incidentally, indicated by the use of the word *payyetan* for the author of a Hebrew liturgical poem, and *piyyut* for such a poem, both derivations from Greek. In fact, the first liturgical poet of the period, Eliezer (or Eleazar) Qalir, lived within the confines of the Byzantine empire, and probably in the Holy Land, at the very time the young Muslim empire absorbed large parts of Byzantium.

Once begun, the liturgical additions to the prayer book grew in number and variety. Saadiah, for example, included in his prayer book some of his own poems. But, the *piyyut* came to real fruition in Spain. Joseph ibn Abitur, who is often termed the first native Hebrew poet in Spain, wrote hundreds of *piyyutim*. And so did the giants of the Golden Age, and the exegete-scientist Abraham ibn Ezra. There is one basic difference between the *piyyut* and Spain's secular Hebrew poetry. While the secular poetry lavishly borrowed its metric forms from contemporary Arabic poetry, the *piyyut*, with very few exceptions, strictly followed the purely Jewish biblical literary forms.

The piyyutic contributions of Solomon ibn Gabirol, Moses ibn Ezra, and Judah Halevi were overwhelming. Their deep religiosity led them to lend to their liturgical poems all their talent and passion. It was probably when Solomon ibn Gabirol felt that his trouble-filled life was approaching its end, that he wrote *The Royal Crown*. In this magnificent poem of 40 stanzas, one of the few medieval Hebrew poems to be given a name by the author, Solomon first described God's greatness as Creator, and followed this by a confession, usually recited by a Jew during his last moments. The content of this poem so moved generations of Jews in many lands that it became customary to recite it Yom Kippur night following the regular services. Moses ibn Ezra's main liturgical contribution also focused on the period of the High Holidays. He wrote many *selihoth*, penitential prayers of the type Jews recite during the night hours of the High Holidays season. This contribution became so important that it earned him the title *hasalah*, the *selihoth* writer. The other Ibn Ezra, Abraham, also wrote liturgical poems, which were included in various prayer books. His hymns strike us with their remarkable subtlety and fervent devotion. This, of course, is quite remarkable when we remember how full of humor, sarcasm, and satire his secular poems are.

As in all other fields of poetry in the Golden Age, Judah Halevi's religious poems tower above those of the other poets. Many of them entered the prayer books for the various holidays and are easily recognizable by the beauty and smoothness of their verse. Those known as Zionides made the deepest impression on the Jewish people. In these 35 poems, each beginning with the word *Zion*, Judah gave unequaled expression to the unique romantic attachment of the Jewish people to the Holy Land and to the yearning for its restoration. One of them, beginning with the verse: "Zion! Wilt thou not ask . . ." had endeared itself immensely to the Jewish people. Later Hebrew poets imitated it many times, and it was translated into many languages. It was only natural that these 35 poems became a major part of the prayers of mourning and hope recited by Jews annually on the ninth day of the month of Av, when the destruction of the Temple in Jerusalem is commemorated.

To be sure, the inclusion of the many liturgical poems in the prayer book was not universally welcomed. No less a figure than Moses Maimonides opposed the interruption of the established order of prayers by new hymns. And even after scores of liturgical poems began to be printed in the holiday prayer books, it remained clear that they had no status of real sanctity and were not part of the obligatory prayers. But the liturgical hymns were nevertheless a novel and much-needed instrument for the medieval Jew, who was "breathing religion," to give expression to his deepest feelings. Maimonides' opinion was thus ignored and the *piyyutim* became an integral part of the Jewish worship.

Religious Unrest

So far we have seen that in the orbit of Islam the Jew could serve his God relatively undisturbed. But Jewish religious life nevertheless was not fully peaceful. From time to time the Muslims deviated from the principle of toleration and did force Jews to convert to their faith. For example, such was the case with Jews in the Caucasus on whom the Muslims imposed their religion upon conquering the country in the ninth century. We have also seen (cf. above, Chapter 3) how episodic religious persecutions took place in Egypt in the eleventh century and in Yemen in the twelfth century, and how the Almohades attempted to outlaw Judaism in North Africa and Spain during the many decades of their rule. Still not fully clear is the reason why the number of Jews who did convert to Islam was infinitesimal in comparison with the large masses of Parsees and Christians who turned Muslim. Maimonides' compassionate attitude to those forcibly converted and his assertion that under adverse circumstances charitable deeds and abridged prayer still led to salvation, may have helped the Jewish community to retain its integrity.

Hatred of the dominant religion was not absent in the Jewish community in the orbit of Islam. Since the status of "second-class citizenship" was dictated by the Muslim religion, Jewish resentment naturally turned against Islam. The Quran, in comparison with the Jewish Bible, was considered a very unsophisticated book. Mohammed was often called "the madman," even by such a self-controlled personality as Moses Maimonides. Religious disputations with Muslims were rare and mostly unimportant in content. Obviously, there were incomparably fewer points of contention between Judaism and Islam than between Judaism and Christianity. In addition, the main thrust of the Muslim religious challenge directed itself against Christianity, and interest in attacking Judaism was considerably less. One issue that constantly irritated the Jews was the Muslim accusation that the Pentateuch was not of divine origin but rather a forgery of Ezra the Scribe. Because of this accusation, Maimonides advised his coreligionists to stay away altogether from religious disputations with their Muslim neighbors. Of course, even without such disputations, the Jews had ample opportunities to challenge and contradict Muslim doctrines. Saadiah, Judah Halevi, and Maimonides did this forcefully in their philosophical works.

Challenges to Jewish religious doctrine were also raised on the part of insiders. During the first half of the twelfth century, for example, many doctrines opposing normative Judaism were common among the people. Some were lax in the observance of the Law and attempted to justify their behavior theologically. More serious attacks on normative Judaism had occurred much earlier on the eastern outskirts of the caliphate. A certain Hiwi al-Balkhi, in late ninth century Khorasan, came out with a set of critical attacks on the Pentateuch, which resembled modern critical challenges to Scriptures. The seriousness of this attack can be fathomed by the fact that Saadiah saw fit to denounce it with a strong counterattack. The outlying eastern regions of the caliphate were generally a hotbed of religious dissent, and it was here that a Jewish schism was born, which never healed, the schism of Karaism.

Chapter 7

Karaism and the Karaites

The Emergence of the Sect

There are many divergent theories as to how and when the Karaite sect came into being. What seems to be certain is that the Karaite schism is rooted in events which took place generations before the sect appeared as a separate religious and social body. We have emphasized in the preceding chapter that here and there heterodox tendencies raised their heads repeatedly in defiance of the authority of the geonim and the other religious leaders. Such tendencies were common especially in Persia and neighboring Khorasan, which included Afghanistan and parts of Turkestan. Here religious customs were followed which differed from those of normative Judaism. Even the local Jewish calendar was not fully identical with the one accepted by the bulk of the Jewish people. These religious differences were accompanied by a strong opposition to the aristocratic behavior of the exilarchs and the oligarchic religious rule of the geonim. True, most Jews in these regions probably followed the dual leadership whose center was in Baghdad. But it seems certain that here protest and deviation from the norm were more articulate and keen than in other places.

These tendencies began to harden early in the eighth century. In Isfahan, a city in south-central Persia, a certain Obadiah, mostly known by his Arabic name Abu Isa, seems to have established a Jewish schismatic group, which after his death was led by a certain Yudgan (probably identical with Judah), and later by a third leader, Mushka. The two outstanding characteristics of this obscure group, which seems to have survived to the tenth century, were an active "messianism" and a tendency towards an ascetic way of life.

A few decades later a schism of major proportions developed in Baghdad, the very seat of the exilarchate and gaonate. The gravity of this breakaway was even more serious due to the fact that its main champion was a member of the exilarchal family, Anan ben David. In 767, Anan, obviously a learned man, renounced his allegiance to the Oral Law and its main repository, the Talmud. He maintained that the Oral Law was man-made and that only the Written Law as found in the Bible is of divine origin and obligatory upon every Jew. At the same time he promulgated, or adopted, a previously existing extra-talmudic collection of laws which he called *The Book of Precepts*. These laws were quite different from those of normative Judaism. Whether at the same time he began to emphasize new social and nationalistic ("Zionist") ideas, as well as the principle that every Jew is free to interpret the Holy Scriptures in his own way, is still a matter of debate. Anan's ideas attracted a number of followers, who became known as Ananites.

During the subsequent 100 years various other dissident religious groups surfaced, some of which professed beliefs similar to those of Anan, and some of which opposed normative Judaism but simultaneously also rejected Anan and his teachings. By the middle of the ninth century, however, all these dissident groups began to crystallize and form a more solid anti-talmudic front, even though many of their differences continued to exist. Meanwhile the new sect began to produce scholars and thinkers who laid the foundations for its legal system and theology. Foremost among them were Benjamin Nahawendi, who was active as a writer in the first quarter of the ninth century, and Daniel al-Qumisi, who flourished late in the ninth and early in the tenth century. The progressing uniformity of the sect was further signified by the name *Benei miqra*, or *Qaraim*, "champions of Scripture" now used by the entire movement. This name was coined by Benjamin Nahawendi. The sect was also supplied with a "history," according to which it came into being at the time of King Solomon's death, in the tenth century B.C.E. The movement also began to glorify Anan, probably because he was the first to write or adopt a manual of extra-talmudic Jewish religious law. The later "Zionist" tendencies of the sect were also ascribed to him, and he was erroneously credited with the establishment of the Karaite community in Jerusalem. Anan's descendants were accorded the title of *nesiim*, patriarchs, due to the alleged merits of their forefather.

By that time the Karaites had clearly cut themselves off from the Jewish people and had become a separate religious community. The circumstances due to which this separation became final are still not fully clear. Most scholars are of the opinion that the separation of the Karaites resulted from their uncompromising opposition to the gaonate and exilarchate and to the Talmud on which the authority of the latter rested. Others, however, are of the opinion that the breach would never have become final if not for the over-reaction of the Rabbinic leadership which declared the Karaite schismatics guilty of heresy. Under these circumstances the breach became inevitable and has never healed.

Religious Doctrine and Practice

Benjamin Nahawendi and Daniel al-Qumisi were followed by a galaxy of scholars and authors who turned the tenth and eleventh centuries into a golden age of Karaite literature. These sages made a heroic effort to arrive at some consensus with regard to Karaite doctrine and religious practice. The challenge was great not only because of the composite nature of the group, but it was even more serious due to the principle that every Jew has the right to interpret the Holy Writ for himself. And yet, such a consensus began to replace the doctrinal chaos. This is best evidenced by the encyclopedic character of Jacob Qirqisani's voluminous work *The Book of Lights* (composed in the tenth century), which contains an extensive description of the laws followed by the Karaites. Incidentally, Qirqisani's work was written in Arabic, as were most Karaite writings of the tenth and eleventh centuries. Karaite biblical exegesis, seemingly unnecessary in a society in which every one was supposed to be his own commentator, made great strides forward. In fact, Karaism then produced a remarkable number of grammarians and exegetes. The concentration on the Bible as the only source of the law helped to overcome the original exegetical individualism. Thus, before the tenth century was over, Japheth ben Ali wrote, 100 years before Rashi, what became the major Karaite commentary to the Bible. He also translated the Bible into Arabic.

The consensus, as far as it existed, began with an uncompromising rejection of the Talmud, at least theoretically. The way to derive laws directly from the Bible was by applying to it the instrument of reason. Despite this, the Karaite law emerged from this process as a body of strict, rigorous, and literally interpreted laws. An example of this are the Karaite marriage laws which prohibit marriages between relatives in cases allowed by Rabbanite interpretation. The excessive rigidity of the law compelled the Karaites in later times to "liberalize" it. The deviation from the original Karaite principles went even as far as to accept the surprising principle that religious customs do not need to emanate directly from the Bible. What is needed is merely the certainty that the Bible does not contradict them. Hand in hand with this went a weakening of the opposition to the Talmud. A thirteenth-century writer even ventured to say that "most of the sayings of the Mishna . . . stem from our (Karaite) Fathers." Two hundred years later this view was endorsed by Elijah Bashyatchi, who is considered the final codifier of Karaite law.

The exclusive concentration on the Bible acted as a damper on the development of a philosophical, ethical, and mystical literature. True, Karaism did produce a number of philosophical works. But these can in no way compare with the philosophical literature created by Sephardic Jewry and the pietistic literature produced by medieval Ashkenazic Jewry. Karaite speculative talent, as we shall see later, exhausted itself in an endless controversy with the Rabbanites.

As a whole, the views of the Karaites on God, the universe, and the Jew's role in history were not much different from those of the Rabbanites. If anything, early Karaism put a greater emphasis on the role of the Holy Land in the life of the Jew. It was probably due to the historical situation of the Jewish people that the belief in the coming of the Messiah entrenched itself deeply in the heart of many of Karaism's early leaders, even though the messianic idea is not found in the Pentateuch. The duty of the Jew to tie his personal destiny to the Holy Land became an accepted Karaite view some 200 years before Judah Halevi startled his contemporaries with his decision to emigrate there. As a result, the proportion of Karaites among the *avele Zion*, the mourners of Zion, who made it their life task to pray at the Western Wall for the restoration of the Temple, was much greater than warranted by the size of the sect. In later times, when a prosperous Karaite diaspora established itself in various countries, the fervent Messianism and Palestinocentrism sublimated into prayer for redemption.

Karaite religious practice like Karaite dogma originally was rigorous and uncompromising, but ultimately softened and moved somewhat closer to Rabbanite usage. To begin with, the tendency toward a strictly ascetic life followed by the early adherents of the sect was gradually given up by later generations. The later teachers also realized that an exclusively literal interpretation of the Pentateuch was impossible, and began to tacitly permit the development of a Karaite oral law which became known as *sevel hayerushah*, the burden of inheritance. The religious practice of the Karaites nevertheless remained quite different from that of the Rabbanites. Most striking was the difference in the way the Karaites observed the Sabbath. Abstention from any form of work was much more strict than among the Rabbanites. The prohibition of kindling fire on the Sabbath (Exodus 35:3) was interpreted by Anan as mandating the spending of Sabbath eves in darkness. Similarly, the passage in Exodus 16:29 "... let no man go out of his place on the seventh day" was understood as a commandment not to leave one's house on the Sabbath. After having observed the Sabbath in this manner for centuries, the Karaites of the Byzantine empire and of Eastern Europe began in the late Middle Ages to light Sabbath candles.

Similar developments took place with regard to the calendar. Originally the Karaites rejected the pre-calculated calendar, which had been in use among the Jews for several centuries (cf. Vol. I, Sec. VIII, Chap. 5), because it was produced by talmudic sages. They re-introduced the proclamation of the New Moon by the method of lunar observation, and made the promulgation of a leap year dependent on the ripening of barley in the Holy Land, which they identified with *aviv* mentioned in the Pentateuch (cf. Exodus 9:31 and Leviticus 2:14). This method, of course, presented the outlying Karaite communities with the difficulties encountered in the Antiquity by the Jewish Diaspora, due to which the pre-calculated calendar was introduced in the first place. It is therefore not surprising that the Byzantine and East European Karaite communities began to gradually abandon the *aviv* method of determining the leap year in favor of the nineteen-year cycle pre-calculated calendar. This process was completed in the second half of the thirteenth century. The Karaite holidays nevertheless do not always coincide with the Rabbanite holidays. It should be noted that the Karaites do not observe the Hanukah holiday, since it is not rooted in the Bible. And the number of fast days is much larger than in normative Judaism.

The Karaite prayer book is quite different from the various Jewish religious rites. Originally, the Karaites tended to include in their prayer services solely biblical texts, and especially many of the Psalms. Later, however, new original prayers began to be composed. Some efforts were also made at compiling a standardized prayerbook. The most felicitous attempt in this direction was undertaken in the second half of the thirteenth century by the Byzantine scholar and poet Aaron ben Joseph ("the Elder"). His compilation then became the generally accepted Karaite prayerbook. The East European Karaites also added some prayers in the Turkic dialect in use among them. The use of phylacteries during the morning service on weekdays was also, of course, rejected since there is no clear mention of them in the Pentateuch. The Karaite house of worship is usually called *kenesah* or *kinasah*. The two most important religious functionaries are the *hakham*, scholar, spiritual leader, and the *hazzan*, the reader of the service.

Karaite-Rabbanite Relations

When the adherents of the new sect began to be called Karaites, the believers in normative Judaism began to be designated as Rabbanites. The Karaites also referred to the Rabbanites as *baalei qabbalah*, adherents of tradition. Although it was clear from the very beginning that the Karaite schism was more serious than any deviation since the appearance of Christianity, no systematic fight seems to have developed between the two Jewish camps during the first 100 years. Saadiah seems to have been the first Jewish religious leader to have seen in the new schismatics a serious menace. He then unleashed against them, as we have seen (cf. above, Chap. 5), a relentless literary attack. The seriousness of

the blow the Karaites received from Saadiah's attacks is best illustrated by the endless, and often abusive counter-attacks of Karaite
scholars even hundreds of years after Saadiah's death. Their main
attack directed itself, of course, against the Talmud, in which
they believed they had discovered abominable things. They found
a preferred target in its colorful anthropomorphic aggadoth. Of
course, they did not attack the many anthropomorphisms in the
Bible. Karaite attacks on the Talmud sometimes resembled objec-
tions raised against it by Christians in their religious disputations
with Jews. Jewish mysticism, too, was attacked by the Karaites
and termed idolatry and witchcraft.

And yet, from time to time the heat abated, and Karaites and
Rabbanites lived together in fairly amicable relations. Ironically,
this was the case, more than anywhere else, in Egypt, Saadiah's
homeland. Here even intermarriage between Rabbanites and
Karaites was frequent. Moses Maimonides, then living in Egypt,
treated the Karaites in a friendly manner. His leniency went as far
as to permit Jews to officiate at Karaite religious ceremonies,
whenever these conformed to normative Judaism as, for example,
circumcision and burial. Friendly relations between the two
groups developed also in Byzantium-Turkey. When Aaron the
Elder organized the prayer book, he did not hesitate to include in
it poems by Solomon ibn Gabirol, Judah Halevi, and other Rabbanite *payyetanim*. Here too Karaites did not find it objectionable to
study with Rabbanite teachers. No less a sage than the above-
mentioned Elijah Bashyatchi, the final codifier of Karaite law, had
Rabbanite scholars among his teachers. In such periods of rap-
prochment, each side used to address the other with the appela-
tion "our brothers."

However, reunification was never considered. Daniel al-
Qumisi believed that with the coming of the Messiah Karaism
would have a total victory over Rabbanism. In the fourteenth
century a Cretan-born Rabbanite scholar, Shemaryah of Neg-
roponte, made an attempt to bring about some sort of reconciliation between the two groups. In his commentaries to the Bible
Shemaryah proposed interpretations often acceptable to the
Karaites. His attempt at reconciliation, in behalf of which he
traveled to Spain in 1352, was, however, unsuccessful. Karaite
attempts at missionizing among Rabbanites were largely futile.

The possibly large numbers of Iraqi Jews who in the tenth century joined the Karaite sect probably did it due to their disillusionment with the exilarchal-geonic establishment rather than because of a preference for Karaite doctrine and practice.

The Karaites in the Orbit of Islam

From their cradle in Iraq and Persia, the Karaites began to expand and establish communities all over the caliphate and the breakaway countries. The first target of the Karaite emigrants was the Holy Land. Here they hoped to hasten redemption by their prayers and the very presence of their community, as well as to have a continuous opportunity of observing the ripening of the *aviv*. Here too they were less exposed to Rabbanite wrath in the tenth century when Saadiah's influence was so decisive in Iraq-Babylonia. There is no truth in the Karaite claim that their community was established by Anan. Some of Anan's descendants, however, did settle in Jerusalem and attempted to establish themselves as patriarchs of the Holy Land. The Palestinian Karaite community kept on growing and reached its heyday in the tenth and eleventh centuries. In fact, the community became a seat of learning which surpassed in importance that of the founding communities in Persia and Babylonia. The conquest of Jerusalem by the crusaders in 1099 put an end to the Karaite community, as it did to the Rabbanite. After the Muslims re-conquered the Holy Land, the Karaites returned. However, their community never regained its former glory. It remained small in number and poor, and largely subsisted on donations from the East-European Karaite communities.

More numerous than the Palestinian community was the communities in Persia and Babylonia. The conquest of Jerusalem by the crusaders in 1099 put an end to the Karaite community, as Some scholars are of the opinion that prior to the middle of the twelfth century the Karaites may even have outnumbered the Rabbanites in Egypt. In addition, they were economically prosperous and wealthy. Conceivably, this was the Karaite power encountered by Saadiah in his youth in Egypt which frightened him and fanned his uncompromising attack on the teachings of the sect. Saadiah's attack—so detrimental to the Karaite cause in Iraq-Babylonia—seems, however, to have done little harm to Egypt's Karaite community. Some of Anan's descendants even attempted to set up a Karaite "exilarchate" in Fustat. However, most of the time the Karaites were represented before the government by the Rabbanite *nagid*. As mentioned above, Karaite-Rabbanite relations here were largely peaceful, and intermarriage between members of the two groups seems to have encountered no opposition. In the second half of the twelfth century, Karaism in Egypt began to decline. Maimonides' religious influence was so overwhelming that it could not help but tip the scales in favor of Rabbanism. But although devoid of its earlier glory, the Egyptian Karaite community survived into modern times as one of the major Karaite centers.

Karaism also spread westward into the other countries in North Africa, especially Algeria and Morocco. Karaites possibly were present here already in the last decades of the tenth century. Solid evidence of their presence, however, comes from a somewhat later period, the first half of the eleventh century. Their settlement in western North Africa seems not to have been dense. In eastern Algeria a nomadic warrior tribe adhered to Karaism. The most important Karaite community in Morocco lived in Fez, and in the eleventh century attained the status of an important religio-cultural center. In the twelfth century the Karaites made an effort to strengthen their position in these countries, but only with limited success. We do not know what was the fate of the Karaite settlement under the oppressive rule of the Almohades, but most likely they did not fare better than the Rabbanites. Their communities seem to have survived only in the Atlas mountains. In Morocco we find early in the sixteenth century two Karaite communities in the Atlas region. The warrior community in eastern Algeria also survived, since the Almohades never occupied this area. Some scholars believe the Algerian mountain Jews (known in modern times as Bahutsim) to be descendants of the warrior Karaites of the Middle Ages. Outside of the mountain regions only few, if any, Karaites lived in Algeria and Morocco during the late Middle Ages.

Karaism's road in Spain was quite stormy. We do not know exactly when the Karaites established themselves there. It is certain that in the tenth century the sect was present in Spain, and it may possibly have been there as early as the ninth century. At first insignificant, and possibly in hiding, it became strong enough in the second half of the eleventh century to begin missionizing among the Rabbanites with some degree of success. By then a number of communities existed, both in the Muslim South and the Christian North, the most sizable of which was that of Toledo. The Rabbanites became obviously apprehensive that Karaism might make inroads into the Jewish community. They therefore began to fight the Karaite menace in various ways. Jews holding high office in Christian Spain used their influence and power to persecute the sect. One such Jewish dignitary, the physician Joseph ibn Ferrizuel, succeeded in bringing about the expulsion of the Karaites from the areas of their settlement in Castile and their concentration in a single locality. This action, harsh as it was, seems not to have brought about the downfall of the sect. Other Jewish dignitaries, among whom was Judah ibn Ezra, continued Ferrizuel's anti-Karaite policy during most of the twelfth century. Jewish thinkers too did their share to curtail Karaite influence on the Rabbanite public. Judah Halevi devoted much of the dialogue in *The Kuzari* to the refutation of Karaite doctrine. Abraham ibn Ezra's many sharp attacks on Karaism in his biblical commentaries, though written outside of Spain, surely reflect antagonisms the author had developed in Spain early in his life. It is remarkable that Spanish Jewry's greatest work in the field of Jewish history in this period, Abraham ibn Daud's *Sepher haqabbalah*, was explicitly written to show the unbroken chain of the Jewish oral tradition in the face of the Karaite attack on its authenticity. It is noteworthy that Abraham ibn Daud also wrote an anti-Karaite exegetical work, which is not now extant. Despite all this, the sect continued to exist in Spain, where we still find its adherents as late as the second half of the thirteenth century.

The Karaites in Byzantium-Turkey and in Eastern Europe

Outside of the Muslim countries, the Byzantine empire became an important Karaite center in the Middle Ages. We do not know the date when this center emerged. Some Karaites possibly may have arrived as early as the late ninth century. In the tenth century, no doubt, Karaite communities had come into being in most of the localities where they lived a century later. Karaism seems, however, never to have penetrated the Byzantine possessions in southern Italy. Significantly, a Karaite community existed on the island of Cyprus as early as the tenth century.

All indications are that the Byzantine Karaite community was established by immigrants from Babylonia-Iraq, with the addition of arrivals from Syria and the Holy Land. In their new home these immigrants settled mostly, if not exclusively, in cities and towns where Rabbanite communities already existed. Sometimes the Karaites shared a common quarter with the Rabbanites, as was the case in Constantinople where only a fence divided the Karaites from the Rabbanites. We do not know how large the Byzantine Karaite community was. It was, no doubt, much smaller than its Rabbanite counterpart. In the second half of the twelfth century possibly 500 Karaites lived in Constantinople; the Rabbanite community was four times larger.

The relations between the two groups were not always friendly. From time to time the Byzantine authorities had to intervene to restore peace between them. In Thessalonica (Salonica), for example, such an intervention became necessary when in the second half of the eleventh century the Rabbanites attacked the Karaites for following a calendar of their own. Despite this, Karaite practice was nowhere as much influenced by Rabbanism as in Byzantium. It was here, as we have seen above, that the Karaites began to light Sabbath candles in their homes, and ultimately also to accept the Rabbanite pre-calculated calendar.

In the second half of the eleventh century Byzantium became an important center of Karaite learning. To a great degree this center was created by native scholars who had spent years of study in Jerusalem, then Karaism's leading religio-cultural center.

It was only natural that here the need was felt first to translate into Hebrew some of Karaism's important works composed in the Near East in Arabic. By then the Arabic spoken by the original Karaite immigrants had been forgotten, and replaced by a specifically Greek-Jewish dialect. Hebrew, of course, continued to be the language of the scholars. Thus, original Karaite literature in Hebrew was also written in Byzantium, including Karaism's most important theological work *Eshkol hakopher*, *Cluster of Henna* (cf. Song of Songs 1:14), by Judah Hadassi of Constantinople, who lived in the twelfth century. In this period many Byzantine Karaite scholars had become versed in Greek literature and other aspects of Greek culture. As a result, they also developed an interest in philosophy and the sciences to a degree unknown in other medieval Karaite communities.

The fall of the Byzantine empire in the fifteenth century and its transformation into the Ottoman empire passed without causing harm to the Karaite community. In fact, during the early period of Ottoman grandeur the Karaites experienced a new religio-cultural heyday. Here, as we have seen, the ultimate Karaite code of laws *Adereth Eliyahu, Mantle of Elijah* (cf. II Kings 2:13), was composed by Elijah Bashyatchi (c. 1420–90). Here too one of the greatest Karaite Hebrew scholars-poets, Caleb Aphendopolo (1464–c. 1524), wrote poetry and rhymed prose which still evoke interest today. Among his writings we find some of the most remarkable secular poems ever written by a Karaite author.

During the entire sixteenth century, the Karaite community in the Ottoman empire was still large and enjoyed much prestige, even among its Rabbanite neighbors. The gradual political and economic decline of the empire, especially beginning with the late seventeenth century, had the same unfavorable impact upon the Karaites as upon the Jewish community in general. The Karaite community nevertheless survived into modern times.

A few generations after the Karaites established themselves in the Byzantine empire, some of their descendants emigrated across the Black Sea to the Crimean peninsula and southernmost Ukraine. We do not know the exact date of this event. The fact that the Crimean Karaite community and its offshoot in the Old Polish Commonwealth have been using, down to modern times, mostly a Kipchak dialect, would indicate that the Karaites arrived in the Crimea some time after 1050 when this Turkic tribe occupied the peninsula. At any rate, when the traveler Pethahiah of Ratisbon visited the area in the second half of the twelfth century, he found there a sizable Karaite community. The Karaites of the Crimea continued to be a sizable community until our times despite the emigration of a number of them to Poland and Lithuania. During the entire Middle Ages, and down to the end of the eighteenth century, the Crimean Karaites lived in fairly stable conditions under the domination of the Tartars, who conquered the peninsula in 1237. Their numbers were probably augmented by the immigration of more of their co-religionists from Byzantium and by the conversion to the Karaite faith of certain numbers of Mongolians. Their cultural and religious life was similar to that of their Byzantine brethren. Whether the Jewish Khazars in nearby southeastern Ukraine (cf. further, Sec. XIV, Chap. 2) were Karaites is still a matter of debate. But some Khazars seem to have accepted Karaism, which may further explain the Turkic element in the physical appearance of the Eastern European Karaites.

Karaite communities existed in various parts of the peninsula, both in places where Rabbanite communities existed, as well as in localities with no Rabbanite population. Chufut Kale (meaning Rock of the Jews), a suburb of Bakhchiserai, was an exclusive Karaite settlement and became Crimean Karaism's main religio-cultural center. In the nineteenth century, however, the Karaite center shifted to Eupatoria (also known as Gozlow). Here was the seat of the chief Karaite *hakham*. A Karaite printing press existed here during several decades of the nineteenth century. In the nineteenth century a secular literature also came into being among the Crimean Karaites in Hebrew, Kipchak, and Russian. By the end of the century, the Karaite population in the Crimea numbered over 6,000. After the First World War its number began to decline, and by 1926 it had fallen to about 4,200.

In Poland-Lithuania the Karaites settled in a number of towns in today's East Galicia, Volhynia, and Lithuania. Their most important and largest community was that of Troki, near Vilna. Troki was originally given to the Karaites for exclusive settlement with the idea of keeping out the Rabbanites. For several hundred years the Karaites succeeded in banning Rabbanites and their economic competition from Troki. They had their own central council, but paid their taxes to the government together with the Rabbanites. Whenever a calamity befell Polish-Lithuanian Jewry, the Karaites were affected by it, too. When the Jews were expelled from Lithuania in 1495, the Karaites of Troki and its sister communities were expelled as well. When the Jews were permitted to return in 1503, the Karaites were also re-admitted. The Karaites also shared the fate of Polish-Lithuanian Jewry during the years of the Great Catastrophe (1648–60), when the Ukrainian hordes of Bohdan Chmielnicki massacred the Jewish communities and the Muscovite and Swedish invasions brought additional suffering and destruction to the Jews.

Troki grew continually as a Karaite religio-cultural center, and by the eighteenth century had outstripped in importance the Karaite center in the Crimea. It was, no doubt, the proximity of the gigantic Polish-Lithuanian Jewish community with its enormous cultural activism that spurred Lithuanian Karaism to great cultural achievements. As a result of these factors the immigration of a number of scholars from Troki to the Crimea in the eighteenth century brought about a cultural renaissance there.

During the last decades of the eighteenth century the Crimea and most of the Polish-Lithuanian Karaites came under the domination of the Russian czars. Russia annexed the Crimean peninsula in 1783, and the partitions of the Old Polish Commonwealth gave to Russia almost all areas of Karaite settlement in Poland and Lithuania. The changeover to czarist domination proved to be very beneficial to the Karaites. Already in 1795 Empress Catherine II placed them in a better position than the Rabbanites in matters of taxation. The Karaites speedily realized that their future depended on the degree of their dissociation from the Jews. Their scholars, and especially the greatest of them Abraham Firkovich (1785–1874), promoted the Karaite cause by insisting that their ancestors left the Holy Land at the time of King Solomon's death, and thus should be exonerated from the accusation of having participated in the crucifixion. In addition, they attempted to prove that the Crimean and Russian Karaites were of Turkic and Mongol descent and thus not related to Russian Jewry. These researches, although not always valid, proved strong enough to convince the czars. Nicholas I exempted the Karaites from the calamitous service in the army imposed upon the Jews in 1827, which is known as the cantonist tragedy. In 1840 the czarist government recognized Karaism as a religion independent of Judaism. The civil status of the Karaites continued to improve throughout the nineteenth century, and in 1893 the last of their legal disabilities were abolished and they were accorded full civil rights.

Under these circumstances the gap between the Karaites and Rabbanites in Russia began to widen early in the nineteenth century to a degree reminiscent of the situation in the Near East in the tenth century. The situation became further aggravated after 1835 when the Karaites began to denounce the Rabbanites and to heap upon them various accusations in their petitions to the government. On the personal level the relations between Karaite and Jew may often have been friendlier than on the communal level. There are some indications that although the Karaites held on to their Kipchak dialect, some use of the Yiddish language was noticeable among them. Of course, they used the Hebrew alphabet also whenever they wrote in their Kipchak dialect. The tiny Karaite community in East Galicia, which after Poland's partitions lived under Austrian rule, kept closer to the Rabbanites. Some of its members developed a vivid interest in the *Haskalah* (Enlightenment) movement with its modern Hebrew literature. Other Galician Karaites manifested an inclination to assimilate culturally with their Polish neighbors.

The First World War brought in its wake serious changes in the life of Eastern Europe's Karaites. During the civil war the Crimean community supported the anti-Soviet forces. As a result, several hundreds of them were compelled to flee to Western Europe when the Red Army occupied the peninsula. In this way small Karaite communities established themselves in France and in Germany. Most of the Lithuanian Karaites lived between the two World Wars in the Polish part of Lithuania, and mostly in Troki and nearby Vilna. Troki was the seat of the Chief Hakham. In the restored Polish Republic the Karaites enjoyed a status far more favorable than the massive Rabbanite Community. Some of them held high government positions, and some taught at the universities. Smaller numbers of Karaites lived in the Republic of

Lithuania and in Latvia. It is difficult to determine the number of the East European Karaites on the eve of the Second World War. Their number in Poland is estimated to have been between 700 and 1,300. About 9,000 are said to have lived in the Crimea under Soviet rule. The total number of Karaites the world over was estimated as no more than 12,000, but this estimate seems to be below their actual numbers.

In the Holocaust and After

On the eve of the Second World War the Karaite diaspora lived in fairly stable and secure conditions. In addition to the three major communities in Egypt, the Crimea, and Poland, smaller communities lived in Iraq, Turkey, France, Germany, and the United States.

With the introduction of the Nuremberg Laws in Nazi Germany, the question of the status of the Karaites living in Germany became a matter of deliberation in German governmental circles. In 1938 the Karaites petitioned the government for exemption from the Nuremberg Laws, asserting that they were racially of non-Jewish origin. The German government responded in January 1939 with the recognition of Karaism as a religion separate from Judaism, but was evasive with regard to the racial question. After the occupation of Poland by the Germans in the fall of 1939 and of the Crimea in 1941, the question of whether the Karaites should be considered Jews racially became much more acute, since Poland, Lithuania, and the Crimea harbored about one-half of the entire Karaite people. Simultaneously, the Vichy government in France, having introduced anti-Jewish legislation modeled after the Nuremberg Laws, wanted to apply these laws to the several hundred Karaites living under its control. All the time, however, the German authorities in charge of Jewish affairs were dragging their feet and postponing the decision as to the racial make-up of the Karaites.

In practice, the Karaites were spared everywhere. When in the autumn of 1941 some 20,000 Jews were exterminated in the western Crimea, the local Karaites were left alone. Meanwhile the German authorities in Poland and Lithuania were researching the racial origin of the Karaites. A few leading Jewish historians in Poland were asked for an opinion on this matter, and in Vilna a debate was arranged between the Karaite Chief Hakham Seraiah Szapszal and the Jewish scholar Selig Kalmanowicz. The Jewish scholars purposely bent the historical truth to save the Karaites. This, in fact, seems also to have been the plan of the German racial authorities. The Germans, who hoped to cross the Ural mountains and to establish friendly relations with the masses of Turko-Mongols, did not want to mar these relations with a harsh attitude to the Karaites who vocally claimed to be of Turkic and Mongolian origin. Thus, despite some opposition on the part of racially-minded German writers, the decision was made in the summer of 1943 to recognize the Karaites as racially non-Jewish and exempt them from all legal disabilities of the Jews and from the "Final Solution." The decision of the German government also affected the Karaites in Vichy, France, and they too came out unscathed from the Holocaust.

When the Second World War came to a conclusion, great geographic changes took place in the Karaite world. Many Karaites left the Crimea to settle in Poland and in the western countries. Many must have gone northward to settle in Troki, where the astounding number of 5,700 Karaites lived in 1959 according to the Soviet census of that year. But, the focal point of Karaite settlement became the State of Israel. Practically the entire Karaite community of Iraq emigrated to Israel. Many Karaites from Turkey emigrated to Israel, too, and only about 1,000 Greek-speaking Karaites remained there. The largest number of Karaites emigrated to Israel from Egypt, where they had begun to identify enthusiastically with the Jewish state prior to their emigration. A number of Egyptian Karaites also emigrated to the United States and to other countries. In 1968 the number of Karaites in Egypt had dwindled to about 500. Due to the new immigration to the United States the number of Karaites here has probably doubled from about 500 in 1941 to about 1,000 now. While they settled mainly in New York and in the state of New Jersey, they are found in other states as well. America's Karaite community is mostly composed of prosperous business men and professionals. In some cities they hold Karaite services in private homes, and in other localities they attend services in various

Jewish synagogues. The rate of intermarriage between Karaites and Rabbanites in the United States is quite high.

The true center of Karaism in the post-World War II period has become the State of Israel. Official estimates have it that the number of Karaites in Israel is about 10,000. The Karaite leadership, however, believes that their number is much larger. The most dense concentrations of Karaites are in the cities of Ramleh and Ashdod. In addition they live in about a dozen other communities, including agricultural settlements. The settlement *Matsliah* is inhabited solely by Karaites and is named for a famous medieval Karaite scholar who lived in Jerusalem. There are about ten Karaite houses of worship in the country. The old Karaite synagogue in Jerusalem is functioning again. Karaite religious life in Israel is directed by a Chief Hakham residing in Ramleh and a central religious council which also has its seat there.

IN THE ORBIT OF EASTERN CHRISTIANITY DURING THE EARLY MIDDLE AGES

Chapter 1

In the Byzantine Empire

The Jewish Population

During the entire period of the Early Middle Ages the Byzantine empire was in a state of constant warfare with the Muslims. Its eastern regions were unceasingly attacked from the Muslim center in Iraq, and its outposts in southern Italy and Sicily were attacked and ultimately conquered by Muslims from North Africa and Spain. As a result, the borders of the empire underwent frequent changes. There were times when the eastern part of Asia Minor, Armenia, and Syria were lost and times when they were regained. The only parts of the empire which were firmly controlled most of the time by Byzantium were Greece and a large part of the rest of the Balkan peninsula. Here only the czardom of Bulgaria, which emerged in the second half of the seventh century, removed parts of the country temporarily from Byzantine control.

These territorial changes make it difficult to chart a geographic picture of the Jewish population. The only thing that seems certain is that practically all the time Jewish communities existed in the major cities of the empire. During the first few centuries of the period the Jewish population was very small in number, and probably even decreased due to frequent persecutions, attempts at forcible conversion, and local expulsions, especially under the early emperors of the Macedonian dynasty in the ninth century. The existence of the Jewish state of the Khazars in nearby southern Ukraine (see the next chapter) provided a good opportunity for emigration to a more hospitable country. The expansion of Bulgarian territory in the ninth and tenth centuries also removed temporarily a number of Jews from Byzantine domination. Furthermore, the friendly attitude manifested by Boris I (852–88) and his son Simeon (893–927) attracted considerable Jewish immigration from Byzantium. The cessation of imperial oppression in the middle of the tenth century reversed the trend. The simultaneous deterioration of the general situation in the caliphate resulted in an emigration from there to Byzantium. The Byzantine Jewish community began to grow again and underwent some expansion beginning with the late tenth century. Jewish communities now appeared in certain localities in which they were unknown to have existed earlier. While in the ninth and tenth centuries Jews are found in only about 20 localities, the number of communities rose to almost 30 in the second half of the twelfth century. In addition to Constantinople, Thebes and Salonica had the largest communities.

In comparison with the populous Jewish communities in the orbit of Islam, Byzantine Jewry was numerically very small. The twelfth-century traveler Benjamin of Tudela believed he had found about 9,000 Jews in Byzantium. Modern estimates arrive at a number of between 12,000 and 15,000 in a general population of about 15 million. Over 2,000 Jews lived in Constantinople, and almost as many in Thebes. In the outlying areas in the east and in the Balkans the Jewish communities, as far as they existed, must have been very small. The same holds true of the islands, such as Cyprus, Rhodes, and Crete, in the periods during which they were under Byzantine control.

Political and Economic Conditions

The political destiny of Byzantine Jewry during the first 300 years of the Early Middle Ages was different from that of the latter half of the period. The first 300 years are characterized by recurring persecution on the part of most of the emperors. This was coupled with attempts to isolate the Jews from their Gentile neighbors and to force them to abandon their faith. Emperor Justinian II issued instructions in 692 designed to put a wedge between the Jews and their neighbors. When about 30 years later Emperor Leo III (717–41) began his famous campaign to remove the images from the churches, the iconodulists—that is, those who were in favor of the images—accused the Jews of conspiracy with their opponents, the iconoclasts. Iconodulic resentment of the alleged Jewish role in the removal of the images survived the entire period of almost 120 years until the images were restored to the churches in 842. It was almost "natural" that the restoration of the images was accompanied by severe anti-Jewish riots. The Jewish condition kept on deteriorating, and when Basil I, the founder of the Macedonian dynasty, ascended the throne in 867, he began to persecute the Jews, both in his Greek and south Italian lands, with a ferocity hitherto unknown. These persecutions were renewed again and again until the time of Emperor Romanus I (920–44). They were discontinued close to the middle of the tenth century when Hisdai ibn Shaprut (cf. above, Sec. XIII, Chap. 3) energetically intervened in favor of his oppressed Byzantine co-religionists. The friendship of this Jewish dignitary of the Cordovan state was too important to Byzantium to alienate him by the persecution of Jews.

In addition to political oppression and social isolation, between the seventh and the tenth century Byzantine Jewry survived several major imperial attempts to force it to convert to Christianity. The harshest attempt in this direction was that of Emperor Basil I, which was accompanied by a compulsory religious disputation between Jews and Christians. It is not fully clear why the attempts at converting the Jews always ended in failure. It was possibly the general weakness of the Byzantine state and the preoccupation of the emperors with the Muslim menace that prevented them from implementing their conversion decrees. Be this as it may, beginning with the late tenth century the political destiny of Byzantine Jewry began to improve. Henceforth, and until the capture of Constantinople by the crusaders in 1204, the Byzantine Jewish community experienced a somewhat more tranquil existence. True, Byzantine Jewry was still treated as a pariah people. It still had to supply the imperial judiciary with torturers and executioners. But it was again a community whose religion, although despised and often officially referred to as "vomit," was legal and entitled to the basic protection granted it in the codes of Theodosius II and Justinian I (cf. Vol. I, Sec. XI, Chap. 1).

Under these unfriendly circumstances it is remarkable how diversified the economic structure of this numerically small community was. To begin with, no serious restrictions were enacted on Jewish economic activity. A proportionately large number of Jews made a living by tilling the soil. In the twelfth century there were at least two wholly Jewish settlements engaged in agriculture. Many, of course, engaged in commerce, and there were among them some wealthy merchants. Jewish merchants, as in other Mediterranean countries, were conspicuous in the silk trade. The various crafts were represented among the Jews, too. Again, as in the Mediterranean countries, many worked in the production of silk and in the dyeing industry. Jewish exclusiveness in the tanning industry may have been involuntary and imposed by oppressive governmental design. The only medieval "Jewish" occupation rarely found in Byzantium among Jews was that of moneylending. This business was a governmental monopoly and thus mostly inaccessible to Jews.

Culture and Religious Life

The social isolation of Byzantine Jewry from the Gentile society was strengthened by the fact that Jews everywhere in the cities and towns lived in separate quarters. True, we do not know whether this was a separation by governmental decree or by voluntary action on the part of the Jews. But the isolating influence of segregated dwelling was apparent. The social segregration was accompanied by an almost total cultural isolation. The Jew spoke his own variety of Greek. Jewish interest in Greek culture was evident here to a lesser degree than among contemporary Jews in other countries. This surprising phenomenon may possibly be explained as a reaction to the atmosphere of humiliation in which the Jew was placed. Nor did the Jewish communal organization ever attain the importance and culture-promoting character it had in other countries. Its range of autonomy was narrower than elsewhere. The two elders who generally headed the smaller communities and the five who ruled the larger seem to have taken care of only the barest communal needs. Be it noted, though, that a degree of co-operation between the scholars and laity in communal affairs did exist.

Under these circumstances, and being numerically rather very small, Byzantine Jewry made only a modest contribution to Jewish culture during the 300 years of oppression. The sole area where Jewish culture did flourish was southern Italy. Here a number of poets produced Hebrew poems second to none written in Spain in the period of the Golden Age. The *piyyutim* of Silano, Shephatiah ben Amittai, and Amittai ben Shephatiah, who lived in southern Italy in the ninth and tenth centuries, contributed much to the exalted and moving quality of the *neilah* service of which they are a part. In southern Italy, too, the first European work of Hebrew prose known to us was written by the physician Sabbathai Donnolo (c. 913–82). His commentary on the kabbalistic work, *Book of Creation*, which he named *Hakhmoni*, or *Tahkemoni* (cf. II Samuel 39:8) is written in a blend of biblical and mishnaic Hebrew. He is also the author of a Hebrew work in pharmacology. It was only in the eleventh century that Hebrew literature awakened among the Jews in the Greek areas of the empire. Characteristically, much of this literature was preoccupied with the Karaite challenge and with attempts to refute it. Obviously, the presence of the Karaite community in their midst (cf. above, Sec. XIII, Chap. 7) served as a literary stimulus to the Rabbanites. As far as the Balkan regions north of Greece are concerned, a number of Jewish scholars lived and taught in Bulgaria in the twelfth century.

The lack of cultural excellence did not visibly affect Byzantine Jewry's religious life. The Byzantine Jews were a community which devotedly clung to its faith. Having survived with only insignificant losses several major attempts at its forcible conversion to Christianity (in the years 640, 721, 873, and 920), the community in general followed the tenets of normative Judaism, and was never shaken by the schisms and heresies which created so much turmoil in the Jewish communities in the orbit of Islam. It had withstood the Karaite challenge and had even, as we have seen (Sec. XIII, Chap. 7), mightily influenced Karaite practice in matters of Sabbath observance and calendation.

The iconoclastic movement, if anything, strengthened the belief of the Jews that their faith is the true way of life ordained by God. If it is true, as many scholars believe, that the beautiful poem *Weyethayu kol leovdekha,* "All shall come to worship Thee . . .," was written in Byzantium by a *payyetan* who witnessed the smashing of the statues in the churches, we have significant evidence of the religious elation of the Jews in that crucial moment in Byzantine history. It is therefore not surprising that zealous Jews may have possibly conducted successful missionary propaganda at that time among the Balkan peoples, which is indicated by the appearance of typically Jewish names (David, Moses) among the higher strata of the population in the czardom of Bulgaria. It is noteworthy that in Byzantium proper, despite the deep gap which existed between Jews and Gentiles, religious disputations between members of the two faiths took place without having been imposed upon the Jews by the authorities.

In this period the Byzantine order of prayer known as the Romaniote rite (cf. Vol. I, Sec. XI, Chap. 1) underwent further development. While basically derived from the Palestinian order of prayer, it now absorbed elements from Amram Gaon's (responsum) prayer book. The prayer services were, of course, conducted in Hebrew. Significantly, however, the Greek-Jewish vernacular—that is, Yevanic—played here a greater role in the religious services than did local vernaculars in the other medieval Jewish communities. Curiously, the order of prayer followed in the Balkan countries was not identical with the Romaniote rite, but developed certain local characteristics of its own. The daily religious practice was in general no different from that of normative Judaism. True, there was a laxity in the observance of certain precepts, but this may have been a result of local unfavorable political conditions. A strong interest in a mystical interpretation of the Bible and in the *aggadoth* literature attests to the deep religious feeling which had permeated Byzantine Jewry in the period of the Early Middle Ages.

Chapter 2

The Khazars

The Khazars and Their Land

At the very time the Byzantine Jews were being accused of having masterminded the "Judaizing" iconoclastic reform in the Eastern Christian Church, a part of the people of the Khazars in nearby southern Russia accepted the Jewish faith. The Khazars were a Turkish tribe who originally lived in Central Asia. They spoke a Turkish dialect and were possibly related to the Huns who invaded Europe in the second half of the fourth century. At what time the Khazars appeared in Europe is not certain. By the sixth century, however, and possibly somewhat earlier, they established a state in the southeastern corner of Russia. In the south they bordered on the Caucasus. Their eastern border was the region of the Volga River and in the north and west the Don River was their basic border. At times the Khazars expanded their territory, and some scholars even believe that during a certain period a Khazar empire was in existence, which included parts of western Asia. What seems to be certain is that for some time a part of the Crimean peninsula was under Khazarian control, and that in the ninth century a part of the Ukraine, including the city of Kiev, was occupied by them. During the ninth century, and possibly even later, various Slavic tribes between the Don and the Dnieper paid tribute to the Khazarians.

The population of Khazaria had a pronounced heterogeneous character. In addition to tribes of nomadic and semi-nomadic Khazars, there were survivors of the former Hellenized population, large numbers of people of Slavic origin, and Jews, mostly refugees from Byzantium and the southern Caucasus. The capital of the state, Atil (or possibly Itil), lay at the point where the Volga River empties into the Caspian Sea. Atil's site is roughly identical with the present location of the city of Astrakhan. The Khazars were governed by the dual authority of the *khaqan* (or *khagan*) and the *beg,* who was second in rank. We have no full knowledge of the constitutional order of the Khazarian state. Some scholars are of the opinion that the *beg* was the actual ruler, and the *khaqan* only played the representative role of head of the state. The office of the *khaqan* was originally elective, but became hereditary in the first half of the eighth century.

The Khazar economy was originally that of a nomadic people whose flocks were grazing in the country's vast prairies. Later the cultivation of rice was introduced, bringing much prosperity to the country. The Khazars also exported a variety of articles to the Middle East, especially lumber. The location of the country also made possible the development of a transit trade.

When the power of the Khazar state grew, it came into frequent contacts with Byzantium to the south and the caliphate to the east. The relations with Byzantium were largely peaceful. In fact, Khazaria rendered an important service to the Byzantine empire by holding back Slavic and Viking (Varangian) raiders, who again and again came down from the north on the Don and Volga, tempted by Constantinople's legendary riches. Repeatedly, however, the Khazars had to fight the forces of the caliphate. Some scholars are of the opinion that at the time of the second Arab-Khazar war (722–37), the khaqan saw himself compelled to accept the Muslim faith. Be this as it may, a great change took place in Khazaria when the *khaqan,* his family, and the aristocracy converted to Judaism.

Conversion to Judaism

Neither the exact time nor the circumstances under which the conversion of the Khazars took place are certain. Most probably the conversion occurred in various stages during the eighth century. Some scholars, however, believe that the conversion took place as late as the second half of the ninth century. A story widely circulated in the Middle Ages has it that the *khaqan* Bulan (730–40) invited to his court representatives of the three monotheistic faiths, who then debated the advantages of their respective persuasions in his presence. During the conversations he realized that the "Christian Scholastic" preferred Judaism to Islam, and the "Doctor of Islam" preferred Judaism to Christianity. This convinced Bulan that Judaism was the truest of all the three religions, and he decided to embrace the Jewish faith. Although the story has legendary and apocryphal features, resembling a similar story in connection with the conversion of Kiev's Grand Duke Vladimir to Orthodox Christianity, the possibility should not be dismissed that some sort of religious debate did play a role in the process of the Khazar conversion to Judaism. We have seen (cf. above, Chap. 1) that Jewish influences were common in the nearby czardom of Bulgaria. The iconoclastic movement in nearby Byzantium, even though certainly not engineered by Jews, had clear Judaic motifs.

In addition to the spiritual factors, political considerations must have played a decisive role in the *khaqan's* decision. The country's geopolitical situation was delicate and vulnerable. It was, after all, a small country compared to the size and might of its neighbors, Christian Byzantium and the Muslim caliphate. The *khaqan's* natural interest called for the observance of as perfect neutrality as possible. This of course, precluded conversion to either Christianity or Islam. By embracing Judaism, Khazaria could not only preserve its neutral position but also its own identity. The conversion was limited to the royal family, the courtiers, and the warrior class. And even though the number of Khazar converts to Judaism kept on growing, the Khazar Jews still remained a minority within the population.

We do not know the nature of the Jewish faith adopted by the Khazars. According to a statement of *Khaqan* Joseph in a document of uncertain authenticity, his ancestor Bulan converted to "the faith of Abraham." Some scholars believe that this may have been a "Karaite" form of Judaism even though Bulan died more than a quarter of a century before Anan ben David renounced his allegiance to the Oral Law in Baghdad. Others believe that Khazar Judaism was not anti-talmudic but represented a form of watered-down normative Judaism. Some also believe that the Khazars, being a nomadic people, practiced Judaism in a form similar to that followed by the Israelites in the desert after the exodus from Egypt. Accordingly, the Khazars had a portable sanctuary similar to that built by the Israelites in the desert (cf. Exodus, Chaps. 35 ff). Be all this as it may, the Khazars did become Jews, and old Russian writings called Khazaria "Land of the Jews."

Jewish Khazaria

What happened in Khazaria after the conversion of its royal house and nobility to Judaism is a matter of perpetual debate among scholars. The difficulty in obtaining a picture of what really happened results from the fact that not one single document has come down to us which could be traced to Khazaria with full certainty. According to documents which surfaced in the sixteenth century, Hisdai ibn Shaprut got in touch with the then *Khaqan* Joseph about the year 960. This fact in itself should not be doubted, since such an action was one Hisdai often took with regard to distant Jewish communities. The authenticity of the correspondence between the Spanish Jewish dignitary and the Khazarian king is, however, still hotly debated among the scholars. At any rate we learn from this correspondence that close to the year 800, King Obadiah, Bulan's descendant, imported Jewish scholars to his country from abroad, who taught him and the other Khazarian Jews the ways of normative Judaism and introduced them to the basic texts of the Jewish faith.

By that time, it should be assumed, Khazarian Judaism had shed the remnants of Shamanist pagan customs which it had originally retained from the Turkic past of the Khazarians. "Karaite" customs, too, such as keeping the homes dark on Friday nights, must also have been abandoned at that time. It may also safely be assumed that in the course of time the level of Jewish knowledge kept on rising in Khazaria, in part due to the constant influx of Jewish immigrants from the Byzantine and Muslim empires. Furthermore, for a period of time Khazaria controlled parts of the Caucasus where a considerable Jewish population was living. The Jewish population was especially large in the Caucasian city of Derbent. That the Jewish Khazarians did draw nearer to Jewish culture is also indicated by the fact that the Hebrew script was now in use among them.

How large Khazaria's Jewish population was, and what its proportion in the general population added up to, is impossible to say. The *khaqans*, even after Obadiah, practiced perfect religious toleration and never attempted to impose Judaism by force either on pagans, Christians, or Muslims. The very fact, however, that Judaism was the religion of the upper classes must have helped to attract non-Jews to the Jewish faith. Significantly, Judaism began to attract adherents among the tribe of the Alans in nearby northern Caucasus.

The peak of Khazarian might was reached about the time Hisdai ibn Shaprut corresponded with King Joseph. True, during the first half of the tenth century the Vikings of Russia recurrently sailed down the Volga River to attack the country. But these attacks seem to have made no significant dent in the position of Khazaria. After 960, however, the situation changed. A Russian attack in 965 dealt the Khazarians a decisive defeat and the loss of their strongest fortress Sarkil. The capital city of Atil fell to the Russians no later than 969. What happened afterwards is again uncertain. Some scholars believe that a definite end came then, or early in the eleventh century, to Khazar independence. Others, however, are of the opinion that a small Khazar independent state continued to exist in the Crimea, with the city of Kertch as its center, for almost 300 years more. It was subdued by the Tartars when they inundated southeastern Europe in the thirteenth century.

What happened to the Jewish Khazars is an even greater enigma. It was generally believed that following the annexation of their country by the Russian duchy of Kiev the Khazarians were absorbed within the Russian people. During the past 80 years, however, various scholars have been promoting the idea that the Khazarians spread northwestward and became the ancestors of the Jewish community in the Old Polish Commonwealth. This theory was mainly built on an attempt to identify various localities in Poland, from its eastern borders to Silesia, as Khazarian settlements. The physical characteristics of most East-European

Jews, which are different from those of the Semitic peoples, were used as a further proof for the veracity of the theory. Many scholars, however, reject this theory almost vehemently.

At any rate, a Khazarian "diaspora" did emerge after the downfall of the kingdom. Various sources mention the presence of Khazarians in the Caucasus, Byzantium, Kievan Russia, Hungary, and even distant Alexandria in Egypt. Khazarians are mentioned in the historical sources as late as the fourteenth century. According to a report which seems reliable, some Jewish Cossacks in the czarist army had a tradition that they were descendants of the Jewish Khazars. In the final analysis, however, the history of the Jewish Khazars after their conversion to Judaism and their later destiny basically remains an enigma.

Chapter 3

In Russia

We have seen above (Vol. I, Sec. XI, Chap. 1) that in the Antiquity Jews had been living in the Crimea and on the northern shores of the Black Sea. In the period of the Early Middle Ages, Jewish settlement expanded farther to the north and northwest. To begin with, Jewish settlement spilled over northward from Khazaria. Other Jews came from the Byzantine empire in the period of the persecutions and attempts at their forcible conversion to Christianity. Smaller numbers of Jews possibly also came from the areas of mass Jewish settlement in Babylonia and the neighboring countries. Individual Jewish settlers may even have come from Western Europe. The center of Jewish settlement was the city of Kiev, which rose to prominence economically and politically. It seems certain that Jews lived here during the last decades of the tenth century. Although a story telling of Jewish attempts to convert the Kievan Grand Duke Vladimir (980–1015) to Judaism is probably untrue, it implies at any rate that the existence of Judaism as a religion was noticed in general society.

The Kievan Jewish community became more numerous in the twelfth century. Jews lived in two sections of the city, and contemporary sources mention a Jewish gate. Jews were even involved in certain political activities, the nature of which is not fully clear. Jewish communities seem to have existed in a few other localities, too. The Jewish settlement, never too numerous during the entire period, seems to have gone out of existence in the first half of the thirteenth century in the turmoil of the Mongol invasions.

Little is known of the inner life of the Jewish community. Although composed of immigrants from diverse regions, it seems to have integrated linguistically and to have spoken "the language of Canaan," a term used by medieval Jewry for the Slavic languages. The only other thing that can be said is that the study of Torah was pursued in Kievan Russia. Some of the local talmudic scholars had contacts with the great centers of Jewish learning in the Near East and in Western Europe.

Section XV

IN THE ORBIT OF WESTERN CHRISTENDOM DURING THE EARLY MIDDLE AGES

Chapter 1

The General Scene

On the threshold of the Middle Ages the general chaos in Western Europe which followed the collapse of the Roman empire began to give way to events which resulted in the establishment and solidification of a series of new states. These states still constitute the basic national and political entities in present-day Europe.

The two most remarkable events in the history of the early Middle Ages are the re-conquest of Spain by the Christians and the formation of the Carolingian empire. Only a few years after the Muslims completed the conquest of Spain, the Christian state of Asturia came into being in the northwestern part of the peninsula. Later, more of northern Spain was reconquered from the Arabs, and the kingdom of Navarre was established. About the year 860 the County of Castile ("Old Castile") emerged in the territory of Asturia. Out of this nucleus the major kingdom of Castile developed, so named for the many frontier forts built in the wars against the Muslims. In 1035 a prince of the royal family of Navarre established in the northeastern region of the peninsula

121

the kingdom of Aragon. The Aragonese state kept on expanding and in time annexed to its territory the kingdom of Navarre, as well as Catalonia, and the city of Barcelona. In the first half of the eleventh century, the nucleus of the Christian kingdom of Portugal had also come into being on the west coast of the peninsula.

In the middle of the eleventh century the Christian states had become sufficiently strong to begin a decisive effort to expel the Muslims from the peninsula. The Castilians wrested from the Muslims the center of the peninsula, and in 1085 captured the city of Toledo and made it their capital in 1087. The Aragonians continued to expand their possessions on Spain's east coast, and with the capture of the Balearic Islands between 1224 and 1233, and of the important city of Valencia in 1238, became the virtual rulers of eastern Spain. When the Muslims were decisively defeated in 1212 in the battle of Las Navas de Tolosa, the way was open for the Castilians to capture Andalusia, the heartland of Muslim Spain. The occupation of Cordova in 1236 and of Seville in 1248 virtually concluded the re-conquest of Spain from the Muslims. Henceforth the tiny kingdom of Granada remained the only Muslim foothold on the Iberian peninsula.

Further north it was Charles Martel, ruler of Frankland, who saved France from Muslim conquest. Under him and his son, Pepin the Short, Frankland grew ever stronger, and it became a mighty empire under its next ruler, Charlemagne, who ascended the throne in 768. By conquering the Spanish March and Lombardy, and by extending his rule in Germany over Bavaria and Saxony, Charlemagne created an empire which stretched from the Ebro River in northern Spain to the Elbe River in eastern Germany. Despite the multiplicity of nationalities inhabiting his dominions, a remarkable tranquility and cohesion existed in the empire. Economically and culturally, too, Charlemagne's empire underwent a process of significant growth, so that some historians feel justified in speaking of a Carolingian Renaissance. It was only natural that Pope Leo III crowned Charlemagne in the year 800 as Roman Emperor.

After Charlemagne's death in 814 his son Louis I the Pious followed him. Although Louis lacked his father's talents as warrior and statesman, the empire survived intact all through his reign. A few years after his death the empire was divided in 843 among his three sons: Charles the Bald became the first king of France, Louis became king of Germany, and Lothair became ruler of a new state comprising Lorraine, Burgundy, Provence, and Lombardy. Lothair's state, due to its artificial nature, quickly disintegrated into a multiplicity of principalities. France and Germany, however, basically inhabited by homogenous populations, developed into major states in Western Europe.

To be sure, under Charles the Bald and his successors, France was constantly weakened by the increasing power of regional rulers and by the recurring attacks of the Vikings ("Normans") on its Atlantic coast. In 911 the Normans established themselves on one of the peninsulas, which henceforth became known as Normandy. The royal power shrank until its control was limited to the area between Paris and Orleans. Thus, in 987 a coalition of regional lords found it easy to depose King Louis V and replace him by one from among themselves, Hugh Capet.

The Capetians ruled France under more favorable conditions. After Duke William of Normandy conquered England in 1066 his main interest was diverted to his new kingdom. Other regional rulers lost their influence in France, when in 1096 they went on the First Crusade to the Holy Land. This gave the Capetians the opportunity they were waiting for, and under Louis VI (1108–37) and Philip II, Augustus (1180–1223), the royal power was greatly strengthened and important administrative, judicial and fiscal reforms were introduced. Philip Augustus also regained control over most of the fiefs possessed by the kings of England in France, including Normandy and Anjou. By defeating the counts of Toulouse through a crusade launched in 1209 against the Albigensian heretics, who were numerous in the county, Philip Augustus initiated a process which led to the reunification of the county with the crown lands about 50 years after his death. These developments, as well as various events during the reign of his grandson Louis IX (1226–70), greatly contributed to the consolidation of the kingdom. In the 1270s France had thus become a first-class power in Western Europe.

In Germany, too, the power of the Carolingians was quite limited, and often inferior to that of their vassals, the dukes of Bavaria, Swabia, and Saxony. Only after the end of the Carolingian era, was Henry I (919–36) of the new Saxon dynasty able to restore the royal power to a significant degree. His son, Otto I (963–73), further strengthened the kingdom and even extended his rule by gaining control over Bohemia on the Slavic border in the east. He was crowned emperor in 962, thus restoring in part the empire of Charlemagne.

Otto's most important inner reform was to delegate to the bishops governmental powers in their dioceses. While this reform gave the country a body of able administrators in a period of almost universal illiteracy, it spelled a great danger to the future of the state. It promoted the division of the state into a multiplicity of ecclesiastical and lay principalities, and weakened the position of Otto's descendants at the time of the great struggle between emperor and pope on the issue of investiture of bishops. Pope Gregory VII (1073–85) insisted on his right to appoint the bishops, despite the fact that they were not only spiritual heads but also temporal rulers of their dioceses. The tragic fate of emperor Henry IV (1056–1106) and his humiliation by the pope at Canossa belong to the most pathetic episodes in the history of the Middle Ages. Henceforth the imperial power remained continuously curtailed by the feudal lords and the Church. The energetic emperors of the Hohenstaufen dynasty, Frederick I Barbarossa, his son Henry VI, and his grandson Frederick II, were not able to arrest the erosion of the imperial power. In the middle of the thirteenth century, the Great Interregnum (1254–73) was a period of a total breakdown of law and order. And when the new Hapsburg dynasty emerged to rule Germany, its limited power resembled that of the last Carolingians in the ninth century.

Before William, duke of Normandy, conquered England in 1066, the country had lived for several hundred years under Saxon and Danish rulers. William's conquest brought the island country closer to Europe, and especially France. French was the official language of William's administration, and henceforth greatly influenced the English language. The union with Normandy and the other French possessions of later English kings brought about important developments in the spheres of culture and economy. The incessant struggle between the kings and the barons brought England closer to constitutional government than any other country in medieval Europe. Henry II (1154–89), William the Conqueror's great-grandson, ruled England efficiently despite his continuous involvement with his possessions in France, which were much larger than his English kingdom. He conquered Wales and parts of Scotland and Ireland. He introduced important judicial innovations, including the institution of the grand jury. His youngest son, John Lackland (1199–1216), so named for not having been assigned any territory in his father's will, was compelled by the barons to grant the country in 1215 the *Magna Carta Libertatum*, the Great Charter of Liberties. The Magna Carta guaranteed the basic liberties to the people and so became the foundation of England's constitutionalism for many centuries. The long reign of Henry III (1216–72) was a period of prosperity and growth, but the reign of his son, Edward I (1272–1307), was full of turmoil and warfare. However, by convening what historians call the "Model Parliament," Edward laid the foundations for England's parliamentary system.

Carolingian rule in Italy disintegrated even more rapidly than in France and Germany. More stability obtained in central Italy ("The Papal States"), where the popes reigned as temporal rulers. Southern Italy was often an object of contest between Byzantines, Muslims, Lombards, and German emperors. Most of the time, however, the Byzantines controlled the country until it came under the rule of the Normans in the middle of the eleventh century. Shortly thereafter the Normans wrested Sicily from the Muslims and united it with their possessions in southern Italy in 1127. In the tenth century Germany re-established its rule over northern Italy. Here no feudal lords contested German rule, but the cities gained more and more power in the recurring political vacuum. In the second half of the twelfth century the cities became so powerful that their league successfully thwarted the attempts of Emperor Frederick I Barbarossa to assert his authority. In fact, in 1183 Frederick, was compelled to recognize in a treaty the virtual autonomy of the cities.

The Norman dynasty was much more successful in asserting its power in southern Italy and Sicily, and turned their state into a model of a well-organized political entity. South Italy-Sicily became even stronger when Henry VI, the son of Frederick Barbarossa, acquired the country by marriage. Under his son, Emperor Frederick II, the country became a great center where Christian and Arabic elements harmoniously mingled to create a unique blend of culture with "modern" colorations. The rule of the Hohenstaufen dynasty lasted until 1268, when it gave way to another dynasty, that of the Anjou.

On the eastern borders of Germany two Slavic states entered the stage of history: Bohemia in the ninth century and Poland in the tenth century. The Bohemians were converted to Christianity in 867 and the Poles about 100 years later. Most of the time Bohemia was united with nearby Moravia, and from time to time controlled parts of Silesia. German influence was always strong, and there were times when the country was under direct German control. In the middle of the thirteenth century, however, Bohemia became very strong and gained much additional territory under Premysl Ottokar II (1253–78).

Poland accepted Christianity under its first historical king, Mieszko I (962–92), of the Piast dynasty. Under his son Boleslaus I (992–1025), the kingdom grew to a position of considerable strength. But after the death of his descendant Boleslaus III in 1138, the country was divided between his sons and so lost much of its strength. In 1241 the Tartars invaded the southern regions of the country causing great devastation. As a result, Poland was opened to a large-scale immigration from Germany. Most of the regions were reunited in the first half of the fourteenth century.

Hungary, east of Bohemia and south of Poland, had a much longer history than its Slavic neighbors. Its territory, partly identical with the Roman provinces of Dacia and Pannonia, was invaded during the late Antiquity and Early Middle Ages by various migrating peoples. Hungary received its ultimate character in 895 or 896 when it was invaded and settled by the Magyars. The country was ruled by kings of the Arpad dynasty and in 975 was converted to Christianity. In the second half of the eleventh century the territory of the kingdom increased, but the twelfth century was a time of inner strife out of which a feudal state emerged. In 1222, however, the power of the great feudal lords was curbed by the "Golden Bull," which strengthened the position of the lower gentry.

Chapter 2

The Jewish Population

We have seen (Vol. I, Sec. XI, Chaps. 2 and 3 and above, Sec. XIII, Chap. 3) that in the waning days of the Antiquity, the Jewish population in northern Italy and in Western Europe was undergoing a process of numerical decline. With the advent of the Early Middle Ages this process reversed itself and the size of the Jewish population began to rise again. Northwestern Europe especially attracted many Jewish immigrants who came from many directions.

We do not know with certainty what attracted Jews to these regions from such distant countries as Byzantium, North Africa, Muslim Spain, and Babylonia. Jews of these countries possibly wished to flee the areas of continuous warfare between Christians and Muslims. In addition, as we have seen, economic opportunities for Jews in Byzantium were rather limited, and were steadily declining in Iraq when the outlying areas began to break away from the caliphate. Western Europe with its rising urban centers thus became a logical target for Jewish immigrants from the East.

If a recent theory that between 1007 and 1012 the forcible conversion of Jews to Christianity was decreed in parts of France and Germany is valid, it had little effect on the settlement and number of Jews in these two countries. In the first half of the twelfth century Germany, at least, had become so attractive to Jewish immigrants, that the kehilloth saw themselves compelled to apply the *herem hayishuv*, a ban on newcomers to settle in a community without the permission of its leaders. The ban enabled communities to protect their members from economic competition; also, the communities could limit their size and thus avoid becoming unacceptable to their Gentile neighbors. The ban also made it possible to prevent socially undesirable immigrants from settling in the communities. And yet, despite the *herem hayishuv* and the growing Christian religious fanaticism all over Western Europe, the Jewish population in Western Europe at the end of the Early Middle Ages and on the eve of the expulsions from England (1290) and France (1306) was incomparably larger than at the beginning of the period.

It is impossible to say which country in Catholic Europe had the largest Jewish population in this period. Some historians are of the opinion that Spain harbored Western Europe's largest community, and that the Norman kingdom of southern Italy and Sicily had the second largest aggregation of Jews. An analysis of the data about the Jews in France (see below) would indicate that France had a Jewish population equal to, if not larger, than that of Spain.

At the time the Christians began to re-conquer Spain from the Muslims, the Jewish population in Asturia, Leon, and Navarre was quite sparse. But, as more Muslim territory was occupied by the Christians, the Jewish population in Christian-held Spain, of course, increased. Whenever a city or region was taken from the Muslims, a considerable part of the Muslim population fled, leaving sections of the cities or rural areas completely or partly vacant. It therefore became the policy of both Aragon and Castile to promote Jewish settlement in vacated areas by granting the Jews land, vineyards, and houses abandoned by the Muslims. In 1247 the Aragonian government promised protection to all Jews who would come by land or sea to settle in the Balearic Islands, Catalonia, and Valencia. The Jewish element thus played a major role in the re-colonization of the newly acquired areas, and the Jewish population in Christian Spain steadily grew. Most of the new Jewish settlers came from southern, Muslim-held Spain.

The weakening of the Muslim states in southern Spain beginning with the middle of the eleventh century, which resulted from the acceleration of the *Reconquista,* gave a new impetus to Jewish emigration to the north. In the middle of the twelfth century, when the Almohades took over southern Spain (cf. above, Sec. XIII, Chap. 3), Jewish emigration from the south to the north assumed the character of a massive flight. From time to time Jews from other countries made use of the new opportunities and immigrated to Christian Spain. This was the case, for example, when the Almohades took over the control of Morocco. Many Jews then immigrated from there to Aragon, and especially to the region of Catalonia. Moroccan Jews, as well as Jews from Marseilles and other cities in southern France, also immigrated to the

Balearic Islands when these were reconquered by the Aragonese in the years 1224–33. Of course, when the *Reconquista* neared its end, the Christian kings no longer needed Jewish cooperation and the support for Jewish immigration weakened. By then, however, the entire peninsula, including Portugal, had a considerable number of Jewish communities.

The question of the absolute number of the Jewish population in Christian Spain is still a matter of debate. Some historians, impressed by reports of contemporary Arab authors who described in glowing terms the grandeur of Spanish Jewry in the period preceding the *Reconquista*, believe that Spain had a Jewish population reaching into the hundreds of thousands. Other historians arrived at the conclusion that up to the fifteenth century Spanish Jewry was of a rather modest size. Spain was then a sparsely populated country, with only a few major urban centers. Most of the Jewish communities were in rural areas and therefore very small. The largest Jewish community in Castile was in Toledo, while Burgos in the north was the other major community. Aragon's largest Jewish community was in Saragossa. Barcelona and Valencia, too, had large Jewish communities. But even Toledo's Jewry numbered only between 200 and 400 families. In Portugal the largest communities were in Lisbon and Oporto. But these were rather small in comparison with Toledo and Saragossa. A computation based on extant tax rolls would indicate that by the end of the Early Middle Ages the combined number of Jews in Aragon, Castile, and Portugal was in the range of about 40,000.

Much smaller, but continuously rising, was the Jewish population in Frankland. While it seems certain that in its French parts the Jewish population of the Antiquity had by and large survived into the Early Middle Ages, opinions are divided as to its German parts. Most historians believe that the Rhineland communities, if there were any in addition to Cologne (cf. Vol. I, Sec. XI, Chap. 3), had disappeared in the turmoil of the waning Antiquity. With the advent of the Carolingian dynasty, and especially in the eighth and ninth centuries, the number of Jews was rising in the French and Italian areas of the empire. The Jews were welcomed, and even invited, due to the role they began to play in international trade.

In Italy the size of the Jewish population underwent many

changes in the period of transition from the Antiquity to the Early Middle Ages. To begin with, between the fifth and ninth century many Jews left the declining city of Rome to disperse to all other parts of the peninsula. In the tenth century Rome's Jewish population sank to its smallest number ever. In the latter part of the Early Middle Ages its number rose again. In northern Italy, where Judaism was outlawed by a Langobardian king in 661 (cf. Vol. I, Sec. XI, Chap. 3), Jews appeared again under the benign rule of the Carolingians, as we have seen above. But this Jewish community remained very small in number. Most of the time we learn of the presence of individual Jewish families in certain localities. Somewhat larger communities existed in post-Carolingian times in Pavia, Verona, and Lucca. Here too the Jewish communities became more numerous and larger in size towards the end of the period. A few local temporary expulsions did not halt the process, and by the end of the period, with the start of immigration of Jews from Germany, north-Italian Jewry was on its way to becoming a community of importance.

The Jewish community in southern Italy and Sicily in this period was much larger. It grew in size especially under Norman rule. In fact, there is reason to believe that Jews were present in practically every city and town both on the mainland and in Sicily. Communities of hundreds of Jews were no rarity here. Palermo, and possibly also Naples, had communities of more than 1,000 Jews. Jews were also found on the islands of Malta, Gozzo, and Sardinia. Only Corsica seems not to have had any Jewish population. It has been estimated that Italy's total Jewish population numbered about 40,000, among a population of about 8,000,000.

When Germany emerged out of the division of the Carolingian empire in 843, few, if any, Jews lived within its confines. Soon, however, and especially during the tenth century, Jewish communities began to spring up in the western regions of the kingdom. Jews arrived from various countries, and especially from Italy. The ban against polygamy issued in the second half of the tenth century by Rabbi Gershom of Mayence, as well as other evidence, strongly suggest that immigrants had been coming to Germany also from the Near East. The invitation issued in 1084 by Bishop Ruediger Huozmann of Spires (Speyer) to Jews to settle in his city on quite favorable conditions indicates that on the eve of the First Crusade Germany was open to Jewish immigration and settlement. The massacres and mass suicide of the Jews of the Rhineland during the preparations for the First Crusade (see below, Chap. 5) dealt a severe blow to Germany's Jewry.

In the twelfth century, however, German Jewry recovered from the disaster through increased immigration, and by the thirteenth century it had become a community of considerable numbers. At that time about 100 localities can be identified as having had Jewish communities. Most of the communities were small in size. There were, however, communities inhabited by hundreds or even as many as 1,000 to 2,000 Jews. The greatest concentration of Jewish communities was in the southern and central areas of the western half of the country. The geographic expansion within Germany also widened. Jewish communities now began to appear in the newly acquired territories in the east. Austria, where Jews had appeared as early as the tenth century, received in the late twelfth century many Jewish immigrants from Bavaria. In the west, too, Jewish communities appeared in the Netherlands and in the Duchy of Brabant, today's Belgium. Brussels had a Jewish community by the middle of the thirteenth century. The absence of Jews in appreciable numbers from this region earlier in the period can be, at least in part, explained by the recurring devastating invasions of the Vikings between the ninth and eleventh centuries into the Low Countries.

When France was separated from the former Carolingian empire in 843, the bulk of its Jewish population was still concentrated in the south, and especially in the Rhone valley. Here, too, the Viking menace may have discouraged Jews from settling farther west and north. But as we proceed deeper into the Middle Ages, we find more and more Jewish communities in the northern parts of the country. Also, the absolute number of the Jews increased. Some estimates have it that on the eve of the expulsion in 1306 no less than 100,000 Jews lived in France. The numerical growth of French Jewry can be attributed to a high birthrate and to the remarkable absence of anti-Jewish violence even during the preparations for the First Crusade. The Jewish population lived in several hundred communities, among which were most of the major cities of the country. The communities were generally small in size; larger concentrations of Jews were found in the big cities. In 1283, under Church pressure, King Philip III ordered the removal of the Jews from the small towns and their transfer to big cities. The ecological structure of French Jewry thus underwent a basic change some 20 years before the expulsion of 1306.

In England, too, Jews, most likely mercenaries in, and suppliers to, the Roman armies, were present in the Antiquity. It is very doubtful, however, that this resulted in the establishment of a Jewish community in these remote times. There are reasons to believe that a more permanent Jewish settlement emerged in England, when new cities began to rise after the Anglo-Saxon conquest, which began in the fifth century. This settlement probably did not grow, and possibly even disappeared in the turmoil of the incessant Viking raids beginning with the last years of the eighth century. Documentary evidence of the existence of a Jewish community in England is available only from the period following the Norman conquest in 1066, which established more peaceful conditions in the country.

The first Jews whom we find at that time in England were immigrants from Normandy, either brought, or permitted to come, by William the Conqueror. The number of the Jews in eleventh-century England was quite small. In the twelfth century, however, their number grew by additional immigration from France, and from Germany, Italy, Spain, and Morocco. Especially large was the group of French Jews who arrived in 1182, after being expelled by King Philip II Augustus. At that time English Jewry numbered about 2,500. The area of Jewish settlement, however, was limited to the southeastern regions, and few Jewish communities existed west of Exeter or north of York.

The tragic events at York in 1190 (see below, Chaps. 3 and 5), during which about 150 Jews died for the sanctification of the Holy Name, obviously caused a diminution of the kingdom's Jewish population. Nevertheless, the Jewish population again increased in the thirteenth century, mostly through natural growth. On the eve of the expulsion of 1290, about 3,000 Jews resided in England. Over 100 localities can be identified as places of Jewish settlement during the entire period between 1066 and 1290.

The Jewish population on the eastern edge of Catholic Europe—that is, Hungary, Bohemia, and Poland—was quite small. Some Jews had been living in Hungary prior to the Magyar conquest of 895, and under the Arpad dynasty, and especially in the eleventh century, their number had increased by immigration from Germany, Bohemia, and Moravia. But even then Jewish communities existed only in a handful of localities. In Bohemia and Moravia Jews must have appeared somewhat later; their presence is attested beginning with the early tenth century. Jewish settlement in the capital city of Prague can be documented from the eleventh century. Somewhat later we find Jews also in other localities, such as Olmuetz and Pilsen. The rather small Jewish population decreased somewhat in 1098 when many fled to nearby Poland to avoid a crusader army which threatened Bohemian Jewry.

The beginning of Jewish settlement in Poland has been a matter of debate among historians for nearly a century. Some historians have forcefully promoted the idea that the first Jewish settlers were Khazarians who had left their country for Poland after its subjugation by the Russians. Other historians have been equally persistent in rejecting this theory. At any rate it seems certain that some of Poland's early Jewish settlers had come from the east, from Russia, the Byzantine empire, and possibly Khazaria. There may also be truth in the legendary traditions about the presence of Jews in Poland as early as the tenth century.

In western Poland the provinces of Pomerania and Silesia seem to have received the first Jewish immigrants from Germany. Small numbers of Jews came from Germany, probably in the eleventh century, and we have seen that by the end of the eleventh century refugees fleeing before the crusaders came from Bohemia. The twelfth century saw an increased Jewish immigration from Germany. Large numbers of Germans came to Poland after its devastation by the Tartar attack of 1241, and Jews may have come as part of this general movement of immigrants. The German character given to many cities by the new immigrants no doubt served as an attraction to German Jews. By the end of the Early Middle Ages about ten Jewish communities existed in western Poland. There may also have been some exclusively Jewish settlements, as is indicated by the name Zydowo—that is, "Jews' Place"—borne by certain localities early in the thirteenth century.

Chapter 3

Jewish Political Destiny

General Developments

At the start of the Early Middle Ages, Jewish existence under western Christendom was largely tranquil. The Jews were proportionately small in number and therefore did not yet evoke resentments among the Gentile population. In addition, the Roman tradition of recognizing the Jews as citizens had not yet been fully forgotten. Furthermore, the Jews fulfilled the important function as the only professional traders, and were therefore generally welcome.

Little by little, however, the situation began to change. Germanic legal concepts, according to which Jews were considered aliens, began to take root. It therefore became necessary to fashion a new legal basis for the presence of the Jews. Thus various rulers, beginning with the Carolingians in Frankland, started to issue charters, either to Jewish individuals or Jewish groups, which granted them the right of domicile and defined the rules and conditions under which they could live in the various territories. Consequently, the existence of Jewish communities became increasingly dependent on the good will or whims of a given ruler, and was no longer based on public law. In the latter part of the period the social status of the Jews deteriorated in the wake of anti-Jewish propaganda of churchmen (cf., the next chap.). As a result, the Jews became even more dependent upon the person of the ruler, and he began to consider them his personal property. As early as the tenth century, charters given to Jews were broken or revoked at will, and Jews were granted as gifts to vassals, or sold or pawned as collateral for debts.

With all its negative elements and great variety of forms, the system of the charters did obligate the rulers who granted them to protect the life and property of the Jews and their right to practice their religion. As long as there was no strong class of Christian burgesses engaged in commerce, the basic tranquility of the

Jewish communities continued to prevail. Even as late as 1084 the bishop of Spires (Speyer) saw fit to invite Jews to settle in his city as developers of commerce. But, when towns began to multiply and the number of Christian merchants began to grow, the Jewish trading population began to be looked upon as unwelcome competitors. The belief spread that the Jews were guilty of perfidy *(perfidia Judaica)*. Their trustworthiness as merchants was questioned, and Jews began to be administered a degrading text of an oath whenever they had litigation with a Christian. The "Jewish oath," still practiced in some countries as late as the nineteenth century, manifested more than anything else how the once respected and appreciated Jewish trader came to be despised by the Gentiles.

Symptoms of the change began to appear in some places as early as the ninth century. But it was in the late eleventh century, with its heightened Christian religious fervor, that all these developments came to a head. The violent outbreaks against the Jews beginning with the First Crusade clearly demonstrated the change in the status of the Jew. They also showed unmistakably that the charters were no longer adequate to protect the Jewish communities.

As a result, a new system of protection developed and obtained its ultimate formulation in the second half of the twelfth and the first half of the thirteenth century. The basic principle of the new system was that the Jews were "serfs of the Chamber," that is, of the Treasury, while the ruler was obliged to protect them as his serfs. The arrangement, which partly resembles the feudal relationship between sovereign and vassal, has for a long time been a major topic of debate among historians. Historians disagree about the nature of the legal position of the Jews under Frederic I Barbarossa and his grandson Frederic II, who were the first to use the term "serfs of our Chamber" in privileges given them in 1182 and 1237 respectively. It is clear that the condition of the Jews was incomparably better than that of the peasants-serfs. Most of the time Jews could move freely from place to place. Their property could generally be transferred to their heirs, despite a number of flagrant confiscations of large fortunes of deceased Jewish plutocrats. They were not completely excluded from participation in the political affairs of the general community.

They participated in the defense of city fortifications in times of siege, and thus enjoyed in many localities the right of bearing arms. Significantly, in some localities the Jews fought under their own banners.

The use of the term "serfs" was justified, and seemed natural in a society which believed on theological grounds that the Jews, due to their alleged part in Jesus' crucifixion, were condemned to live in perpetual servitude. On a more secular basis it was also believed that the emperors of the Holy Roman Empire, as heirs to the emperors of Rome, inherited ownership rights over the Jews from Vespasian, the conqueror of Judaea in 70 C.E. The Jews accepted almost without protest their status as serfs of the Chamber. They expected the coming of the Messiah at a time when they would have expiated the sins of their ancestors, they believed that their alienation and servitude were part of that process of expiation.

While theoretically the Jews were considered serfs of the Imperial Chamber, their actual lot depended on a multitude of feudal rulers, both lay and ecclesiastical. By the time the idea of Chamber serfdom attained its full force, all the Catholic states were at the peak of feudal decentralization. True, the emperor and the kings still issued patents of privileges to Jewish communities. But realistically the communities also had to make arrangements for their safety with local authorities. Thus a system of contributions, also called bribes by some historians, developed, whereby large sums of money were paid by Jewish communities for their right to exist and for their safety. The size of the contributions and the way they were collected differed from ruler to ruler. But toward the end of the Early Middle Ages the monetary contribution of the Jews to local authorities had become the most important single instrument regulating the relationship between the Jews and the state.

On the Iberian Peninsula

Almost the entire period of the Early Middle Ages was dominated by Christian efforts to reconquer the peninsula from the Muslims, and the Jewish policy of the rulers was geared to this aim. Thus, while the Jews were generally treated with benignity, their situation began to deteriorate when the *Reconquista* came to its virtual conclusion in the second half of the thirteenth century. In the beginning, Christians, Muslims, and Jews were treated alike in the re-conquered territories. Soon, however, it became clear that the Jews were enjoying a political and social status far above that of the Muslims. Although some modern historians believe that the Jews remained neutral during the *Reconquista* wars, the impression is clear that Jewish interest tilted toward the Christian side. In fact, oppression of the Jews in Muslim Spain by the Almoravids and Almohades, beginning with the last decade of the eleventh century, could not help but shift Jewish loyalties to the Christian side.

Jewish participation in military campaigns against the Muslim states was not insignificant, and Jews continued to support the cause of the *Reconquista* even after the attacks perpetrated on them in 1109 by their Christian neighbors in Toledo and in other localities in Castile. Jewish taxes were often used to maintain the Reconquest armies. Jewish financiers played an essential role in financing many *Reconquista* campaigns. For example, the campaign of the celebrated *Reconquista* hero El Cid to retake the province of Valencia was heavily financed by Jews. Jewish financiers became so important that they grew into a courtier class of major significance. They came ultimately to perform a great variety of governmental functions. Their knowledge of languages and their special familiarity with the Muslim South greatly enlarged their opportunities in the diplomatic service. All this gave the Jews a far better social status than that of their coreligionists in other contemporary Christian countries. Jews were usually addressed by the title "Don." In Catalan they were addressed as "En," the title common in Spain's Northeast.

The situation was, however, not without ambiguity. Legally the Jews were considered serfs of the kings and princes. True, in practice this only meant that the Jews had to pay their taxes directly to the king. But in theory, at least, the property of the Jews was not theirs but the king's. The weak Spanish states, preoccupied with the overwhelming issues of the *Reconquista*, were not even able to give the Jewish population effective protection against bands of marauding robbers and the Jews had to live behind fortified walls of self-imposed ghettos. And yet, during most of the period the kings of the *Reconquista* states were able to withstand parliamentary and Church pressures and grant the Jews a degree of freedom fairly high for those times. The absence of a strong burgher class eliminated the element of anti-Jewish economic competition.

During most of the period few differences could be discerned in the situation of the Jews in Castile, Aragon, and Portugal. All three kingdoms availed themselves of the services of Jewish courtiers. These courtiers were a mixed blessing to the Jewish communities. True, they often acted and interceded successfully on behalf of their coreligionists. A shining example is Judah ibn Ezra, purveyor and financial agent in the service of King Alphonso VII of Castile (1126–57). While in command of the frontier fortress of Calatrava, in 1148 he facilitated the massive Jewish flight from Almohade-dominated Muslim Spain to Castile. He also extended his aid to the rufugees in their new homeland. But equally often the influence and wealth of the Jewish courtiers evoked envy and hatred among the populace and nobility, and in Church circles. The fall of a Jewish dignitary was sometimes accompanied by attacks on the entire Jewish population. Occasionally, the enormous wealth of the courtiers also misled the kings into believing that all Jews were wealthy. They thus felt justified in imposing exorbitant taxes on Jewish communities, which often caused their almost total ruin. The generally favorable Jewish situation was mainly due, however, not to intercessions of the courtiers, but to the fact that the Jews' presence was useful to the states. Thus, the introduction of the Jewish-distinctive clothes, decreed by the Fourth Lateran Council held in Rome in 1215, was generally ignored in the Spanish lands.

Later in the thirteenth century things visibly began to change. The *Reconquista* was largely completed and the areas vacated by the Muslims had been colonized. The Jews were no longer unexpendable, and the kings began to listen more attentively to the anti-Jewish agitation of the Church and the *Cortes* (parliament). A blood accusation in 1250, and the imposed religious disputation in Barcelona in 1263, unmistakably heralded the advent of new and less favorable political conditions for Spain's Jewry. In Catalonia the situation of the Jews had already begun to deteriorate in the first half of the thirteenth century, because the region was now fully colonized and the Church stronger than elsewhere on the peninsula.

In Frankland

The political situation of the Jews in Frankland under the Carolingians was even better than in Spain. Pepin the Short (741–68), his son Charlemagne (768–814), and his grandson Louis the Pious (814–40) were all favorably disposed toward their Jewish subjects. The especially friendly attitude of Louis the Pious and his wife Judith was manifested in the face of angry opposition on the part of such a leading churchman as Lyons' bishop Agobard. The basis for the favorable treatment of the Jews was the major role they played in trade and commerce. But it was also the principle of toleration followed by the Carolingians, rulers over a multinational empire, that worked in favor of the Jews. Equally tolerant was the attitude of the Gentile population toward their Jewish neighbors. Rarely was there a place in medieval Christian Europe where Jews and Gentiles mingled so freely as in Carolingian Frankland.

The nature of the legal status of Frankland's Jews is still a matter of debate. Whether the Jews were considered aliens, or a separate religious group, their existence was not covered by the public law of the country. Instead, the system of granting charters to individual Jews seems to have provided sufficiently for their protection and right to practice their religion. A governmental official described as "the master of the Jews" seems to have had the task of providing protection to the Jews whenever needed. The Jews must have felt quite secure if after the death of Louis the Pious they involved themselves in the thorny question of the succession by siding with Empress Judith and her son Charles, later known as the Bald.

Even more debated than the legal status of the Jews is the question of whether a Jewish princedom had existed under the Carolingians in Narbonne and its vicinity. A recent researcher, after thoroughly investigating the question, arrived at the conclusion that such a Jewish feudal princedom really existed. Characteristically, the charters given by the Carolingians to Jewish individuals often resembled feudal agreements between a sovereign and his vassals. It is therefore not inconceivable that the Carolingians were ready to grant to a Jew a region of their state as a free allodium (landed property for which the grantee owes no rent or service to the sovereign). That Narbonne was given to a Jew was probably due to the fact that Jews played a major role in the transfer of Narbonne from Muslim to Carolingian rule in 759.

The man endowed with the princedom by Pepin and his sons in 768 was a certain Natronai-Makhir, a member of Babylonia's exilarchal dynasty. His princedom encompassed Septimania, on the French Mediterranean coast, and Toulouse and its vicinity. Makhir, known as Theodoric (in the French *chansons de geste* he is called Aymeri), was possibly married to Pepin's sister. Nonetheless, their son William of Toulouse was a pious and observant Jew. In 791 the endowment of the Narbonne principality was confirmed by a new patent from Charlemagne and by a resolution adopted at a Church Council then in session in Narbonne. At the same time the princedom expanded into the Spanish Mediterranean coast and its forces participated in the conquest of Barcelona from the Muslims in 803.

The Jewish rulers of the Narbonnaise, Toulousaine, and the Spanish March—that is, Frankland's possessions south of the Pyrenees—continued to play an important role in the politics of the Frankish empire even after its partition in 843. Their involvement in matters of state continued in France almost to the time of the Capetian takeover. Like many other feudal lords almost all of Makhir's descendants were either executed or died on the battlefield. The title "Prince of the Jews" (in Hebrew he was usually called *nasi*) survived into the tenth century.

In France

When France emerged in 843 as a separate kingdom under Charles the Bald, the situation of the Jews deteriorated slightly due to the weakening of the royal power that resulted from the partition of the empire. Basically, however, their situation remained favorable until the overthrow of the Carolingians in 987 and beyond. A friendly Gentile population served as a suitable backdrop to the governmental policy. True, after the year 1000 the tranquility of the Jewish community was sporadically disturbed by anti-Jewish outbreaks, mostly due to growing Christian religious fanaticism. Such was the case in the first decade of the eleventh century when Jews were suspected of attempting to demolish the Holy Sepulchre in Jerusalem in complicity with Muslims, or of helping Christian heretical movements. In 1065 Jews were attacked in southern France by groups of crusaders on their way to aid the Spanish Christians in their struggle to re-conquer their country from the Muslims. These outbreaks were short-lived, and there was a remarkable general absence of anti-Jewish violence in France. Even the preparations for the First Crusade in 1096, so tragic for Germany's Jewry (see below, Chap. 5), left French Jewry largely unscathed.

The twelfth century was a period of increased Christian religious fanaticism, during which French Jewry endured its first ritual murder accusations, often accompanied by riots and local expulsions. It was in this heated religious atmosphere that King Philip II Augustus (1180–1223), who already in his boyhood had manifested a dislike for the Jews, decided in 1182 to expel them from his domains. The expulsion, however, caused little harm to French Jewry since the territory then under royal control was small, and the expelled Jews were readily admitted into nearby feudal territories. When Philip Augustus later in his reign gained control over the English possessions in France, including the regions of Anjou and Normandy, he refrained from expelling their Jews. It was then logical for him to permit the Jews he expelled in 1182 to return to their homes in 1198.

Under Louis IX, the Saint (1226–70), the situation of the Jews took a definite turn for the worse. In Languedoc and Provence, where the Albigensian heresy had been vanquished by a Crusade from the north, Jews could no longer hold governmental offices. In the royal domains and in the feudal territories fiscal demands increased and the methods of collecting the Jewish taxes became ever more brutal. By 1240 the Church was able to compel the Jews to appear for a religious disputation with Nicholas Donin, a

Jewish convert to Christianity. In the wake of the disputation held in Paris, Jewish books were burned at the stake there in 1242 (or possibly 1244).

During the reign of Philip III and Philip IV there was a certain improvement in the situation of the Jews compared with their plight under Louis IX. But the wheel could not be fully turned back in those years when the Middle Ages reached their peak. Thus, first the Jews of the rural communities were transferred to larger cities, and ultimately expelled from the country in 1306. This time the feudal lords, imbued with the religious zeal of the time, cooperated and the Jews had to leave almost all of France. To be sure, they were recalled and expelled several more times in the course of the fourteenth century. But these were the last convulsions in a process of rejecting the Jew which had actually attained its full force already in the expulsion of 1306.

In Germany

In Germany the Frankish policy of giving protection to the Jews was continued even after the Carolingians were replaced by later dynasties. In fact, this policy was followed more intensively here than in France. The bishops, who became the actual temporal rulers of most of the major cities, basically also followed this policy. Here too no serious anti-Jewish outbreaks occurred up to the end of the eleventh century. Even though expressions of hostility on the part of the Gentile neighbors were not totally absent, no real friction existed between Jew and Christian. Indicative of this may be the fact that Jews of that period found it necessary and possible to mourn the death of the bishops of Magdeburg and Metz. In 1084, only 12 years before the horrible events accompanying the First Crusade, the bishop of Spires (Speyer), Ruediger Huozmann, invited Jews to settle in his city and granted them extensive rights, such as the possession of land, employment of Christian labor, and communal autonomy.

In 1090 Emperor Henry IV (1056–1106), always their unswerving friend, confirmed the charter given to the Jews of Spires and granted a similar one to the Jews of Worms. It is therefore not simple to explain how and why Christian mobs fell upon the Jews of major cities, such as Mayence, Worms, and Cologne in the spring of 1096, at the time the First Crusade was organizing itself. In fact, it was in part the element of surprise and bewilderment that drove thousands of Jews to self-immolation (see below, Chap. 5). No doubt, the absence of the emperor from the country greatly contributed to the calamity. Characteristically, no major exodus of the Jews to other countries took place. They only abandoned the smaller rural settlements to move into fortified cities. The authorities also began in 1103 to include the Jews into the *Landfrieden*, the public peace guaranteed to the weaker strata of the population who, being unarmed, needed special protection.

The rule of the Hohenstaufen, beginning with Frederick I Barbarossa (1152–90), was very beneficial to the Jews, although it was they who brought the concept of Jewish Chamber serfdom to its full and clear formulation. No doubt, the Hohenstaufen viewed very seriously their obligation to protect the Jews implicit in the serfdom concept. Frederick I and his successors staunchly defended the Jews whenever a situation developed calling for action on their part. In 1157 Barbarossa confirmed the charter given to the Jews of Worms by Emperor Henry IV in 1090.

It was also thanks to Barbarossa that German Jewry suffered little, if any, damage when the Third Crusade organized itself in 1189. Although his grandson, Emperor Frederick II (1215–50), resided most of the time in his Sicilian kingdom, he extended as much protection to his Jewish subjects in Germany as he could under the circumstances. When Jews of Fulda were accused in 1235 of having committed the ritual murder of several Christian children, he dismissed the accusation as untrue. Simultaneously he ordered a thorough investigation of the ritual murder libel by a committee of clergymen and scholars. When the committee brought in an opinion fully exonerating the Jews, he proclaimed all German Jews innocent of such accusations. About the same time he confirmed, as had his grandfather Frederick Barbarossa, the charter of the Jews of Worms and extended the privileges contained in it to all German Jewry.

We have seen that in addition to royal or imperial safeguards, the lot of the Jews was dependent on the measure of protection given them by local feudal rulers. It is therefore not surprising that a charter given in 1244 to the Jews of Austria by Duke

Frederick II (1230–46) of the Babenberg dynasty was as important for them, if not more so, as the above-mentioned charter granted to the Jews of the entire empire by Emperor Frederick II Hohenstaufen. Nothing attests to this as much as the fact that the Austrian charter, sometimes called a bill of rights, became in the next few decades a model for charters issued by the kings of Bohemia, Hungary, and Poland to their rising Jewish communities. In this charter the duke of Austria gave full and vigorous protection to the life, economic interests, and religious institutions of the Jews. Christians were to be severely punished for doing bodily harm to a Jew, and capital punishment was to be meted out for the murder of a Jew. The desecration of a synagogue or a Jewish cemetery was also to be severely punished. Most of the paragraphs of the charter deal with the moneylending interests of the Jews and attempt to secure for the Jewish lender the capital and interest in every possible way.

The charters and the protection guaranteed by them were paid for by the Jews with huge sums of money. The "regular" taxes imposed on them were also exorbitant. In the middle of the thirteenth century German Jewry paid to the Imperial Treasury 12 percent of the entire revenue collected by it. The sum of the Jewish tax also equaled 20 percent of the revenue collected from the cities of the empire. Since the Jews constituted only a tiny fraction of the general population, this was indeed a very burdensome and unfair tax. Of course, all kinds of special taxes, contributions, and "gifts" were also collected from the Jews on many occasions.

After the storms of the First and Second Crusades blew themselves out, German Jewry did not experience any serious upheavals during the latter part of the Early Middle Ages. It was the following chaotic period of the Great Interregnum (1254–73) that brought insecurity to the life of the Jews as to most people in the Germanic lands. Henceforth the Jewish situation went from tragedy to tragedy. In the Late Middle Ages Germany became to the Jews *erets hadamim*, the bloody land, from which most of them had to flee to find refuge in more hospitable domiciles.

In Italy

The spread of Carolingian control over Italy beginning with 754, was very favorable to the interests of Italian Jewry. The Jews were beneficiaries of the general state of tranquility brought to the country by the Carolingians and of the friendly attitude they manifested to their Jewish subjects everywhere. The German kings of the Saxon dynasty, upon gaining control over Italy in the tenth century, basically continued the Jewish policy of the Carolingians. We have seen that early in the period the Jewish population in northern Italy was very sparse. But in the twelfth century, at a time when the Jewish population began to grow in number, the influence of the German emperors declined and the major cities gained a high degree of independence. As a result, the Jewish situation deteriorated, since the Christian middle class ruling these cities saw in them economic competitors. Venice and Genoa, the mightiest among the cities-republics refused most of the time to tolerate Jews in their midst. Pisa treated its small Jewish community in a much friendlier way. In other cities, such as Verona, Pavia, Milan, Cremona, and Bologna, the Jews were tolerated, but had to endure temporary expulsions. Despite this, the Jewish communities in northern Italy survived, and on the threshold of the Late Middle Ages the region became an area of major Jewish immigration.

In central Italy the popes continued the policy—introduced by their early predecessors—of giving limited protection to the Jews and their religion. No major persecution of the Jews occurred here during the entire period. Even under Pope Innocent III (1198–1216), who is sometimes termed the father of medieval anti-Semitism, the Jewish situation in the Papal States did not essentially deteriorate. Some of the popes, as was the case with Alexander III (1159–81), employed Jews in their financial administration.

Even better was the situation of the Jews in southern Italy and Sicily, both under Norman and Hohenstaufen rule. Basically, Jews continued to enjoy the status of a protected minority, not unlike the status they had as *dhimmis* when Muslims ruled the country. Here and there a royal charter even granted the Jews a status equal to that of their Christian neighbors. Jewish officials are found in the financial administration of both the state and the cities, as well as in the management of royal monopolies. In fact, if not for the Christian oath often imposed on the officialdom, its Jewish contingent probably would have been much larger. Only under Church pressure did the rulers sometimes introduce anti-Jewish regulations. This was the case with Emperor Frederick II, who under perpetual Church accusations of being a heretic, saw himself compelled to implement in 1222 the laws about Jewish-distinctive clothes decreed seven years earlier by the Fourth Lateran Council. At the same time, Frederick never failed to give protection to the life and property of his Jewish subjects. A further chapter will describe how he surrounded himself with Jewish scholars and scientists.

In England

We have seen that the Jewish community in England came into being in 1066 with the approval, or possibly at the initiative, of William the Conqueror. It is therefore not surprising that it enjoyed favorable treatment under William and most of his successors. Although the kings of England considered the Jews their property, an idea which found entrance into a collection of English laws early in the twelfth century, the Jews lived under favorable conditions and enjoyed a high degree of communal autonomy all through the twelfth century. The growing religious anti-Jewish prejudice, which found expression in the blood libel of Norwich in 1144, the first recorded accusation of this type in Western Europe, did not visibly hurt England's Jewish population. Anti-Jewish riots which occurred in about ten localities during the eleventh and twelfth centuries seem to have been of minor proportions.

The Jews who came from Normandy in 1066 were moneylenders, and they continued to engage in banking in their new homeland. Being practically the only dispensers of credit in the country, their role in the economy was significant. The favorable treatment given to them was a response to the importance of the economic role they played. In fact, most of the royal decrees issued to Jews early in the twelfth century clearly aimed to make it possible for them to live in England comfortably. They could move about the country freely and could own real estate. The Jews made use of these privileges and even built stone houses, a great rarity in England in those times. Curiously, ruins of medieval stone houses are still popularly referred to as "Jews' houses."

A serious worsening of the Jews' situation took place at the time of the Third Crusade. During the ceremonies of the coronation of Richard the Lionhearted in 1189 a serious pogrom broke out in London in which a number of Jews lost their lives. Among the victims were members of a delegation of provincial Jewry, which came to pay homage to the new king. This was followed the next year by the bloody massacre of Jews in York, during which practically the entire Jewish community perished, either at the hands of the mob or by suicide (cf. below, Chap. 5). The events of 1189 and 1190, like those in Germany in 1096, caught both government and Jews by surprise. It soon became clear that economic grievances, even more than the heated religious atmosphere of the Third Crusade, lay at the root of the events. The bonds signed by their Christian debtors were no less a target of the attack than the Jews themselves.

Afterwards, the situation of the Jews never again improved. Beginning with the reign of Henry III (1216–72), sums exacted from the Jews in the form of taxes and special contributions became ever more exorbitant, and the means of their collection increasingly brutal and cruel. In 1272 many Jews, including the entire Jewish community of Hereford, were incarcerated in an attempt to collect from them an imposition for that year. Confiscations of the fortunes of wealthy Jews upon their death were a recurrent phenomenon. Some historians have described the role of English Jewry as that of a "sponge" in the service of the crown: first the Jews collected from the populace enormous amounts of money through their credit transactions, and these sums were afterwards taken away from the Jews by the kings. The kings considered the confiscation of Jewish wealth justifiable due to their belief that they possessed an absolute proprietorship over the Jews. The function of the Jews as "sponges" may have been the reason that, unlike rulers on the European continent, the kings of England never ceded to the barons the right of owning or taxing the Jews.

In the course of the thirteenth century the situation of the Jews underwent further deterioration. Indicative of this was the enforcement, beginning with 1222, of the decree of the Fourth Lateran Council ordering Jews to wear distinctive clothes. In the 1230s and 1240s Henry III granted a number of towns the right not to tolerate Jews in their midst (*privilegium de non tolerandis Judaeis*). The 1260s witnessed new outbreaks of anti-Jewish violence. The situation was further aggravated by a combination of developments which made Jewish moneylending both unnecessary and undesirable. Large-scale moneylenders from Italy and France began to penetrate the credit market and to replace the Jews. Also, by acquiring from Jews pledges with landed estates as collateral, some of the barons enlarged their landholdings and thus became stronger in their perpetual opposition to the kings.

A result of these developments was the Statute on the Jews issued by King Edward I in 1275 barring them from engaging in moneylending. Jews, however, circumvented the law and continued lending money to Gentiles under the guise of business-like transactions. Then, in 1290, Edward I issued an order expelling the Jews from his kingdom. The explusion order was issued on July 18, which corresponded to the 9th of Av, a date notorious in Jewish history for repeated calamities. The Jews departed during the late summer and autumn for France, Germany, and Flanders. A small group of them reached Spain. In 1310 Jews negotiated with the English government for permission to settle again in the country, but permission was not given.

In Bohemia-Moravia, Hungary, and Poland

In the first part of the Early Middle Ages the fledgling Jewish communities in this area seem to have lived generally under fairly favorable conditions. The very paucity of the number of Jews precluded the emergence of anything resembling a "Jewish question." True, Bohemian and Moravian Jews were attacked in the period of the First Crusade and some of them were forcibly converted. But these were attacks by passing crusader forces, and the situation of the Jews was not altered by the events. In Poland no specific Jewish legislation is known prior to the year 1200. A number of uniface coins with Hebrew characters from the late twelfth and early thirteenth centuries found in western Poland suggest that the rulers employed Jews as mintmasters. A prohibition against Jews serving in the royal administration or joining the ranks of the nobility decreed in 1222 by Andrew II of Hungary (1205–35) in the statute known as "The Golden Bull," may have been inspired by the heated religious atmosphere following the Fourth Lateran Council.

By and large, however, the Jewish condition remained stable in all these countries till the end of the Early Middle Ages. The main reason for the friendly attitude to the Jews lay in the desire of the various central-European rulers to attract immigrants to their countries, devastated and depopulated by the Tartar invasion of 1241. This is best attested to by the charters given in 1251 to Hungarian Jewry by King Bela IV (1235–70), in 1254 to Bohemian-Moravian Jewry by King Premysl Ottokar II (1253–78), and in 1264 to the Jews of Great Poland by Grand Duke Boleslaus V (1241–79). All these charters were modeled after the "bill of rights" given to Austrian Jewry in 1244 (see above). At a time when the Catholic Church had reached the peak of its might, Jewish communities which obtained these kinds of charters in Catholic countries were indeed living under quite felicitous conditions.

Chapter 4

The Church and the Jews

The Theological Image of the Jew
and Its Consequences

In a period of intense religiosity, such as that of the Middle Ages, the influence of the Church on the destiny of the Jews was as strong as that of the state and sometimes even stronger. This was especially the case under western Christendom. In Byzantium, where the emperor was simultaneously the head of the Church, the influence of the latter was necessarily checked by the interests of the state. In the Catholic West the Church was independent of the state and subject to the central authority of the popes; it was therefore rarely held in check by the state. The Church was thus able to develop its own policy with regard to the Jews.

The medieval Church inherited from the Antiquity the image of the Jew as created in the writings of its early theologians. This theological image portrayed the Jew in the first place as the killer of Christ. A widespread legend had it that one of the Jews present at the crucifixion was cursed by Jesus to be a perpetual wanderer. This wandering Jew was often "recognized," especially toward the end of the Early Middle Ages. The wandering Jew, an immortal witness of the crucifixion, together with the New Testament story blaming Jews for the death of the Christian messiah, kept the deicide guilt of the Jews perpetually before the eyes of every pious Christian. And since the corporate consciousness of medieval man perceived every human being as a member of a group, the guilt of deicide was easily placed at the threshold of the entire Jewish community.

The theological image of the Jew endowed him with additional faults. He was considered not so much an infidel as a heretic. True, early Christian thought and legislation considered Judaism a separate religion. They even ascribed to Judaism the role of a *preparatio evangelica*—that is, of having paved the road for the true Christian faith. But in the mind of the average medieval Christian this concept was replaced by the idea that the Jew was rather a heretic; that he knew that Jesus was the true messiah and the son of God, and that even forefather Abraham was a professing Christian. But the Jew was stiffnecked and stubbornly clung to his Jewish "vomit." He was thus not a member of a different religious denomination, but a renegade and a heretic. Jews were therefore suspected of fomenting heresy, including that of the Albigensians. In addition, the nervousness of the Christian West in face of the overwhelming Muslim ("Saracen") success made the Jews suspect of being secret allies of this arch enemy of Christianity.

The theological image of the Jew found increasing acceptance in Western Europe with the progressing Christianization of its peoples. It also assumed more and more frightening forms. Ultimately the Jew came to be considered as an inhuman creature, perpetually plotting in complicity with sorcerers, or even the devil, the destruction of Christian society. It was only logical to connect the Jew in some way also with the Antichrist. The Antichrist, an eschatological figure, embodying evil in its extreme, was expected to appear at the end of days to oppose Jesus. There was hardly an Antichrist story without a Jew figuring in it. Most portray the Jew as waiting for the coming of the Antichrist in order to help him in his rebellion against the true messiah. Other stories have him even being born of a Jewess. The Jew-monster was popularized by the most potent media of communication of those times, the sermon, sculptures and paintings in the churches, and the passion plays. The lower clergy, unmindful of the attempts of the popes to preserve the physical existence of the Jews (see below), kept on harping in their sermons on the perfidy of the Jews and the evil of their character. The then very popular mystery plays, which had as their central theme the crucifixion, assigned a conspicuous role to the Jewish Christ killers. Often the devil was hovering over the Jew in the play. By developing such an image of the Jew the Church created, albeit not fully intentionally, the backdrop against which many atrocities were perpetrated against the Jewish minority, including the massacres at the time of the Crusades, the blood libel, and the accusation of host defamations (see below, Chaps. 5 and 6).

As mentioned above, the church sermon was a major vehicle in the dissemination of the image of the diabolical Jew. An additional source of anti-Jewish propaganda arose with the organization of new monastic orders in the latter part of the Early Middle Ages. The mendicant friars, who depended on broad contacts with the population for their very subsistence, were able to fan anti-Jewish sentiments in the course of their activities. To be sure, rulers interested in the well-being of their Jewish subjects, such as the kings of Frankland and the Reconquista sovereigns of Spain, were often successful in preventing the clergy from doing too much harm. But, wherever the secular powers were weak, the clergy had a free reign in inciting the populace against the Jews. The hierarchy only rarely followed this line. The activities of Bishop Agobard of Lyons in the first half of the ninth century and of his successor Amulo can only be understood as the reaction of frustrated Church princes to the unusual favors bestowed upon the Jews by the Frankish emperors and the amity between Christians and Jews.

Jewish-Christian fraternization in ninth-century Frankland had reached such a point of intensity that it evoked protests from the pope himself. The Church was apprehensive of too much rapprochement between Christians and Jews for two reasons. First, it was sincerely worried that Judaizing influences might infiltrate Christian society. And second, if Christians were to be permitted to mingle with Jews socially, it would look as if Jews were equal to Christians, while Church dogma assigned to the Jews the status of pariahs. What most worried the Church was the possibility of romantic relations between Jews and Christians. Carnal relations with Jews, who were considered inhuman, were viewed by the Church as sodomy. In fact, such relations were called in Latin *bestialitas*, and were punishable by death, as was the crime of sodomy.

The efforts of the Church at isolating the Jews from their Christian neighbors, not very successful in Carolingian times, gained momentum in later generations. Early in the thirteenth century, when the might of the Church reached its peak, it became easy to promote the idea of the unity of Christendom in the midst of which no place was left for the Jew-heretic. It was then a logical step for the Fourth Lateran Council to adopt the ordinance obliging the Jew to wear distinctive clothes. To be sure, years passed before the Christian princes began to enforce the ordinance in their dominions, but the "yellow badge" became the undeniable symbol of the deep, and for centuries unbridgeable, gap which the Church had opened between its adherents and their Jewish neighbors. True, it is not inconceivable that in the atmosphere of the Middle Ages the Jew would have been driven into total isolation even if the Church would not have played its part in the process. But it is equally undeniable that for theological reasons the Church saw fit to place itself in the forefront of the action to deny the Jew his rightful place in human society.

In subsequent chapters (Chaps. 5 and 6), the major Church-related and Church-inspired calamities that befell the Jews, the massacres at the time of the Crusades, and the various libels hurled at Jews will be discussed. Here, mention should be made of a series of insults and attacks which were directed at the Jews as a reaction to their alleged role in the crucifixion. Characteristically, these actions already appeared early in the Middle Ages when Jew and Gentile still lived amicably side by side. Most of these anti-Jewish actions occurred during the Lenten season, and especially during the Holy Week. The most common occurrence was the stoning of Jews and their houses in commemoration of Jesus' stoning by the Jews (cf. John 8:59). In some places a Jew was slapped on Good Friday, a custom known as "Jew's Slap." Such actions often made Jews inclined to stay indoors during the Holy Week. In some localities Jews were even forbidden to step out of their houses in the days preceding Easter. We shall see further that most of the blood libels also occurred in this period of the year with its heated religious atmosphere.

Attitudes of the Church Councils

One of the mightiest institutions in Christendom was the Church Synod or Church Council. Regional Church Councils, in which the local clergy participated, met fairly frequently in all the countries of Western and Central Europe. Ecumenical Councils, convened and presided over by the popes, met at longer, at sometimes very long, intervals. Both the regional and ecumenical

Councils dealt extensively with the Jewish question in their effort to lead Christian society according to principles and rules
found or implied in the law books of the Church known as the
"canon law." The Jewish issues which came up for debate and
resolution before the councils were mostly of a practical nature
and reflected the attitude of the clergy to various aspects of the
Jewish condition at a given time.

The regional Councils which met during the period of the
Dark Ages all dealt, with certain modifications, with the problems of Jewish ownership of slaves, the service of Christians,
especially women, in Jewish homes, the already-mentioned problem of Jewish-Christian social fraternization, and that of Jews
holding public office. The Councils registered their opposition to
all these phenomena, but their resolutions remained largely on
paper. The role of Jews as international traders in the Carolingian
state and as colonizers and financiers in *Reconquista* Spain made
the rulers of these countries inclined to overlook the wishes of
the clergy. The ordinances issued by the Councils nevertheless
came to be included in the canon law and thus became potentially
harmful to the Jews in later times.

In the period of the Crusades a clear change became noticeable in the Jewish agenda of the Church Councils. They no longer
discussed the question of Jewish slave ownership, since such
ownership disappeared with the declining role of Jews in international trade and their gradual withdrawal from agriculture, where
slave work was mostly needed. Early in the thirteenth century the
Councils (Avignon, 1209, and Paris, 1213) began to discuss the
problem of "Jewish usury," since more and more Jews had entered
the field of credit transactions. Simultaneously, the resolutions of
the Councils began to assume more practical significance, since
the secular powers now faced a much stronger and more aggressive Catholic Church. The Church Councils of this period not
only re-enacted old, unenforced anti-Jewish ordinances, but they
now even boldly demanded that Jews pay tithes to the Church for
all their real-estate holdings.

The peak of synodal influence on Jewish life under Western
Christendom was reached by the Fourth Lateran Council which
met in Rome (in the Lateran Palace) in 1215. Convened by the
mightiest of the medieval popes, Innocent III (1198–1216), it re-

vived old anti-Jewish ordinances, came out against the Jewish loan business, and made the decisive step toward the social isolation of Jews (and Muslims) within Christian society by obliging them to wear distinctive clothes. Jewish society and Jews as individuals resented no other Church-inspired disability as much as they resented the "yellow badge." No anti-Jewish Church law was as often broken as the obligation to wear the "Jewish badge." This law, which took effect in England and in the kingdom of Sicily in 1222, was not enforced in France until the late thirteenth century.

The many regional Councils which repeated the obligation to wear the badge during the thirteenth and fourteenth centuries only underscore the degree of Jewish resistance to it and of the Jews' success in preventing its enforcement. But, even though some countries never enforced the Church law of 1215, the yellow badge became in the Late Middle Ages a distinctive feature of the appearance of the Jew. It also, of course, became the mark of the Jew under Nazi domination in the 1930s and 1940s.

The Attitude of the Popes

The impact of the popes on the destiny of the Jews was much greater than that of the Church Councils. Throughout the Early Middle Ages the power of the popes vis-á-vis the secular states was growing, and their role in shaping the life of the Jews grew along with it. By and large the popes manifested an attitude of toleration toward the Jews. Some of them even saw fit to protect the Jews. Cases of outright papal persecution were a rare occurrence in this period. Characteristic of the relationship between the Jews and the popes was the way in which Rome's Jewish community paid homage to every new pope upon his ascension to the Holy See. A Jewish delegation presented him with a Torah scroll, which the pope accepted while adding the following remark: "I revere the Law of God but condemn your futile interpretation and the religious practices based on it."

The principles of a Jewish policy established by Fathers of the Church, such as Augustine and Pope Gregory I the Great (cf. Vol. I, Sec. XI, Chap. 2) still guided the actions of most of the popes of this period. Popes who were legal-minded insisted on the enforcement of the anti-Jewish ordinances in the canon law. Some went so far as to threaten the secular powers with excommunication for failing to fashion their Jewish policy in accordance with the canon law.

When the situation of the Jews underwent a sudden deterioration in the period of the First Crusade, and the physical extinction of the Jews became potentially possible, the papacy stepped in to save the Jews. This is clearly visible in the bull of Pope Calixtus II (1119–24) issued about 1120. While the bull insisted on the retention of the Jewish disabilities introduced by the early Church, it equally insisted on preserving the privileges Jews possessed theretofore. It stressed the obligation of the Church to protect Jewish life and to prevent forced baptisms. It was a sign of the time that Calixtus also called for the protection of Jewish cemeteries. Many of the men who subsequently occupied the papal throne confirmed Calixtus' bull, so that it became a basic instrument for the protection of the Jews in an increasingly hostile environment.

The attitude of the popes was based on the belief that the people who brought forth the Christian messiah was entitled to live among his adherents until his second coming. Had the Jews totally disappeared, the hope that the very people from which he was born would join the masses of his Gentile followers in recognizing him would have faded forever. Furthermore, had the physical existence of the Jews been terminated, the only testimony to Jesus' incarnation would have been a mere literary one, the New Testament. Therefore the Jews had to be kept alive *ad testimonium fidei*, as a testimony to the faith.

Biblical support for this attitude was found in a prayer in which King David implored God to humiliate his enemies (Psalms 59:12): "Slay them not, lest my people forget, make them wander to and fro by Thy power, and bring them down, o Lord our shield." Thus, while Jews were to be kept in a state of lowliness, they still should not be slain. Even Pope Innocent III, who is credited by some historians with systematizing all the anti-Jewish attitudes of the Church, basically held on to this principle. The very fact that he challenged the right of the German emperors to consider the Jews serfs of their Treasury, and wished the

Jews to be "subject" to the papacy, implied his obligation and readiness to give to the Jews that protection inherent in the institution of chamber serfdom.

Religious Disputations and the Offensive Against Jewish Books

Hand in hand with the attempts at isolating Jew from Christian went an unceasing effort at converting Jews to Christianity. A major instrument used by the Church in this attempt was the forced religious disputation. To be sure, religious debates between Jews and Christians often took place in a spirit of amity, when both sides tried to clarify to each other and themselves where the two religions differed. In the latter part of the Early Middle Ages, when the religious atmosphere became heated, such debates became by necessity less friendly and more aggressive. A special literature emerged, first among the Christians and later among the Jews, which aimed at providing prospective disputants with questions and answers for use in their debates. In literary dramatizations of imaginary disputations the debaters were sometimes called *Ecclesia*, Church, and *Sinagoga*, Synagogue.

Toward the end of the period, and to a much greater degree during the Late Middle Ages, the Church began to force the Jews to appear at public disputations sponsored by it, for the purpose of proving the truth of Christianity. It was believed that such disputations would induce Jews to convert en masse. Such a public disputation took place in Paris in the summer of 1240. This disputation resulted from an action undertaken in 1236 by a renegade Jew, Nicholas Donin, who entered the Dominican order. In a memorandum submitted to Pope Gregory IX (1227–41) he listed over 30 complaints with regard to the Talmud, including that it was full of sorcery, magic, and superstitions, and that it contained blasphemous statements about Jesus. The Pope evidently had faith in the apostate, and in 1239 he ordered the confiscation of all Jewish books in various Catholic countries so the Dominican and Franciscan friars could expurgate from them any anti-Christian statements. This order was carried out only in France, where the Pope also instructed the Jews to send representatives to a public trial of the Talmud to be held in Paris in 1240.

At this trial, which became the first major Jewish-Christian disputation, the Jewish delegation was headed by Rabbi Yehiel, a noted Parisian talmudic scholar, and by Rabbi Moses of Coucy, an equally great scholar and animated religious leader. A perusal of the records of the disputation shows that the Jewish representatives tried to avoid being dragged into a substantive debate. They knew, as was amply shown in the many disputations of the Late Middle Ages, that the Jewish side had few chances, if any, to win the debate, but ran the dangerous risk of unwittingly insulting Christianity or its messiah. Characteristically, the accusations hurled here at the Talmud often resembled those raised against it centuries earlier by Karaite thinkers and theologians. As could be foreseen, the Talmud lost out and was condemned and forbidden to be studied.

Connected in some way with the trial-disputation of Paris was the burning of Jewish books which took place there in 1242 (or possibly in 1244). Simultaneously, Jewish books were then possibly burned in Rome too. What a shocking experience the event was to Western Jewry is shown by the poem *Shaali seruphah baesh*, (Ask, o thou consumed of fire) composed on the model of Judah Halevi's most famous Zionide (cf. Sec. XIII, Chap. 5) by Rabbi Meir of Rothenburg, who probably witnessed the burning scene in Paris.

Chapter 5

In the Crucible of the Crusades

On the Threshold of the Crusades

The Crusades were the holy wars which Christianity as a whole conducted in the Middle Ages against its mortal enemy, the Muslims. The name derived from the cross which the Christian warriors attached to their garments as a symbol of their dedication to the cause of their faith. The first opportunity for a Crusade presented itself when the Christian states on the Iberian peninsula set out in the eleventh century on the campaign to re-conquer the country from the Muslims. Groups of Christian warriors then entered the peninsula from France to assist in this holy war.

Shortly thereafter a much greater goal which called for a Crusade began to loom before Christianity. The Seljuk Turks made themselves rulers of the caliphate and in 1071 dealt a decisive blow to the Byzantine army. They thus not only became a great menace to the easternmost outpost of Christianity, but were also able to conquer Jerusalem in 1085.

These events caused great alarm in Western Europe. The second half of the eleventh century was a period when the religious fervor fanned by the movement initiated earlier in the monastery of Cluny (France) reached its peak. Everybody suddenly became aware of the fact that the Holy Sepulchre in Jerusalem was under the control of Muslim infidels. This was especially so since the new intense religiosity sent ever larger groups of pilgrims to the Holy Land, some of which numbered in the thousands. The idea then began to spread that it was necessary to wrest the Holy Land from the Turks so that its holy shrines would be under Christian control and always accessible to the pilgrims. By then it had become customary for the pilgrims to bear arms, and an armed Crusade was therefore considered logical and possible.

The sincere religious desire which lay at the root of the movement was matched by equally strong economic interests. Many landless knights looked to the possibility of acquiring fiefs in the areas to be liberated. The Italian commercial cities, such as Venice, Genoa, Pisa, and Amalfi, desired to extend their mercantile enterprises to the eastern shores of the Mediterranean. The peasant serfs, too, the unhappiest lot in Europe, had in their midst young men who were ready to answer the call to a crusade which would extricate them from the monotony of their life, toil, and servitude.

When Pope Urban II (1088–99) called for a crusade to the Holy Land on the closing day of the Church Council which met in Clermont (France) in 1095, the response was overwhelming.

Curiously, the way the Pope characterized the crusade resembled Muslim calls for a holy war (*jihad*). The promises given to the prospective volunteers also resembled in part Muslim rewards for *jihad* warriors. The Council of Clermont thus initiated a major happening in the history of the Middle Ages, which was to last 200 years. It is no exaggeration to state that during the entire 200 years the mind of every Christian from pope and emperor to the lowly serf was occupied with the Crusades and the many complex issues and problems which were their backdrop or their result.

It is therefore not surprising that the Crusades had a deep impact upon the life of the Jews in Europe and in the Near East. We have seen (above, Chap. 4) that the Jew was suspected of plotting the destruction of Christianity in complicity with the Muslims. Therefore it seemed justified to attack that Jewish "fifth column" in the midst of Christianity, even prior to the encounter with the Muslims. This was surely the thinking of a crusaders' force which came to aid the *Reconquista* armies in Spain in 1063. The massacres the crusaders perpetrated against the Jews both in France and Spain were so severe that Pope Alexander II (1061–73) found himself compelled to intervene in favor of the Jews. The danger to the Jews was incomparably greater when the Crusade to the Holy Land was proclaimed in 1095. Its main objective, as we have seen, was to redeem the Holy Sepulchre from the hands of the Saracens. The story of the crucifixion therefore had to come to the mind of anyone who was connected in any way with the Crusade and so the alleged Jewish role in the crucifixion was recalled. In addition, the populace instinctively felt in the tense moments of the Crusade that an opportunity was given to it to vent its many frustrations in a form that could appear as pious and even laudable. The stage was thus set for a major and bloody attack on Western Europe's Jewry.

The First Crusade

Almost from the moment the First Crusade began to be organized it became apparent, at least in France, that a great danger to the Jews was inherent in it. The preachers, who spread out all over the land to urge the people to take the cross, used in their sermons the writings of the Fathers of the Church, which are full of a venomous hatred for the Jews. In addition a rumor, probably not wholly untrue, spread that Godfrey of Bouillon, one of the important commanders of the Crusade, was of the opinion that the Jews-Christ killers should be punished prior to the start of the campaign. First and foremost among the preachers was Peter of Amiens, known as Peter the Hermit, and wherever he arrived with his followers, Jews began to be attacked. This was the case in Rouen (in Normandy) and in Metz. Some Jews lost their lives and some were forcibly converted to Christianity.

While French Jewry was justifiably alarmed by these events, the Jews of Germany felt fully secure. They proclaimed a day of fast and prayer in behalf of their French coreligionists. But they believed that the good will of Emperor Henry IV, their devoted protector, and the friendly attitude of their Christian neighbors would preclude any outbreaks against them. They nevertheless sent one of their leaders to the emperor, who at the time was sojourning in Italy. Two of the major communities, Mayence and Cologne, also contributed a considerable sum to the war chest of the Crusade to gain the crusaders' good will.

Soon, however, German Jewry was brutally awakened from its sense of security. The blow came from bands of peasants who set out on their own to the Near East prior to the departure of the main crusader armies. These bands of peasant crusaders, whose march is sometimes called "the preliminary expedition," began their campaign with mass attacks on the Jews. The bishops who administered the cities for the emperor were responsible for the safety of the Jews. The emperor, indeed, urged them in a letter to use all their power to protect the Jews. The burgesses, too, were generally opposed to any disturbances in the cities. But it soon became clear that the forces available to the bishops were not sufficient to halt the angry onslaught of the mobs of peasants turned crusaders. In Treves (Trier) and Spires the damage was moderate. Some Jews were murdered and others were persuaded to convert in order to save their lives.

But things were totally different in the three largest communities of Worms, Mayence, and Cologne. A large band, under the command of a certain Count Emicho of Leiningen, driven by religious fanaticism and greed for spoils, attacked the Jews in these cities during the month of May 1096. The bishops made an attempt to protect the Jews in various ways, but to no avail. In Worms about 800 Jews perished, partly by suicide, and partly massacred by the crusaders. The bishop of Cologne tried to save the Jews by dispersing them to the nearby rural communities. Nevertheless, hundreds lost their lives. In Mayence, where the Jews had barricaded themselves in the castle, they even tried to defend themselves with weapons. But all this was in vain. Hundreds of them were massacred by the attackers who were joined in their assault by the local mob. Most of the Jews, however, upon realizing that all hope was gone, chose to die by their own hand rather than by the knife of the enemy. In a ritualistic manner, and after reciting a blessing, they slaughtered their wives and children, and then took their own lives. When the storm was over, a total of about 5,000 Jews had lost their lives in the Rhineland and elsewhere in Germany. An additional several hundred were forcibly converted, including all the Jews of Ratisbon, who were dragged to the Danube to be baptized.

From Germany the bands of irregulars crossed into Bohemia. Here too the Jews were attacked in various localities including Prague. We have seen above (cf. Chaps. 2 and 3) that some Bohemian Jews saved themselves by fleeing to nearby Poland. Ultimately, near Vishehrad a combined force of Bohemians and Jews dealt the bands a severe blow. The irregulars were also beaten in Hungary. Their remnants, upon arriving in Byzantium were not very well received, and were quickly shoved off into Asia Minor. Thus, they were unable to do any damage to Jews living on the Balkan peninsula and in Asia Minor. Byzantine Jewry also escaped damage when the main forces of the Crusade arrived. Byzantine Jewry was nevertheless deeply touched by the Crusade and experienced a resurgence of the hope for the imminent coming of the Messiah. Whenever Christian and Muslim armies fought for the possession of the Holy Land, the expectation emerged that their armies would destroy each other, or would be destroyed by a cataclysmic supernatural event, after which the true King Messiah would appear and the land would be returned to its rightful owners, the Jewish people.

Upon his return from Italy, Emperor Henry IV endeavored to

punish those guilty of the pogroms, but few could actually be apprehended, since most of the perpetrators were gone, and local attackers could not easily be identified. As for the bishops, they could in some cases be blamed for passivity. In other cases, however, the bishops were in danger themselves and had to flee for their safety. And since it became clear that the Jews were henceforth in the need of special protection, they began to be included, as we have seen (cf. above, Chap. 3), early in the twelfth century in the *Landfrieden*, General Peace, designed for the protection of the weak strata of the population. In 1097 the emperor at the risk of incurring the wrath of the pope, permitted all forcibly converted Jews to return to Judaism. King William II of England, in his capacity as the ruler of Normandy, also permitted the forcibly converted Jews in Rouen to again openly profess the Jewish faith.

The Later Crusades

When the news reached Europe that Edessa, the easternmost region of the crusader Kingdom of Jerusalem, was re-captured by the Muslims in 1144, Western Europe rose to organize the Second Crusade in the years 1146–47. The preparations for the Second Crusade were quite similar to those of the First. Preachers again reminded the masses of the presence of Jews, the killers of Christ, in their midst. One of them, Peter of Cluny, attacked the Jews with great ferocity and demanded that all Jewish property be confiscated to finance the expedition. Despite this and despite the outbreak of anti-Jewish riots in many localities, the Second Crusade was far less tragic for the Jews than the First. All Jewish property was not confiscated, and the Jews got away with contributing a considerable sum of money to the expenses of the new holy war. Now both the Jews and the authorities were more alert, and the number of victims was rather small. Again, French Jewry fared better than its German counterpart. French Jewry's greatest sage, Jacob ben Meir (popularly known as Rabenu Tam), was wounded, but recovered. In Germany most of the victims were Jews who chanced to travel on the highways. Only in Wuerzburg (Bavaria) did 22 Jews lose their lives. The number of the Jews who perished in Bohemia, about 150, was disproportionately large.

Carinthian Jewry too sustained a number of losses, when the crusader army reached this southeastern region of the German empire.

This time the Church played a more active role in the efforts to protect the Jews. Bernard of Clairvaux, the great French churchman who is considered the spiritual leader of the Second Crusade, energetically demanded that the Jews be left alone. He reminded his fellow Christians that it was in the vital interest of the Church to preserve the physical existence of the Jews, the living testimony to the historicity of the Christian messiah (cf. above, Chap. 4). Other churchmen acted likewise, and sources even report a German priest who helped forcibly converted Jews to escape to France where they could openly live again as Jews. As in the First Crusade, the anti-Jewish riots were limited to France, Germany, and Bohemia. In England no anti-Jewish sentiments were apparent, which is quite remarkable in view of the fact that only two years earlier the Jews of Norwich were accused of having murdered a Christian child for ritual purposes, the first known blood libel in Western Europe.

In 1187 the Kingdom of Jerusalem suffered a disastrous blow with the fall of its capital to the Muslims. As always, the news of a setback to the crusader state evoked repercussions against the Jews in Europe. And yet, during the preparations for the Third Crusade no real harm occurred to the Jews either in France or in Germany. France, as we have seen, did not produce any serious anti-Jewish riots during the two former Crusades, and the same was the case now during the Third Crusade. As for Germany, due mainly to the precautions taken by Emperor Frederick I Barbarossa, peace for the Jews was secured both during the preparations for the Crusade and after the emperor left to lead an army to the Near East.

This time hitherto tranquil England became the scene of bloody events for the Jews. A combination of deep economic resentment and religious frenzy, fanned by the direct English participation in the Third Crusade, was responsible for the ferocity of the outbreak. We have seen (cf. above, Chap. 3) that a pogrom against the Jews broke out in London in 1189 during the days immediately following the coronation of Richard the Lionhearted. After the king's departure on the Crusade, the Jews were attacked in such towns as Stamford, Lynn, Norwich, and Bury St. Edmunds. The pattern of events vividly resembled what had occurred on the continent during the first two Crusades: many Jews were massacred, and some converted to Christianity to save their lives. Only in Lincoln did the authorities succeed in saving the Jews.

In York, more than anywhere else, the events matched what had happened in Worms, Mayence, and Cologne in May 1096. Upon sensing the tension in the city, the Jews entered the castle and barricaded themselves there. A long siege began, during which the hostility of the mob and the lower gentry rose to a fatal point. When the besieged Jews realized that all hope was gone, they decided to die by their own hands rather than to be massacred by their enemies. On the Great Sabbath, preceding Passover (March 16/17, 1190), they first set fire to their belongings and then sacrificed their lives for the sanctification of the Holy Name. About 150 Jews perished in York. The fact that after storming the castle the lower gentry and the mob destroyed the register of debts owed by Christians to Jews underscores the complex nature of the causes underlying the York tragedy.

Several more Crusades were organized after the year 1200. First came what is called the Fourth Crusade, which never reached the Holy Land but resulted in the capture of Constantinople by the crusaders. When the city was stormed, Constantinople's Jewish quarter was sacked. However, the situation of the Jews under crusader ("Latin") rule (1204–61) did not fundamentally change. Since most of the time Latin rule was limited to the city of Constantinople, Greece, Thrace, and the Aegean islands, the crusader regime did not affect the destiny of all Byzantine Jewry. By comparison, the Jews of France endured much more between 1209 and 1229, when a series of Crusades attempted to eradicate the Albigensian heresy in southern France. Many Jews, and especially those of Beziers, were slain, and many fled for their lives to Spain. The Jewry of northwestern France, too, had to endure riots and massacres when bands of volunteers assembled there in 1236 for another Crusade. To be sure, the fear that the riots would spill over across the Channel into England did not materialize.

The Jews in the Crusader Kingdom
of Jerusalem

Although the forces of the First Crusade lost many of their men on the march through Asia Minor, they were still strong enough to occupy most of the Holy Land and parts of Syria. Jerusalem fell into their hands on July 15, 1099, and with the conquest of Haifa months later the goal of the Crusade seemed to have been reached. Two important cities in the south, Ashkelon and Gaza, remained under Muslim control till 1153. The conquest in 1124 of Tyre in today's Lebanon, then an important coastal city, strengthened the crusaders' hold over Syria. The country, henceforth known as the Latin Kingdom of Jerusalem, was organized as a feudal monarchy on the Western European model. Godfrey of Bouillon became the first crusader ruler in Jerusalem and three other leaders of the Crusade were invested with the duchies of Tripoli, Antioch, and Edessa, respectively.

The arrival of the crusaders in 1099 spelled disaster for Palestine's flourishing Jewish community. On receiving the news of the crusaders' approach, the Jews of Jaffa and Ramleh fled to Ashkelon. They obviously were aware of what the crusaders had done to their co-religionists in Germany and Bohemia. It is therefore also understandable why the Jews of Jerusalem participated in the defense of the walls, and especially those protecting their own quarter, when the crusaders laid siege to the city. The vengeance of the crusaders was as brutal as the attack of the "irregulars" on the Jews of the Rhineland three years earlier. Most of the Jews were burned alive in the synagogues into which they fled, many others were sold into slavery, and a small number were left alive at the price of conversion to Christianity. The Jews of nearby Hebron were expelled, and the Jewish rural communities in the northern Negev, Judaea, and Transjordan were obliterated. When the crusaders approached Haifa, its sizable Jewish community had every reason to defend the city to the utmost. When the city finally fell, its Jews were all massacred. The Jewish rural communities in Galilee, however, somehow escaped destruction.

The reign of terror against the Jews lasted till 1110, and then it began to subside. The crusaders, mostly Frenchmen and Normans, constituted only a thin layer of the population. The kings

of Jerusalem saw fit, therefore, to establish in the country a regime of toleration. The Jews were among the beneficiaries of this
policy, and Jewish life began to re-awaken everywhere. In fact, in
time the political situation of the Jews in the Kingdom of
Jerusalem turned out to be more favorable than that of their
brethren in the Catholic states in Western Europe. When Tyre
was occupied in 1124 and Ashkelon and Gaza in 1153, their
Jewish communities remained intact since these cities were
taken without battle.

It was the policy of the kings of Jerusalem to permit Jewish
settlement everywhere in their realm, except in Jerusalem. The
ban on Jewish settlement in the Holy City was somewhat relaxed
in the course of the twelfth century, but few Jews lived in the city
prior to its conquest by Saladin in 1187. All in all, some 20 localities in the Holy Land had Jewish communities at one time or
another during the existence of the crusader states between 1099
and 1291. Among them were Ashkelon, Ramleh, Caesarea,
Tiberias, and Acre. In the course of the twelfth century, increasing numbers of Jews came both as pilgrims and immigrants from
the East and the West. The improved lines of transportation, developed by the crusaders, made immigration from Europe much
easier.

In the thirteenth century, too, more Jews arrived from abroad.
About 1210 a group of some 300 Jews came from France, and
possibly England, even though by then the size of the Kingdom of
Jerusalem had already been reduced by Egyptian conquests. In
fact, the *olim* of the thirteenth century were so numerous that
some historians are of the opinion that they were surpassed in
number only by the *olim* of the sixteenth century and by those of
modern times. The immigrants who arrived in the thirteenth century settled mostly in the coastal cities still controlled by the
Europeans, but some settled in the interior, then again under
Muslim rule. Of the two most famous immigrants, the first,
Rabbi Yehiel of Paris, went directly to Acre upon arriving in 1257.
The other, Rabbi Moses ben Nahman (the Ramban), first settled
in 1267 in Egyptian-held Jerusalem, but he too ultimately settled
in Acre. A *nagid* of the Maimonidean family also immigrated to
Acre.

Historians are still debating the question of Jewish economic life in the Latin Kingdom of Jerusalem. Some are of the opinion that generally it was rather hard for Jews to make a living. But other historians believe that the Jewish community was economically well off. As before, Jews still had a sort of monopoly in the dyeing industry. Some Jews served in the management of certain royal monopolies. The greatest economic opportunity, however, came to the Jews who lived in the coastal cities. Here the Italian mercantile republics had established a network of agencies which maintained lucrative trade relations with Europe. Many Jews found an opportunity to earn their livelihood in the framework of this foreign trade. The Jewish communities of Acre and Tyre even attained a position of wealth.

Culturally, too, the Jewry of the Latin Kingdom attained a degree of success. Its culture was no longer Babylonia-oriented. In Acre, Rabbi Yehiel of Paris established a school for the study of Rabbinics which became known as "The Yeshivah of Paris." The name of the school clearly indicates that it transplanted to the shores of the Holy Land the teachings of the French Tosafists (see below, Chap. 9). Rabbi Moses ben Nahman also brought to Acre "western" ways and methods of the study of Torah. Here he also completed some of his great works.

After the Mameluks made themselves rulers of Egypt in the second half of the thirteenth century, they set out on a successful campaign to curtail the possessions of the crusader states. It now became increasingly clear that the days of the Latin Kingdom were numbered. The end came in 1291 when Acre fell to the Mameluks. In the storm of conquest its flourishing Jewish community was almost totally destroyed.

Sanctification of the Holy Name

Mass suicide as a means of reacting to an attack from outside and of sanctifying the Holy Name appeared for the first time among Jews in the Rhenish cities in 1096 and again in York in 1190. Sacrificing one's life for the sanctification of the Holy Name and mass suicide were not unknown phenomena in the Jewish past. Many Jews died for their God during the short periods of religious persecution when Judaea was under Hellenistic and

Roman rule (cf. Vol. I, Sec. V, Chaps. 1 and 2). All these martyrs did not die by their own hand but were massacred by the enemy. The mass suicide of Jews in the fortress of Masada (cf. Vol. I, Sec. VIII, Chap. 1) was committed not as a reaction to religious oppression, but as an act of desperation due to the collapse of the First Revolt. The mass suicide of the Jews on the Rhine and in York in the period of the Crusades was a new way designed by medieval Ashkenazic Jews to demonstrate their unflinching devotion to their God and to sanctify His Name. The full significance of this horrifying and simultaneously grandiose act in which men found it possible to slaughter their wives and children and then themselves can only be fathomed when we remember that the act was performed with a ritual slaughter knife and was accompanied by the recitation of a blessing and by sprinkling of the blood of the victims on the pillars of the holy ark. Obviously, the Ashkenazic Jews followed the procedure of the sacrificial service in the Temple, with the holy ark substituting for the altar.

Many reasons could account for this new and bizarre religious act. To begin with, medieval man, Jew and Gentile, lived in a perpetual state of mental tension and therefore was inclined to perform extreme and drastic acts. In addition, the Jews in the Rhine cities and in York felt fairly safe, and when overwhelmed by the suddenness and unexpectedness of the attack panicked into a state of mind in which self-destruction became a "natural" reaction. Their uncompromising devotion to God also led them to self-sacrifice. In the manner of medieval man, they viewed the world as a perpetual battleground between God and His adversaries. They considered themselves warriors for God who were born into the world to demonstrate that they were on God's side. The conviction of medieval men that they were laden with an endless burden of sin may have led at least some of these Jews to actively seek death in order to expiate for their real or imaginary sins.

The Jews of the generations following the First Crusade came to realize that they had hitherto lived with a false sense of security and that they and their children would increasingly face situations in which they would be called to demonstrate "who belongs to God and who to His adversaries." They therefore developed a system of education and propaganda designed to steel the character of the Jew in preparation for the great encounter. This propaganda never tired of pointing out how lowly and miserable life in this world was in comparison to the splendor into which they would enter once they had sacrificed their life for God. They were also convinced, and tried to convince others, that once a Jew had made up his mind to make the supreme sacrifice and die for his God, he did not suffer at all and felt no pain at the time of his martyrdom. In addition, a sort of public climate was created by the "Pious Men of Ashkenaz," the religious extremists of the period (cf. further, Chap. 10), in which a Jew who did not possess the courage to go through with his martyrdom to the bitter end was looked down upon as a kind of second-class Jew. It should be noted, however, that most of the great religious leaders, from Rabenu Gershom about the year 1000 to Rabbi Meir (Maharam) of Rothenburg in the second half of the thirteenth century, disagreed with this attitude. They had much compassion for, and understanding of the plight of, Jews who submitted to forcible conversion to save their lives. These rabbis sternly admonished Jewish society to abstain from criticizing these marranos once they had returned to Judaism.

Contemporary Jewry, as well as later generations, stood in awe before the great sacrifice of those who sanctified the Holy Name. Their deed was compared to Abraham's heroic act in binding his son Isaac for slaughter to follow the will of God (cf. Genesis, Chap. 22). In fact, some considered the sacrifice of the Rhenish Jews to have been superior to that of Abraham, since they actually sacrificed their lives and their children's while Isaac's life was ultimately spared through God's intervention.

Rashi, the great commentator of the Bible and Talmud, who as an old man witnessed the events of the First Crusade, interpreted the verse (Psalms 47:10): "The princes of the peoples are gathered together, the people of the God of Abraham" as referring to those "who gave themselves to slaughter and death for the sanctification of His Name." Chroniclers described the heroism of the martyrs, and liturgical poems were composed in which many a name of a martyr was immortalized. The days of the months Iyar and Siwan in which the events in Rhineland took place were commemorated for centuries as days of mourning. The lists containing the names of many of the martyrs were henceforth read publicly in many, many Jewish communities. Indeed, the memory of the martyrs of 1096 was indelibly etched on the consciousness of the Jewish people.

Chapter 6

The Accusations

The Blood Libel

We have seen (cf. above, Chap. 4) that medieval Christian religious fanaticism was a fertile soil on which a thicket of mistrust of, and accusations against, the Jews was growing. In addition to the general accusations against the Jews, such as being in complicity with the devil, several specific accusations were being hurled against them which had a devastating impact upon their lives and security. First and foremost among these was, and still is even in modern times, the blood libel.

The accusation that Jews kidnap and murder Christians, and especially children, first appeared, as far as we presently know, in England. It is likely that when the Jewish community of London was sentenced in 1130–31 to pay an enormous fine for having killed "a sick man," it was due to a blood libel. A full-blown blood libel was staged against the Jews of Norwich in 1144, alleging that they had murdered a Christian child. Several times more similar accusations were hurled against the Jews of England in the course of the twelfth century. In France, the Jews of Blois were accused of the same crime in 1171, and 31 of them were burned alive. In Spain, too, the accusation appeared in the twelfth century, when in 1182 the Jews of Saragossa were hit by it.

We do not know why the blood accusation occurred in the generally tranquil twelfth-century Jewish community in England with greater frequency than anywhere else. Similarly, we do not know why German Jewry was spared this calamity until 1235. It was the good luck of German Jewry that when Jews in Fulda were accused in that year of having murdered five boys for ritual purposes, the case was brought before Emperor Frederick II. Being free of prejudices, this almost modern man of the thirteenth century convened, as we have seen, an international commission of outstanding churchmen and Christian Hebraists to opine on the question. When the commission declared ritual murder to be a myth, the imperial diet which met in Augsburg in 1236 completely exonerated the Jews of Fulda. Several more blood libels are known to have occurred in Western Europe before the end of the Early Middle Ages.

At first no clear motive was ascribed to the Jews accused of killing Christian children. It was probably assumed that it was due to the hatred of the human race supposedly prevalent among the Jews, and to their alleged devilish character. Later, however, the blood accusation began to be connected more and more with certain "goals" allegedly pursued by the Jews. One of these "goals" was to re-enact again and again on the body of an innocent Christian child the passion of the crucifixion. Another "goal" was to use Christian blood in preparing the dough for the *matsoth*, the unleavened bread eaten by Jews on Passover, or to mix it with the wine used in celebration of the *seder*, the Passover night meal. Still another "purpose" was to use Christian blood as a remedy against specific afflictions believed to have plagued the Jews because of their rejection of Jesus, such as the *fetor Judaicus*, the bad odor allegedly emanating from their bodies. The pain of a Jewish child following circumcision could also be soothed, according to popular belief, by the application of Christian blood.

Of all these motives ascribed to the Jewish killers of Christian children, the one connected with the baking of *matsoth* became the most popular. This was due in part to the fact that more and more often the blood accusation appeared close to Passover time. The Christian Holy Week and Easter, commemorating Jesus' passion and resurrection, mostly occur close to the Jewish Passover. The alleged repetition of Jesus' passion could thus easily be associated with ceremonies of the Passover holiday.

The belief that Jews were murdering Christians specifically at this time of the year was also possibly nurtured by the custom of Jews to stage Purim performances in which Haman, their arch-enemy, was hanged in effigy. Such a "Haman" had, of course, to look and be dressed like a Gentile, and since he had to be hanged on a tree (cf. Esther 7:10), the hanging could easily have been mistaken for an act of crucifixion. All these elements of the libel did not appear at the same time and in the same place. But this composite picture in all its bizarre forms had its origin in the early history of the accusation which unfolded in this period.

Modern scholarship has made many efforts to uncover the sources of the libel that by now has haunted the Jewish people for more than 800 years. Some believe it to be rooted in the story told by the anti-Semitic Greek writer, Apion, in first century C.E. Alexandria, that when Antiochus IV Epiphanes entered the Temple in Jerusalem (cf. Vol. I, Sec. V, Chap. 1), he found there a Greek man who allegedly was being fattened in preparation for slaughter as a sacrifice. The prospective victim also told Antiochus, according to Apion, that the sacrifice of a Greek man was celebrated annually by the Jews.

While it is not impossible that a faint echo of this Greek accusation against the Jews reached down to the Christian society of twelfth-century Western Europe, the theological image of the Jew (cf. above, Chap. 4) was in itself a sufficiently fertile ground to produce the accusation. What is remarkable was its unconditional and unshaken acceptance by the population. Characteristically, it was the lower clergy which were among the main promoters of the myth, despite a denunciation issued by Pope Innocent IV (1243–54) in 1247. The idea that parish priests were directly interested in supporting the accusation in order to enhance the local church by the presence of a martyr's tomb cannot be dismissed. Nor was the intervention of the secular authorities successful in eradicating the myth. The charter given to the Jews of Austria in 1244 by Duke Frederick II of Babenberg, which served as a model for similar charters for the Jews of Hungary, Bohemia, and Poland (cf. above, Chap. 3), clearly promised them protection against the libel. But this neither made a dent in the popular belief, nor did it prevent the appearance of the accusation in the following decades. And so the blood libel survived not only into the later Middle Ages, but practically to our own times as a terrible calamity which has caused Jewish communities everywhere untold suffering.

Other Libels

Another major accusation which came to haunt the Jewish people down to the nineteenth century was that they were stealing the holy wafer, or host, used in the celebration of the Eucharist. According to Christian belief, the wafer, upon consecration, becomes the body of Jesus. It was therefore believed that much in the way Jews murder a Christian child to re-enact on its body the passion of the crucifixion, they also steal, stab, mutilate, and profane the holy wafer for the same purpose. The host libel appeared for the first time in 1243 in Germany. The appearance of the accusation at this time may be explained by the fact that the Fourth Lateran Church Council, held in Rome in 1215, greatly strengthened the idea of the identity of the wafer with Jesus' body, and the wafer thus gained in sanctity and popularity. The accusation of 1243 seems to have been the only one which occurred during the Early Middle Ages. However, it became a real scourge to the Jews in the Late Middle Ages and beyond.

Another libel, too, grew out of the Christian belief in the perpetual urge of the Jew to re-enact Jesus' crucifixion. According to this, Jews were removing images of Jesus from churches to "wound" them by stabbing and mutilation. It was also believed that the images in such a case would begin to bleed or issue a sound and so reveal the misdeed of the perpetrators. In fact, the accusation of mutilating images chronologically preceded the other accusations. As early as 1062 the Jews of Aterno, near Pescara in Italy, were accused of having profaned and mutilated an image of Jesus in the synagogue on the eve of Good Friday. It would be correct to assume that the Jewish abhorrence of images (cf. Exodus 20:4-5) led the Christians to believe in this myth, as it led many to believe that Jews were behind the iconoclastic revolution in Byzantium (cf. above, Sec. XIV, Chap. 1). This libel too came to its full fruition in later times.

The Jews were also repeatedly accused of two misdeeds perpetrated not against Jesus and his memory, but against the Christians amidst whom they lived: arson and poisoning of the wells. In the medieval towns where almost all houses were built of wood, consuming fires were a frequent occurrence. The people, helpless against the elements and deeply steeped in superstition, believed that a sinister force was conspiring against them to rob them of their dwellings. It was therefore natural to suspect the Jews, the devil's allies. It was even more plausible to suspect the Jews of arson in view of the fact that they themselves often lived in stone houses, as was the case in England, and were less frequently victimized by fires.

One of the most popular and most devastating accusations against the Jews was that they were poisoners causing terrible epidemics by poisoning the wells. This accusation was hurled for the first time in 1096 against the Jews of Worms, when they were being attacked by the crusaders. This libel appeared in its bloodiest form in 1348–49 when it was universally believed that the Jews brought on the bubonic plague, known as the Black Death, by poisoning the wells and rivers.

An additional sinister element in the accusations was the practice of making all the Jews of a locality, or even the whole country, responsible for the alleged crime of one or a few Jews. It was a general medieval custom to view an individual solely as a member of his group. It goes without saying that this approach was consistently followed with regard to the Jews. Thus, the accusations not only resulted in the execution of many Jews when a blood libel or host accusation occurred, but quite often led to the destruction of entire communities.

Chapter 7

Community Government

Jewish Communal Autonomy

The Jewish communal organization, the *kehillah*, in the period of the Early Middle Ages assumed an ever-growing importance in the life of Western Jewry. Already the rulers of Frankland granted the Jews the right to conduct their internal affairs and their judiciary on an autonomous basis. Jewish communal autonomy, dating back to Roman times (cf. Vol. I, Sec. XI, Chap. 2), now received an additional boost from the Germanic principle that every man is entitled to be judged according to his own ethnic law. Thus, being basically considered aliens (cf. above, Chap. 3), the Jews were assured of their communal autonomy. Curiously, the kehillah grew in strength precisely during the times when the general Jewish situation deteriorated in the latter part of the period. Characteristically, Church interference with, or opposition to, Jewish communal autonomy was rare and rather mild.

The second half of the tenth and the first half of the eleventh century was the period when the kehillah developed into an institution of major importance. This coincided with the emergence of many new cities in France and in Germany and with the development of their governing institutions. In general, the kehillah played a role in the life of the Jew similar to that of the city administration. The kehillah not only cared for and administered the religious affairs and institutions of the community, but also regulated, and sometimes controlled, the conomic activities of its members. It also, of course, represented the interests of the Jews at the courts of the rulers, regional, royal, or imperial. The governments generally supported the Jewish communal authorities. Since they insisted that the Jews be collectively responsible for the acts of individuals, and attempted to collect Jewish taxes in lump sums on a local or national basis, the governments could not help but lend their unconditional support to the Jewish communal organization. This was the case in the successor states to the Frankish empire as well as in Spain. Broad imperial support for Jewish communal autonomy was given by Emperor Henry IV in the privileges he granted in 1090 to the Jews of Spires and Worms, as well as in similar privileges given in 1157 by Emperor Frederick I Barbarossa to the community of Worms.

Privileges given by the kings of Castile and Aragon to the Jewish communities included even broader communal autonomy. Here the Jewish communities, which retained the old Arab designation *aljama*, even possessed the right of imposing capital punishment in the enforcement of their regulations. To be sure, the Spanish communities administered capital punishment only with regard to informers. But a system of monetary fines, flogging, and the ban (*herem*) was used everywhere by the kehilloth to enforce their authority. The ban, resembling excommunication practiced in the Catholic Church, afflicted its victim with total social isolation. In the twelfth century its effectiveness was greatly strengthened by an ordinance of Rabbenu Tam which gave the rabbinic courts authority to order compliance with a ban. In fact, the threat of the ban was so formidable that in practice it had to be used only rarely.

The kehilloth, imbued by lofty Jewish ideals and by the necessity of maintaining peaceful relations with the Christian community, strove to impose upon their members a way of life of high moral standards. Attempts by individual Jews to be exempted from the control of the kehillah were not infrequent. Jewish courtiers in Spain especially made many efforts in this direction. By and large, however, the kehilloth, through the use of the threat of *herem*, succeeded in checking all serious centrifugal tendencies in their midst.

Despite the use of the ban and of other means of coercion, the kehillah north of the Pyrenees possessed a basically democratic character in comparison with its counterpart in the orbit of Islam. Here no tradition of communal administration existed, and for a long time the scholarly circles were groping for forms of leadership based on talmudic principles. In practice, most of the time the leadership was of an aristocratic nature, based on learning and patrician lineage. In the latter part of the period more blunt oligarchic tendencies began to surface, as was also the case in the contemporary Christian municipality. But even then the very small size of the local community guaranteed at least a semblance of democracy.

Much less democratic was the Spanish *aljama*. Oligarchic rule was here deeply entrenched. There were cases where community leadership was vested in one and the same family for as long as an entire century. Attempts by the lower strata of the Jewish population late in the period to gain influence on the conduct of the affairs of the *aljamas* had only minor success.

The opponents of oligarchic rule in the communities found allies in the circles of the *hasidim* in Germany and France and among the mystics in Spain. These circles, which insisted on honesty and decency in the conduct of private and public affairs, could not remain neutral in the face of attempts by individuals to impose their will on the Jewish communities, often with outside help. While it is not possible to fully determine the degree to which the moralists were able to influence kehillah government, it must be assumed that they did succeed at least in part in stemming the trend toward totalitarian rule by a few.

The most important feature of Jewish communal life was the absolute independence of the local community. Each community viewed itself as if it were the Jewish people in miniature. True, as we shall see later, attempts were made by governments late in the period to centralize the community leadership for fiscal purposes. But precisely for the same reasons the Jewish population opposed such attempts. And although late in the period the basic deterioration of the Jewish political situation began to work in favor of centralization, the local community existed most of the time as an autonomous and independent entity. In fact, the cluster of autonomous Jewish communities was not unlike the feudal state of those times. Like the feudal unit, the local Jewish community jealously guarded its authority with all the means at its disposal. From time to time, however, it reluctantly yielded its independence, when such a course appeared compelling in the interest of *kelal Yisrael*, the larger Jewish community.

Community Administration

Membership in the Jewish community was acquired either by birth or through formal admission by the community leadership. However, most of the time participation in elections or decision-making was not open to all the membership. Only in very small communities were decisions made at what may be called a general assembly. But even in such cases it is doubtful whether members not enjoying the "respect" of the community had any say.

When a community was small, its affairs often were cared for by a single officer. Larger communities were often governed by a board consisting of seven members ("the seven best men in town"), called *parnasim*, aldermen. The aldermen were aided by a variety of other officers, such as tax assessors and supervisors of weights and measures. The new communities which emerged in the Slavic countries late in the period mostly imitated the administrative set-up of the German communities whence most of their members came. The authority which the community administration wielded over the Jewish population on the Iberian peninsula was well established by tradition, and further buttressed by the above-mentioned system of enforcement which had governmental backing. In the Ashkenazic countries, however, the authority of the communal administration was slow to gain recognition. It took a long time until everybody agreed that a minority in the community was obliged to submit to decisions passed by the majority.

It is easily understandable that the most fought-over issue in every community was the fair apportionment among the members of the regular and many special taxes which the community had to pay to the government. The situation was aggravated by the fact that the community had to pay the taxes for the poor who were unable to pay any share of the lump sum for which the community was responsible. Still worse was the already-mentioned fact that wealthy individuals, on the Iberian peninsula more than in the Ashkenazic communities, often used their influence with the governments to be exempted from taxation. The communities fought these attempts of the mighty at least with partial success. Taxes were collected by the communities in various ways, including a sales tax on meat and wine.

Sporadic attempts at centralizing Jewish communal administration, or at least discussing Jewish affairs on an inter-communal basis, appeared all through the period in various parts of the area. Such was the case with meetings of Jewish communal leaders attending the fairs, and especially those of Cologne, who used the opportunity for discussing issues of general Jewish communal interest. True, it was clearly understood that the "ordinances" resulting from such meetings were to be valid only where the local kehillah gave its consent. And yet, although these meetings occurred only by chance, their significance was far from negligible. After all, the communities of the Rhineland did have common interests both vis-á-vis the government and the Jewish population. It is worth noting that the Jewish super-community which emerged in Poland-Lithuania in the sixteenth century under the name of the "Council of the Four Provinces" grew out of such incidental meetings of Jewish communal leaders at the fairs of Jaroslaw and Lublin. It is not improbable that had Germany not undergone a process of feudal fragmentation, an institution similar to that of Poland's super-community might have grown out of the informal meetings at Cologne. The acceptance by Ashkenazic Jewry of the various religious ordinances connected with the names of the communities of Spires, Worms, and Mayence (the "SHUM ordinances," cf. below, Chap. 10) may well have received decisive impetus at the Cologne meetings.

Of greater importance were the synods of French Jewry which met in Troyes beginning with 1150. Curiously, representatives of some German communities also showed up at the first gathering. True, no central communal organization emerged from it, but this and the following assemblies surely contributed greatly to the strengthening of the communities by firmly promoting the principle of the unconditional acceptance of, and adherence to, exclusively Jewish courts. That these Troyes synods were cognizant of their importance is indicated by the fact that they felt it safe to threaten with the ban individuals or communities refusing to submit to their ordinances. Important Jewish inter-communal interests brought together at Saint Gilles leaders of the communities of southern France in 1215 when it was feared that the Fourth Lateran Church Council then meeting in Rome might pass legislation harmful to the Jews. Only in Portugal did a fully organized central Jewish authority emerge in the thirteenth century, led by a chief rabbi and seven *dayyanim*, regional judges. This type of Jewish central communal administration became much more common in the period of the Late Middle Ages.

We have seen above that governments, too, were interested in central Jewish authorities in their respective territories for the purpose of streamlining the collection of taxes from their Jewish subjects. The first attempt of this kind of which we know was made in England when a congress of communities, curiously designated "Parliament of Jews," met in 1241 in Worcester for the avowed purpose of apportioning a tax then imposed upon the Jewish community as a whole. The larger among England's 21 Jewish communities were represented by 6 delegates each, and the smaller by 2 each. The question as to whether the office of the *rab de la corte,* rabbi of the court, a sort of head of all the Jews in Castile had come into existence in this period cannot be answered with certainty. The investiture by King James I (1213–76) of the Alconstantini family as "supreme rabbis and judges" over all the *aljamas* of Aragon was of short duration and limited significance.

The ever-increasing scope of communal affairs necessitated the employment of various salaried, or otherwise remunerated, functionaries. Rabbis appeared with increasing frequency as the twelfth century progressed, but no clear evidence is available that they were then part of a salaried communal personnel. It may be assumed that in small communities a single functionary performed the tasks of rabbi, cantor, teacher, and ritual slaughterer. This was the case, at least, in the fledgling communities in Poland during the waning decades of this period. Larger communities, of course, had to employ several functionaries to be in charge of the basic communal institutions, such as synagogue, slaughter house, ritual bath, and cemetery.

Chapter 8

The Economic Scene

Major Trends

No area of Jewish life in Western Europe in this epoch offers such a picture of perpetual change as does the economy. Early in the period Jewish economic opportunities in Frankland were almost unlimited. In fact, the Jewish role in international trade was the raison d'être of this Jewish community. Some historians even believe that this role was more important than the role played by Jews in the semi-capitalist economy of the caliphate and its successor states. In addition to commerce, Jews were still active in agriculture and in a variety of other occupations. Jews were employed in the management of royal monopolies not only in *Reconquista* Spain, but in other countries as well. They were also conspicuous as mintmasters and coin distributors in Central and Eastern Europe. Coins with Hebrew inscriptions have been yielded by archeological excavations in the entire area. In western Poland very large numbers of uniface coins were found with what are quite probably Hebrew inscriptions. These coins, coming from the twelfth and thirteenth centuries, suggest the presence of Jewish coiners in the duchies of Great Poland and Mazovia.

All these phenomena can be traced to various areas in the orbit of western Christendom practically to the end of the Early Middle Ages. But a progressive narrowing of opportunities open to the Jews can be observed to have developed parallel to the creeping deterioration of the Jewish political situation. The end result of this process was that in the waning years of the epoch moneylending had become the major Jewish occupation in practically all of these countries. In Spain, where moneylending occupied a less consequential position in Jewish economic life, the narrowing of opportunities resulted not only in a decline in Jewish wealth, but also in the emergence of a class of small shopkeepers and craftsmen as the largest social group among the Jews. Indicative of the new situation was the evergrowing application, beginning with the twelfth century, of the *herem hayishuv*, the ban on settlement. This ban was used by the authorities of the local kehilloth not only as a means of keeping out socially undesirable elements, but also to protect the members of the community against an influx of potential competitors for a slice of the shrinking economic opportunities. To be sure, the *herem hayishuv* was controversial and unpopular. But the economic realities seem to have justified its increasing use.

By and large, however, the Jews of Western Europe did not belong to the poor strata of the population. The picture which emerges from the circles of the Tosafists in Germany and France (cf. the next chapter) is that of a rather prosperous society. To an even greater degree, English Jewry lived most of the time as an affluent society which could afford the greatest luxury of those times, living in stone houses. Wealth was then considered by most Jews a real blessing, since only enormous bribes, euphemistically termed "gifts," or special taxes, could shield them from many calamities, including confiscation of their property and expulsion.

In a period when uncompromising religious devotion produced among the Jews the phenomenon of mass suicide for the sanctification of God's Name, the question of the permissibility of maintaining economic relations with their Christian neighbors had to come up for debate. Talmudic law imposes restrictions on the Jew in his economic dealings with pagans. Many Jews, and especially those who chose to die rather than to save their lives by conversion to Christianity, believed that the latter was equal to idolatry. Had the Jewish community acted in accordance with this belief, Jewish economic existence in Christian countries would have become impossible. It was therefore an act of great courage and of responsible community leadership when the scholars, beginning with Rabenu Gershom in the tenth century, decided to bypass the law and to bend to the necessities of life by explicitly permitting economic intercourse with Christians.

Another issue which occupied the Jewish communal and religious leadership was the question of honesty in Jewish-Christian economic relations. Since the principle of *maarufiah* (a term of uncertain origin) gave a Jewish merchant or artisan communal assistance in retaining a customer against possible competition on the part of another Jew, the former actually possessed a sort of monopoly in his relations with Gentile customers. It is understandable that such a monopoly could often be abused to the detriment of the Christian. Dishonest behavior could also easily occur in the handling of credit transactions whenever a pawn was given as collateral. There is no doubt that acts of dishonesty by the Jewish party to a transaction did occur. Communal leaders, and especially those imbued with the ideals of the Pious Men of Ashkenaz (see below, Chap. 10), saw in such behavior a danger to the religious integrity of the lender as well as a cause for anti-Jewish sentiments in Gentile society. The literature of the time is therefore full of admonitions to the Jew to conduct his business affairs with perfect honesty.

The Jews in Commerce

Jewish participation in commerce in the countries of the western Mediterranean in the late Antiquity continued into the Early Middle Ages. But for the time being the Jewish role in commerce, and especially in international trade, was rather limited. In Gaul, Syrian merchants played an almost monopolistic role in supplying the upper strata of the population with luxury articles imported from the East.

After the Arab conquests of the seventh and eighth centuries, the situation changed radically. Syrian merchants could no longer sail unhampered on the Mediterranean, which had now become a perpetual theatre of war between Muslim and Christian fleets, and Muslim and Christian pirates. Jewish merchants were now the only "neutral" group able to traverse the sea with at least a minimum of security. In fact, even when captured by pirates, Jewish travelers had far better chances than Christians and Muslims to be ransomed by their co-religionists on either side of the "front." The presence of Jewish communities in the lands controlled by both Christians and Muslims created a golden opportunity for the establishment of business contacts between Jewish firms in Western Europe and in the Near East. Naturally, also, the Hebrew language could play a certain role in facilitating the maintenance of such contacts. How serious Jewish competition had become to long-established maritime trade can be fathomed from the fact that in 945 the Venetian government ordered its shipowners not to carry Jewish passengers.

The curtailment of traffic on the Mediterranean called for the development of an alternate connection to the East. Such a new connection was the overland route from Western Europe through the Slavonic countries eastward. The staging point of this route was Ratisbon in Germany and its destination was Kiev in the Ukraine. Jews frequented this route, too, and the Rabbinic literature of the period mentions the *holkhai Russia,* the travelers to Russia. The above-mentioned Radhaniya (cf. above, Sec. XIII, Chap. 3) had in addition to their staging point in Morocco also a staging point in northern France. As will be recalled, their destinations were India and China. There is also reason to believe that Jewish merchants from Western Europe reached Korea and Japan in this period. On all these routes the Jewish merchants traded in amber, textiles, hides, arms, spices, precious stones, and other luxury articles. Their clientele consisted mainly of royal and ducal courts and the aristocracy, both secular and clerical. From the Slavic countries on the overland route they also brought slaves to Western Europe.

Jews were not the only group engaged in international trade, nor did they play the dominant role in it. But the function they performed was important enough to make them desirable as settlers and to earn them many of the privileges granted to them by various rulers. All imperial charters between the ninth and twelfth century given to the Jews provided for the regulation and safeguarding of their commercial interests. Characteristically, beginning with the tenth century it became customary to refer in German legal documents to "Jews and other merchants" (*Iudei et alii mercatores*). In the cities re-conquered from the Muslims in Spain, Jews played a decisive role in the revival of commerce and industry, and especially in the production and merchandising of clothing. Even England's Jewry, which engaged in moneylending from its very inception, played a certain role in commerce, too.

After the year 1100 the Jewish role in international trade began to decline. As usual, a variety of factors brought about the change. The Crusades again opened the Mediterranean to Christian traffic, and the Italian merchant republics of Venice, Genoa, and Pisa eagerly usurped the new opportunities for themselves. On the overland route the Hansa cities began to replace the Jewish traders. Their caravans were heavily armed, and the unarmed Jews were no match for them.

Jewish participation in the slave trade during the Early Middle Ages has been much debated among historians. Some believe that Jews all but controlled the slave trade. Such an impression may indeed be obtained when one becomes acquainted with the sources telling of the stiff opposition of the medieval Church to Jews trading in slaves. Jews were even accused in the Middle Ages of kidnapping Christian children and selling them to Muslims in southern Spain. Jewish historians, on the other hand, often sound apologetic when discussing this sensitive question. In reality, the proportion of Jews among the slave traders was probably smaller than their proportion in international trade. The opposition of the

Church effectively served as a real damper on Jewish endeavor in this field. Jewish trade in Christian slaves was certainly very limited, even though it was sometimes protected by a Christian ruler, as was the case with Emperor Louis the Pious of Frankland. Jewish trade in slaves is attested to during the ninth century in Frankland, the tenth century in Germany, and later in Bohemia and Silesia. The slave trade virtually came to an end when the Slavic peoples converted to Christianity.

Jews had their share of the local trade, also. Although their role here was less important than in international trade, it was by no means negligible. They were a familiar sight at, and helped in the development of, various local and regional fairs, such as those of the Rhineland and the Champagne region in France. They dealt in clothing, salt, agricultural products and wine, the latter despite clergy opposition. In Spain, where a considerable number of Jews were shopkeepers, their role in the local market may have been even greater than in Germany and France. The information available about Italy also shows that both in the north and south Jews engaged in merchandising. The Jewish local trade evoked more resentment among Christian competitors than did Jewish participation in international trade. This is clearly indicated by the chagrin of Bishop Agobard when about 825 the market day in Lyons was moved from Saturday to a weekday in order to accommodate the religious needs of the Jewish merchants.

Ultimately, the Jews had to partly retreat from this branch of the economy, too. After the year 1000 local Gentile industry and trade had begun to make great strides. With the expansion of the towns and cities in the latter part of the period, the class of the burgesses became even stronger and they were now able to cause real harm to the local Jewish trade. The Christian merchant guilds were often so strong that they succeeded in almost monopolizing for their members the exclusive right to deal in certain wares. The ever-rising special Jewish taxes (cf. above, Chap. 3) also contributed to the undermining of Jewish mercantile activities and the local Jewish merchants, too, had to turn more and more to moneylending for a livelihood.

Jews in the Crafts

While Jews were engaged in commerce practically in every Catholic country, this was not the case with regard to the crafts. There were few, if any, Jewish craftsmen in Germany and northern France. Rabenu Tam, a keen observer of Jewish life in this area, clearly stated that Jews did not engage in manual labor. Nor do we have information on Jewish craftsmen, except the coiners, in the fledgling communities in the Slavic countries. Curiously, we find in 1198 in England's wealthy Jewish community men who worked in the tin mines in Cornwall. When King Edward I attempted to re-structure English Jewry economically through the *Statutum de judeismo* (cf. above, Chap. 3), he recommended to them that they engage in crafts. It is doubtful, however, whether many Jews took to crafts in the remaining 15 years of their stay in the country.

By contrast, craftmanship was a major field of Jewish economic endeavor in Italy. There were many artisans among the Jews of central Italy, even more in the south of the peninsula and very many in Sicily. Here, in fact, a majority of the Jewish population engaged in the crafts. A major area of Jewish craftmanship in Sicily was the production and dyeing of silk. Emperor Frederick II Hohenstaufen, who resided many years in Sicily, was aware of the traditional Jewish skill and experience in this field and encouraged the Jews to continue engaging in it. In fact, much of Jewish commerce in Sicily consisted of merchandising silk.

The country in which masses of Jews, if not their majority, earned their livelihood as artisans was Spain. Here the Jewish craftsmen did not concentrate in one area like their counterparts in Italy and Sicily, but rather worked in many branches of the crafts, including blacksmithery. Jewish engagement in the crafts in *Reconquista* Spain resembled that of the Jewish craftsmen in Poland several hundred years later.

Jews in Agriculture

At the same time, Jews were also engaged in agriculture in most of the Catholic countries. Early in the period a majority of the Jews in Christian Spain earned their livelihood by tilling the soil. And, although with the progress of time a trend toward urbanization and urban occupations set in, agriculture remained for a long time one of the principal areas of economic endeavor among the Jews of Christian Spain. There were many Jewish families in which the same piece of land was held for several generations. In nearby Frankland too a considerable part of the Jewish population engaged in agriculture. The number of Jewish farmers here was probably larger than that of the Jewish merchants. Some Jews of Frankland, and especially in its French regions, owned large estates, including *allodia*, estates for which they paid no taxes. In Italy, too, Jews engaged in farming. As in the crafts, there was a greater Jewish concentration in farming in the southern parts of the peninsula and in Sicily. In northern Italy only few Jews engaged in farming, and the same holds true of Germany.

While Jewish landowners engaged in many branches of farming, including cattle raising, they manifested a special predilection for viticulture. The reason for this may have been the fact that this branch of agriculture required intermittent supervision by the landowner rather than continual labor. In the face of waning safety for Jews in the countryside, viticulture could be continued by Jews preferring to live in the towns. Characteristically, France's two greatest sages, Rashi and his grandson Rabenu Tam, both owned vineyards. Jewish preference for the production of wine also resulted, of course, from the prohibition on drinking wine prepared by non-Jews.

Jewish agriculture was attacked from time to time by the Church. Bishop Agobard of Lyons in the ninth century objected to Jewish ownership of large landed estates because he looked askance at Jews who owned slaves and employed Christian laborers. The Church was only partially successful in denying Jews the possession of large estates and they continued to own such estates in France as they also did in other countries. On the island of Majorca, Jews worked their large estates by the employment of

Muslim slave labor. In England Jewish moneylenders came to own land given to them as collateral by creditors from the nobility. In fact, in the twelfth century Jews sometimes owned entire villages.

Little by little, however, Jews were phased out of most of agriculture. The feudal system, which was becoming the backbone of the medieval western state, was based on land granting and land ownership. The feudal state was structured like a pyramid, and in the pyramid of the Christian state there was no place for the Jew. In England, as we have seen (cf. above, Chap. 3), Jewish acquisition of land even led to their expulsion from the country in 1290. Jewish ownership of small farms and of vineyards had better chances to survive. But even in Christian Spain later, fewer Jews remained in farming and, as we have seen, most had become shopkeepers and craftsmen.

The Jewish Moneylenders

In the latter part of the Early Middle Ages, Jews increasingly began to engage in lending money on interest to Christians, and at the end of the period this had become one of their major occupations in most of the Catholic countries. To be sure, some Jews were moneylenders early in the period, and in France even in the time of the last Merovingians. But these were only exceptions. Moneylending was then almost a monopoly of the monasteries.

After the year 1000 the situation changed radically. The Church began to look at moneylending as a sinful occupation and the monasteries had to phase out of it. This was also the time when, as we have seen, Jews began to lose their hold on commerce, both international and local. It was thus a natural development that the Jews, in need of a livelihood and in possession of the capital withdrawn from commerce, entered the loan business abandoned by the monasteries. New Jewish arrivals from the Near East with its semi-capitalist economy brought along their capital, and this too became available to the credit market.

The attitude of the Church to the Jewish moneylenders was ambiguous. On the one hand, it realized the existence of a need for credit. On the other hand, it considered every loan transaction as usury. In the twelfth century, the attitude of the Church hardened, and early in the thirteenth century the Fourth Lateran Church Council came out with an outright condemnation of the Jewish loan business. Later, the Franciscan monks began to advocate the replacement of the Jewish loan business by Christian charitable credit institutions, an activity in which they persisted for hundreds of years. To be sure, all the time Christians, too, engaged in moneylending, and Jews never had a monopoly on it. In fact, the capital at the disposal of the Christian moneylenders was incomparably larger than that of their Jewish counterparts.

The attitude of the state was more friendly and more realistic. It by and large protected the interests of the Jewish lenders, and attempted to regulate the business in a way that might be workable for the benefit of both the Jewish lenders and the Christian borrowers. Almost half the paragraphs of the charter given to the Austrian Jews in 1244 by Duke Frederick II (cf. above, Chap. 3) dealt with regulating the relationship between the Jewish lender and his Christian client. Only occasionally did Christian rulers, concerned with the evil inherent in usury, attempt to divert the Jews to other occupations.

The spread of the loan business among the Jews in the various countries was not uniform. Wherever agriculture and the crafts were pursued by a considerable part of the Jewish population—as was the case in Spain, southern Italy, and Sicily—the loan business spread only slowly. In Germany, France, and the new Jewish communities in the Slavic countries it spread more rapidly. In the small communities in Germany, probably most Jews loaned money on interest to Gentiles. In England, where its first Jewish settlers in 1066 were, it seems, all moneylenders, the loan business among the Jews played a greater role than elsewhere.

The Jewish moneylenders provided credit to virtually all strata of the population. Even in England, most of the Jewish money was loaned to small landowners and the lower middle class. People turned to a Jewish moneylender mostly when faced with a crisis. When the crop was meager, the farmer found himself in need of credit. When townspeople were stricken by misfortune, they too needed a loan from the Jew. In the closed economy of medieval Western Europe, little could be done with capital to increase one's profit. The Jewish credit transactions were thus almost always of a consumptive rather than productive nature. As a result, the borrower rarely felt gratitude to the lender. On the contrary, borrowing money was always connected with unfortunate experiences, and the Jewish moneylender became in the mind of the borrower a steady reminder of his misery. In addition, most lending was done on pawns as collateral, and the ordinary man often had to deposit with the Jew the only precious thing that he possessed. Small wonder that in the mind of the populace the widely-believed Jewish alliance with the devil (cf. above, Chap. 4) was applied also to the loan business. In the passion plays and in the visual arts, the Jewish usurer began to be depicted in the company of the devil as an actual partner in Jewish financial dealings.

Jewish money loaned to the gentry and the magnates also had an outspoken consumptive character. When preparing for a Crusade, or for service in the ranks of the feudal overlord, the vassal-knight needed money to procure equipment for himself and his men. If he had no ready cash, his only resort was to borrow money from the Jew. His acquisition of imported luxury articles from a Jewish merchant also necessitated borrowing money or buying on credit. Jewish merchants thus often functioned also as moneylenders to their aristocratic customers. Basically, this was also the nature of the credit transactions between Jewish moneylenders and the royal courts. Only the size of the sums borrowed by royalty distinguished such transactions from those between the Jew and the ordinary man. The collateral that the moneylenders received from the aristocracy and the monarchs was in one way or another connected with mortgages on land. It was in this way that Jewish moneylenders often found themselves in possession of large estates.

The consumptive nature of the Jewish credit operations was not their only negative aspect. Equally bad, if not worse, was the enormity of the interest paid on loans in those times. Beginning with the early twelfth century, interest rates were regulated by the governments and varied from place to place. In some countries it was legal to charge between 20 percent and 160 percent per annum. But in such an important charter as that issued in 1244 by

Duke Frederick II of Austria, the interest rate was set at 173⅓ percent.

The reasons for the variations and for the often exorbitant legal rates are not fully clear. It is likely that the truly exorbitant rates of interest were mostly charged in cases of deferred payment of the principal. Similar interest rates were also charged by Christians who loaned money to Christians. It was probably the extreme risk involved in such transactions, as well as taxes bordering on confiscation which were collected by the governments, that were mainly responsible for the unreasonably high interest rates. Not in vain was it customary in later times to look at the Jewish moneylenders as a "sponge" conveniently used by royalty to squeeze out from the populace sums of money which they would never have been able to receive by way of regular tax collections.

We have seen (cf. above, Chap. 5) that during the riots in York in 1190 the bonds held by the Jewish victims were destroyed together with them. As a result it became obligatory in England beginning with 1194 to execute each bond in two copies, one to be kept by the Jewish lender and one by a special official whose title was Exchequer of the Jews. In this way the king of England wanted to make sure that in case the Jew and his bonds were destroyed, he would be able to collect the inheritance of the Jew, the "serf of his chamber." When Aaron of Lincoln, the wealthiest Jewish moneylender in England, if not in all of Europe, died in the 1180s it became necessary to appoint a special official ("Aaron's Exchequer") to liquidate his outstanding loans. Characteristically, after years, only half of his loans and mortgages were collected.

The morality of the Jewish loan business was also questioned from within. In the circles of the Pious Men of Ashkenaz (cf. below, Chap. 10) a strong opposition arose against engaging in moneylending in general, and especially against the high interest charged to the borrower. Here too, as with regard to Jewish commerce, the pietists insisted on absolute honesty by the Jewish party. The sages and communal leaders, however, aware of Jewish economic realities, abstained from criticizing the business too harshly. But their approval was reluctant and applied only to cases where no other way could be found to earn a livelihood.

This was obviously the case with those of the scholars who themselves earned their livelihood through moneylending. The Jewish awareness of the moral problem involved in usury had its impact, and by and large the Jew practiced his credit business with a greater degree of honesty than was found among his Christian competitors. The honesty of the Jewish moneylender was not unknown in Christian society, and many a Gentile preferred to turn in his moment of need to the Jew, rather than to his own co-religionist.

Despite the opposition of the Church and of Jewish pietists, Jews continued to engage in moneylending during the entire following period of the Late Middle Ages and beyond. Only in France and England did the Jewish loan business decline in the thirteenth century due to the invasion of the credit market by the Christian leading moneylenders known as Lombards and Cahorsins. The first group consisted of immensely wealthy Italian financiers who had their base in Lombardy, and the second also of Italian bankers who had their headquarters in Cahors in southern France. The appearance of the Christian financiers made it possible for King Edward I to eliminate Jews altogether from the English credit market in 1275. Although some Jews continued to lend money to Christians under various legal disguises, the ordinance of 1275 did put an end to the most conspicuous Jewish moneylending community in the period of the Early Middle Ages.

Chapter 9

The Cultural Experience

General Developments

While politically and economically the entire Jewry in the orbit of Western Christendom during the Early Middle Ages presented a fairly uniform picture in which the differences were not very sharp, this was not the case in the area of its cultural experience. Here the differences were quite clear and their traces are still visible now. The cultural experience of its northern branch became known as the Ashkenazic tradition and that of its southern flank became known as the Sephardic. The differences between the Ashkenazic and Sephardic cultural patterns grew ever sharper after the year 1100, when each group developed its own Hebrew cursive writing and its own set of customs.

The Sephardim were generally better educated in the secular sciences and they were more successful in the establishment of a cultural symbiosis with their Gentile neighbors. In the areas located between the flanks, and especially in Provence, cultural experiences developed which bore characteristics of a transition between, or blend of, those of the North and the South. Italian Jewry had its own cultural physiognomy, while simultaneously drawing inspiration and learning from, and following some of the patterns of, Sephardic culture. At the same time, Italian Jewry was also one of the sources that contributed to the shaping of Ashkenazic culture. While the Jewish communities in the Slavic countries were culturally an offshoot of Ashkenazic Jewry, they also had elements of an indigenous Slavic Jewish culture. Nor were they missing elements of Byzantine Jewish culture, brought by immigrants from Byzantium, Khazaria, and Kievan Russia. In addition to its Italian, and thus Palestinian source, Ashkenazic Jewry found in Babylonian Jewry another source for the shaping of its culture. As for Sephardic Jewish culture, it to a great degree paralleled the cultural patterns developed by Spanish Jewry under Muslim rule. It was not before the second half of the thirteenth century, on the threshold of the Late Middle Ages, that Sephardic Jewish culture began to change and assume certain Ashkenazic characteristics.

Little is known of Jewish cultural life in the early times of the period. The curtain begins to rise late in the eighth century when a school of Rabbinics is said to have existed in Narbonne in southern France. In the following century, lively Jewish cultural activities are reported to have taken place in various localities in the border region of France and Spain. When we enter the tenth century, Jewish cultural life already blossoms in Germany, France, and Italy. In Germany, Jewish cultural activity was most noticeable at that time in the communities of the Rhineland. In France, which had been experiencing a great cultural upsurge since the eleventh century, Jewish culture had blossomed for a short while in the eleventh century in the center of the country. But then it receded here, and the communities of Champagne in the north and Narbonne and Montpellier in the south took over the cultural leadership. In Italy, the city of Lucca in the north was the most important cultural center. In Christian Spain, Barcelona and Saragossa in Aragon, and Toledo in Castile, became important Jewish cultural centers in the eleventh century. But Christian Spain as a Jewish cultural center attained its true greatness in the twelfth century, when Almohade oppression in southern Muslim Spain (cf. Sec. XIII, Chap. 3) drove many intellectuals from there to the Christian North. Intellectual creativity experienced a great expansion within Spanish society at that time, and the newly arrived Jewish scholars thus found themselves in an atmosphere very favorable to all their endeavors.

When the calamity of the Crusades struck, Jewish cultural creativity in Germany and in France had already become so much a genuine part of the Jewish experience that the tragic events of 1096 and 1146–47 could not undermine it. On the contrary, the time of the Crusades was the period of the Tosafists, one of the golden ages of Jewish learning. It is worth noting that the second half of the twelfth century was for German Gentile society, too, a time of great expansion of learning and culture, energetically promoted by the many feudal princes. Italy too had in the latter part of the Early Middle Ages important centers of Jewish learning, and Hebrew poets who, although unable to match their Spanish colleagues, established for themselves a niche in Jewish literary history.

English Jewry received its intellectual inspiration mainly from French Jewry, but was still able to create its own scholarly climate with a non-negligible community of scholars and authors. Little still occurred in the young Jewish communities of the Slavic countries, which as we have seen, did not begin to grow numerically until the end of the period. Why Portuguese Jewry remained culturally backward during the entire period and long thereafter is not fully clear.

The communities of Provence and of Sicily played a unique

role in Jewish cultural life in the Catholic countries. Provence lay geographically between the Ashkenazic and Sephardic cultural spheres, and thus became a natural intermediary between the two. At first Provence was culturally not much different from Muslim Spain, but when the area was incorporated into Frankland in the eighth century, it began to lose its former cultural character. In time Ashkenazic influences from the north began to penetrate it with ever-increasing strength. But when in the middle of the twelfth century many refugee scholars arrived from Almohade-dominated Andalusia (cf. above, Sec. XIII, Chap. 3), the southern Jewish cultural influences were on the rise again. All these processes resulted in the emergence of Provence's transitional Ashkenazic-Sephardic culture.

Sicily, by the fact that it was occupied by the Muslims for a very long period, also was able after its return to Christian domination to serve in a similar capacity, although to a lesser degree. Unlike the other western countries, Provence had a relatively open society, and this climate was conducive to the development of broad intellectual interests. Thus, many Jewish scholars devoted themselves here to the translation of Arabic works into Hebrew, so making them accessible to the Ashkenazic cultural sphere. Of utmost importance was the contribution of several generations of the Tibbon Family, who lived in the twelfth and thirteenth centuries. Their combined work added a whole library to the cultural treasures of western Jewry and included such Jewish classics as *The Duties of the Hearts* by Bahya ibn Paquda, *The Kuzari* by Judah Halevi, and *The Guide of the Perplexed* by Moses Maimonides (cf. above, Sec. XIII, Chap. 5). Other Hebrew translations from Arabic done in Provence, Christian Spain, and Sicily opened to Ashkenazic Jewry much of the world of classical Greece whose main philosophical and scientific works had been rendered into Arabic at an earlier time. Jewish scholars in Spain, Provence, and Sicily also engaged in translating philosophical and scientific literature from Arabic into Latin, and in Spain also into Spanish. In southern Italy and Sicily such activity took place especially in the first half of the thirteenth century during the reign of Emperor Frederick II Hohenstaufen. Be it noted, however, that with all its wide scope, the role of Jewish translators in the transmission of Greek and Arabic culture to Christian Europe was limited in comparison with that of the naturally more numerous Christian translators.

The above-mentioned school which existed in Narbonne late in the eighth century was endowed by its founder, the Jewish count of Toulouse (cf. above, Chap. 3), with a library. It is understandable that with the rise of Jewish intellectual activity, books and libraries multiplied among western Jewry. In fact, at least among the Ashkenazim in France books were proportionately more common in the thirteenth century than among their Gentile neighbors. Assuming, as the case seems to have been, that the average Jewish library contained about 30 volumes, it must be concluded that between 1,000 and 2,000 Jewish families possessed libraries which were confiscated and burned in Paris in 1242 (or 1244).

It seems, however, that the need of, and hunger for, books was greater than the supply available to the scholars and the students. Books were, of course, handwritten until the invention of the art of printing in the first half of the fifteenth century. They were therefore very expensive and rare. One of the anonymous authors of the *Sepher hasidim, Book of the Pious,* (cf. Below, Chap. 10), therefore came out with a stern demand that the wealthy owners of books should not refuse to lend them to scholars and students. Furthermore, he warned against including several books, or even several tractates of the Talmud, in one volume. Each book, or tractate, should instead be bound separately, so that many students could use them for study. While we do not know to what degree such admonitions were heeded, it must be assumed that the call of the moralists did contribute to the availability of Hebrew books among western Jewry, and thus to the progress of learning.

Education of the young, too, was promoted on a communal basis and Rabbinic ordinances sought to secure sufficient funds for it. If we are to believe the testimoney of a Gentile writer in twelfth-century France, Jews cared for the education of their daughters, too, a phenomenon uncommon in those times. Some historians are of the opinion that the general level of education in those times was higher among the Jews than among their Gentile neighbors.

Linguistic Conditions

The Jewish communities in the Western countries spoke in a great variety of languages. These were mostly, but not always, the languages of the countries in which they dwelt. Some time early in the period the Jews began to change, and add their own additions to, the local vernaculars. At this point the Jewish dialects, or Jewish languages, began to develop. Latin, Arabic, French, Italian, Spanish, German, and primarily Hebrew were the sources out of which the entire linguistic experience of Western Jewry emerged during the period of the Early Middle Ages.

Latin was still in use alongside the local vernaculars among the Jews of Frankland as late as the ninth century. In later times, Jews in the various countries adopted the languages which grew out of the Latin of the late Antiquity, and transformed them into their own dialects. This was mainly done by enriching these languages with the host of Hebrew words needed for the expression of their specific Jewish interests. Often a Hebrew noun or verb was "vernacularized" by the addition of a prefix or suffix from the local language. Equally often, grammatical rules borrowed from Hebrew were forced upon the local language, so giving it a Jewish character.

The Jewishness of these new dialects was further strengthened by the practically exclusive use of a Hebrew cursive. Thus, more than half a dozen Jewish Romance dialects came into being including Judeo-Italian, Judeo-Catalan, Judeo-Portuguese, and two Judeo-French ("Zarphatic"), the Provençal and the northern. Exactly when all these linguistic entities attained the nature of distinct Jewish dialects cannot be determined with certainty. Some, no doubt, had appeared as early as the tenth century. Others appeared later, as was the case with Judeo-Italian, which emerged in central and southern Italy in the twelfth and thirteenth centuries. Whether Ladino, also known as Judesmo or Spaniolic, spoken down to the nineteenth century by most Sephardic Jews, was originally a distinct Jewish language, is not clear. While it is certain that by the end of the Early Middle Ages Ladino was common among the Jews of Spain, it is nonetheless possible that it assumed its specific Jewish character only in the Sephardic Diaspora after the expulsion from Spain in 1492.

Yiddish, which became the most widely used Jewish language, emerged in the tenth century out of middle-high German spoken in an urban environment. One theory has it that Yiddish originated among Zarphatic-speaking Jews who had immigrated to Germany. This would explain the presence of many Romance elements in Yiddish. The possibility, however, should not be overlooked that the Romance elements are rather a remnant of the Latin spoken in Germany in the late Antiquity before the collapse of Roman colonial rule.

The use of the various Iberian Jewish dialects and of Judeo-Italian was limited in the period of the Early Middle Ages to the countries in which they originated. Judeo-French and Yiddish, however, underwent a process of geographic expansion already in those times. English Jewry, an outgrowth of French Jewry, continued to speak its dialect in the new homeland. This was facilitated by the fact that the Norman aristocracy continued to speak French upon settling in England after the conquest of 1066. The use of Yiddish expanded into Bohemia-Moravia and Poland with the ever-increasing immigration of Jews from Germany to these countries. Here, too, the use of the language brought by the immigrants was facilitated by the large-scale immigration of German colonists after the devastation of the region by the Tartar invasion of 1241. For the time being, however, the spread of Yiddish here had not yet resulted in the elimination of the use of the Slavic languages among the Jews of the region. The presence of many Slavic words in the contemporary Rabbinic literature amply attests to this fact. At the other end of Western Jewry's linguistic spectrum stands Arabic. The re-conquest of Spain by the Christians did not eliminate the use of Arabic, and many Jews continued to speak and write in this language under Christian rule. The survival of Arabic was continuously strengthened by the stream of Jewish refugees coming to Christian Spain from Almoravid- and Almohade-dominated Muslim Spain. Nor did Arabic as a spoken language disappear from among the Jews of Sicily, when the island reverted to Christian rule in the second half of the eleventh century. For centuries the Jews of Sicily were in a sense a trilingual community, using Arabic in addition to Judeo-Italian and Judeo-Greek.

Hebrew was nowhere a spoken language among Western

Jewry. Its influence, however, on the various Jewish dialects was immense. It became an integral part of the Jewish dialects and the most conspicuous element that distinguished them from their parent languages. At the same time, a reverse process took place and Hebrew, as far as it was still used in the western countries, was influenced by the languages of the environment. From Latin, Hebrew borrowed most of its geographic terminology. In Spain it absorbed many elements from the Arabic spoken by Gentile and Jew alike.

Hebrew was the main language in which Western Jewry expressed itself in writing. The styles employed by its poets, as we shall see later, to a great degree followed patterns established in the Near East and in Muslim Spain. But there was distinct innovation in its Hebrew prose. The translators of the Provence created for the first time a philosophical and scientific Hebrew style. Having no model on which to fall back, they had to create a terminology for the various disciplines of the "seven wisdoms." True, in their efforts to render as literal as possible a translation, they developed a style which was dry and rigid. It also inevitably abounded in Arabisms. But it was still fit for literal expression in the sciences and it was used profitably by later generations of Jewish philosophers and scientists.

The Hebrew style created in northern France and in Germany by Rabbinic authors was less innovative. Here, where talmudic studies dominated the Jewish cultural scene, the Hebrew style had by its nature to be based on the language of the Mishnah. The countless Aramaic words skillfully woven into the linguistic tapestry are not surprising. In fact, the language of the Mishnah was even employed in the rich Ashkenazic literature of biblical exegesis, due to the preoccupation of its authors with the *midrashim*. This Rabbinic style came to dominate Rabbinic literature in the following centuries.

The necessity of creating new literary styles prompted Western Jewry to give much consideration to the study of Hebrew grammar. It was by far less creative in this field than its counterpart in the Muslim world, but its practical interest in Hebrew grammar was probably greater. This can be seen from the fact that Rashi's commentaries to the Bible and Talmud abound in grammatical expositions and that his grandson, Rabenu Tam, took time out from his halakhic studies and communal activities to write a treatise on Hebrew grammar. It is also noteworthy that the least intellectual Jewish community in the region, that of England, produced significant works in the field of Hebrew grammar. Some Ashkenazic scholars were even known as *dayqanim* (grammarians), a description attesting to their penchant for linguistic studies. It was in Provence, however, that Western Jewry's greatest grammatical work was written. David Qimhi (ca. 1160–1235), about whom more will be said further as a commentator of the Bible, authored here the work *Mikhlol* (Completeness), which in addition to being a treatise on grammar also contains a dictionary of biblical roots. More than other works written in the orbit of Western Christendom, *Mikhlol* parallels the great works on Hebrew grammar written in Muslim Spain.

A considerable contribution to Western Jewry's grammatical studies was also made by Abraham ibn Ezra during the decades of his sojourn in Italy, France, and England. Upon his arrival in Italy about 1140 he seems to have sensed the keen interest in grammatical studies, and immediately undertook to do what seemed needed: the translation into Hebrew of various works on Hebrew grammar originally written in Arabic. By this he made accessible to Italianic and Ashkenazic Jewry a body of much-needed information in a field in which their interest was much greater than their creativity. Abraham ibn Ezra further extended his contribution by writing a number of treatises on specific grammatical issues. True, in these treatises he was more a popularizer than an innovator, but it was exactly this which Western Jewry really needed in the field of the Hebrew language for the successful promotion of its cultural interests.

It is worth noting that Abraham ibn Ezra was the only one among the giants of the Golden Age who did not write any works in Arabic. He left Spain in the prime of his life to throw in his lot with the Jewry living in the orbit of Western Christendom. Keen observer that he was, he immediately realized that Latin, the language of the scholars in these countries, was not going to occupy in the Jewish scholarly community the place Arabic occupied in Jewish literature in the orbit of Islam. A Jewish-Christian symbiosis simply did not exist here. Therefore, Hebrew and only Hebrew could become the language of Jewish literary and scientific expression. And so the refugee-scholar and poet from Spain fell in line and wrote all his works in Hebrew.

Talmudic Studies and Talmudic Literature

Western Jewry's greatest cultural experience and literary achievement during the Early Middle Ages was in the field of talmudic studies. Already in the late eighth and early ninth century, as we have seen, the study of the Talmud was pursued in Narbonne and enjoyed the support and patronage of William-Isaac, count of Toulouse. He is said to have imported to Narbonne leading scholars from abroad. Narbonne, as well as Lunel, Montpellier, and other cities in southern France, were seats of yeshivoth throughout the entire period. As in many other areas of Jewish experience, the transitional character of the Provence also manifested itself in the field of talmudic studies. From the Sephardic yeshivoth in Muslim Spain, the Provençal sages learned to engage in the formulation of general principles for use in the interpretation of talmudic texts. From Rashi and the Tosafists in northern France they learned the method of commenting on, and discussing, single passages and even words crucial to a text. With the appearance in the thirteenth century of Hebrew translations of Maimonides' commentary to the Mishnah, the use of this commentary spread in Provence as well as in Spain.

In Italy, too, the study of the Talmud was cultivated at an early date. An important seat of learning was the city of Lucca, where talmudic scholarship flourished in the tenth and eleventh centuries. In later times talmudic schools existed in Verona, in the north, in Rome, and throughout the south of the peninsula. Southern Italy achieved its greatest fame as a center of talmudic studies in the twelfth century, when no less an authority than Rabenu Tam paraphrased Isaiah 2:3 to proclaim that "out of Bari shall go forth the law and the word of God from Otranto."

But it was in Germany and northern France that a golden age of talmudic studies emerged in this period. True, Torah learning came to these regions at a later date than in southern France, but once it entrenched itself, it became practically a universal Jewish preoccupation. Groups of men, young and old, engaged in the informal study of Talmud everywhere. This was the case in England, too, whose Jewish community in many respects was an offshoot of French Jewry. Talmudic schools existed in many cities in Germany and France, with a special concentration in the Rhineland, Champagne, and Paris and its vicinity. Some of the schools had hundreds of students, as was the case with that of Mayence, headed by Rabenu Gershom (ca. 960–1028), that of Troyes, headed by Rashi, and the one in Rameru, headed by Rabenu Tam (ca. 1100–71). Students came to the latter school even from far away Bohemia and Ukraine. It is not possible to explain fully why Germany and France became the area where talmudic studies were persued with such extraordinary intensity. It is probable that the first talmudic sages to set foot here came from Italy. But the main contribution to these developments must have come from immigrants from the Near East (cf. above, Chap. 2), who brought along the living tradition of the teachings of the geonim. It has been correctly suggested that when Ashkenazic Jewry bestowed upon Rabenu Gershom the title *meor hagolah*, "light of the Diaspora," it was modeled on the title used by Babylonian Jewry *rosh hagolah*, "head of the Diaspora."

The first generations of talmudic teachers led by Rabbenu Gershom and Rashi dedicated themselves to introducing their students to an accurate text of the Talmud, purged of errors, and to its systematic explanation and interpretation. The generations that followed in the twelfth century instead undertook the task of dialectically discussing actual or imaginary contradictions in the great work with a view to harmonizing the text by way of a penetrating analysis. In fact, the way in which they argued their ideas resembled the method by which the Amoraim discussed the law in the Talmud. These scholars became known as "Tosafists," those who added (their glossae to Rashi's basic commentary). The Tosafists dominated the study of the Talmud for fully 200 years, from ca. 1100 to ca. 1300. Several of Rashi's descendants were among the founders of this new school of learning; his grandson Rabenu Tam is considered the foremost Tosafist, and is mentioned in the period's Rabbinic literature more than any other Ashkenazic sage. The Talmud had so deeply entrenched itself within the Ashkenazic community that its study survived the terrible shock of the Crusades. In fact, its most flourishing period

falls between the First and Third Crusades. The study of the Talmud began, however, to decline when Church intervention endeavored to eliminate it. In 1242, as we have seen, not only were
thousands of Hebrew books burned in Paris, but Pope Gregory IX
also issued a ban on the study of the Talmud. At the same time,
be it noted, talmudic studies awakened in the southeastern region
of the German empire, Bohemia and Austria.

Christian Spain in this period presents a less spectacular picture in the area of talmudic studies. True, there is evidence that
some form of organized Jewish elementary education did exist. It
is also likely that, at least in the first half of the thirteenth century, *midrashim*—that is, informal schools for the study of
Rabbinics—were not uncommon. But the place that the study of
the Talmud occupied within Jewish society was not very prominent. In fact, there were circles which treated talmudic scholars
with open contempt. Yeshivoth of the type found in the other
countries, or earlier in Muslim Spain, seem not to have existed.

A decisive change took place after the year 1200, especially in
the northeast of the peninsula. Scholars from France, both from
the Provence and the Ashkenazic North, came to Spain and began
to disseminate the knowledge of the Talmud in the specific
methods followed in the French schools. Spain's two most prominent talmudists of this period, Jonah ben Abraham of Gerona (ca.
1200–63) and Moses ben Nahman (Ramban, Nahmanides), obtained directly or indirectly instruction in the Talmud and in the
Rabbinic literature from French scholars. Also, a disciple of the
Tosafists opened a talmudic school in Barcelona. The school established by Jonah ben Abraham in Gerona attained much fame,
even though its founder excelled in the moralistic literature more
than in the halakhic. Closer to the middle of the thirteenth century, a revival of talmudic studies took place in Toledo when
Jonah of Gerona and a scholar from the Provence settled in the
city.

But it was the personality of Moses ben Nahman more than
anything else that symbolized the new interest in talmudic
studies which had emerged in Spain. Moses was born in Gerona in
1194. As we have seen, he was trained like his compatriot Jonah
by French scholars. But much more than Jonah, Moses became a

decisive admirer and adherent of the method of Torah study developed by the Tosafists. His novellae on the Talmud are not unlike the glossae of the Tosafists, even though he was not unmindful of the manner of Talmud study practiced in the eleventh and twelfth centuries in Muslim Spain. It was this felicitous synthesis of the Sephardic and Ashkenazic ways of study which made Ramban's novellae a major text used in Spain's talmudic academies down to the expulsion of 1492. Although a physician by profession, he succeeded in training in his school in Gerona what became the cream of Spanish talmudic scholarship in the next generation. We shall see later that Nahmanides was also the author of an important and novel commentary to the Bible. The sum total of his writings and activities made him the greatest luminary among Spanish Jewry in the waning years of the Early Middle Ages.

Western Jewry's Rabbinic literature of this period closely parallels its efforts and contributions in the field of the academic study of the Talmud. Its Ashkenazic sector was dominated by Rashi's commentary to the Talmud and by the glossae of the Tosafists. Solomon ben Isaac, popularly known as Rashi, was born in 1039 or 1040 in Troyes, in the Champagne region of France. After years of study in the talmudic schools of Worms and Mayence, he returned to his native Troyes, where he lived to the end of his life in 1105. It seems that he never held an official rabbinic position, and made a living as an owner of a vineyard. We have seen that his school in Troyes attained great fame. The same holds true of his commentary to the Talmud, one of the greatest Rabbinic works ever written. It covers most of the tractates of the Babylonian Talmud. The Talmud, originally designed as a work to be studied and transmitted orally, was written in a concise style and was therefore very difficult to understand. If it was ever to become a work to be studied and understood by people other than outstanding scholars, it needed a commentary that would add words or sentences to transform it into a lucid text.

This was exactly what Rashi's commentary supplied. It was written in a simple Hebrew replete with many Aramaic words familiar to the student of the Talmud. The blend of Hebrew and Aramaic was devised by Rashi in such a skillful way that the reader rarely notices the different linguistic elements. In order to explain less familiar expressions, Rashi often supplied the translation in the French spoken in his days. It is no exaggeration to say that by writing his commentary Rashi enabled his generation and all later generations to understand the Talmud and the environment in which it came into being, even though they lived in societies and countries quite different from those of Babylonia. All scholars agree that Rashi's commentary is the most outstanding among the hundreds of commentaries written on the entire Talmud or on its various tractates. In fact, it became the basis of practically all subsequent Rabbinic literature in the countries of the West. It is thus not surprising that the commentary was printed in virtually all editions of the Babylonian Talmud. Rashi's own generation, recognizing the greatness of the work, named it *Perush* (*The Commentary*), and *Quntres* (a variation of the Latin word *commentarius*). It became customary to print the commentary of Rashi's grandson Samuel ben Meir (Rashbam) to certain chapters of tractates Pesachim and Bava Bathra to which Rashi's commentary is not available.

The literary output of the Tosafists consists of an immense collection of mostly short texts resembling the glossae found on the margins of medieval law books. All these texts are anonymous and are works of about 100 sages of Germany, northern France, and England. The point of departure for the analyses contained in these notes is mostly Rashi's commentary, and they are therefore called *Tosafoth (Additions)*. The sharp and pointed notes of the Tosafists aim at clarifying textual variants in the Talmud as well as issues and specific halakhoth discussed in it. The *Tosafoth* too were printed in almost every edition of the Babylonian Talmud.

The Rabbinic literature of the period also includes a large number of responsa. Rabenu Gershom, Rashi, and to an even greater degree Jacob ben Meir, whose popular name Rabenu Tam was mentioned above, wrote responsa. These responsa were, however, very different from the original type of responsum designed by the Babylonian geonim. They were lengthy essays and their authors not only gave solutions to the problems submitted to them, but endeavored to justify their decisions with elaborate discussions of the relevant talmudic material. We shall see in a later chapter that this type of responsum was proper for the time and place in which it developed.

In the same period, Rabbinic writers in the Ashkenazic countries began to compose compendia of laws. These were not systematic and elaborate codes of the type of Maimonides' *Mishneh Torah*. Instead they either described the laws in accordance with the order of the tractates of the Talmud or listed the laws connected with the basic 613 precepts of the Jewish religion. The most important of these are *Roqeah (A Compound of Spices)*, by Eleazar of Worms, and *Sepher mitswoth gadol (The Greater Book of Precepts)*, by Moses of Coucy, both of the first half of the thirteenth century. The book *Roqeah*, despite its brevity, covers the full spectrum of the Jewish religious law. *Sepher mitswoth gadol* describes the 613 precepts of the Jewish religion by following Maimonides' *Mishneh Torah*. No other Ashkenazic halakhist of the period made such an extensive use of Maimonides' *Code* as did Moses of Coucy. It is possible that Moses wrote his work to supply his compatriots with an instrument for the study of the Jewish law after the Talmud was burned and its study prohibited. Another Rabbinic work of great importance was *Or zarua (Sown Light*, cf. Psalms 97:11) by Isaac ben Moses of Vienna (ca. 1180–1260).

Less spectacular but still quite important was the contribution to Rabbinic literature of the Provençal, Spanish, and Italian talmudists. Outstanding among the Rabbinic writers of the Provence was Abraham ben David of Posquiers (1125–98), known as Rabad. He wrote responsa, and possibly a commentary to the entire Talmud. His fame, however, rests on his massive critical notes (*hassagoth*) on the *Code* of Moses Maimonides. No one among the many commentators of the *Code* subjected it to such a thorough and penetrating review as Rabad. This work became so popular with the scholars that they came to refer to him as Rabad, The Critic (*baal hahassagoth*).

The community of talmudic scholars in Spain was smaller in number in this period than that of Provence. Its outstanding member, however, Moses ben Nahman (1194 or 1195–ca. 1270), ranks among the giants of Rabbinic literature of all times. He was a prolific writer, and among his works are responsa and monographs on specific talmudic issues. The bulk of his writings consists of the already-mentioned *Novellae on the Talmud.* In the Spanish talmudic schools these occupied a place similar to that of the Tosafoth in the Ashkenazic academies.

Italy, too, had its outstanding talmudic writers. Some historians are of the opinion that Isaiah da Trani the Elder (ca. 1180–ca. 1250) occupied among the Italianic Jews a place comparable to that of Maimonides among the Sephardim and Rabenu Tam among the Ashkenazim. However, Italy's main contribution to Rabbinic literature in this period was the *Arukh (Lexicon)*, by Nathan ben Jehiel of Rome (ca. 1030–1106). This work, completed in 1101, is a lexicographical and encyclopedic reference book to the Talmud. Its importance lies in the method of comparative philology followed by the author. It is this modern characteristic of the work that made it the basis for all lexicographical research in the Talmud undertaken with the emergence of the Science of Judaism in the nineteenth century.

Biblical Exegesis

Western Jewry's achievement in the field of biblical exegesis was virtually unparalleled during the Early Middle Ages. No other epoch in the history of the Jewish people produced commentaries to the Bible of such superb quality as the commentaries of Rashi, Abraham ibn Ezra, David Qimhi, and Moses ben Nahman, all written in Western Europe between the eleventh and thirteenth centuries. As Rashi's commentary to the Talmud was the first encompassing most of its tractates, so also his commentary to the Bible was the first to cover almost all of the Scriptures. The other three major commentators also probably wrote commentaries to the entire Bible, although only commentaries to certain biblical books are extant. In addition to these four commentators, many other sages devoted their skill and labor to the elucidation of the Book of Books. Even the Tosafists made their own contribution to this field. Rashi's two grandsons, Samuel ben Meir (Rashbam) and his brother Rabenu Tam wrote biblical commentaries, the first probably to the entire Bible and the latter to the book of Job. Other scholars mentioned in the *Tosafoth* wrote short notes to biblical verses resembling their glosses to specific passages in the

Talmud. In addition, there were other scholars, especially in France, who concentrated their commentaries on one or another biblical book. But Rashi, Abraham ibn Ezra, David Qimhi, and Moses ben Nahman put an indelible imprint on the eternal effort to understand the Bible and to fathom its ideas.

As in the commentary to the Talmud, Rashi's main objective in his commentary to the Bible was to create an instrument with the help of which a fairly educated man would be able to independently study the Bible and to teach it to the less educated and even to school children. A major source from which he drew his material were the old Aramaic translations. Another source was his own penetrating erudition in the philology of the Hebrew language. The commentary is also permeated with a mass of material from the *midrashim*, a necessary element in a biblical commentary designed for the many in a period when books were still handwritten and very rare.

Rashi's commentary was the first of its sort and it remained till our times first and foremost in the massive literature of biblical exegesis. The part which contains the commentary on the Pentateuch became, as far as we can ascertain, the first Hebrew printed book. It was translated into various languages, and over 200 supercommentaries were written on it. Characteristically, the most important among the supercommentaries is that of Elijah Mizrahi, a Byzantine-Turkish scholar. Jewish communities other than the Ashkenazic also realized the overwhelming importance of the commentary and accepted it. A grateful posterity interpreted the name *Rashi* not only as an abbreviation of Rabbi Solomon ben Isaac but also as a symbol of the words *raban shel Yisrael*, the teacher of all the Jewish people.

In a close, often contradictory, relationship to Rashi's commentary stands the commentary of his grandson Samuel ben Meir (Rashbam, ca. 1085–ca. 1174). Although one of the most sophisticated Tosafists, always eager to put forth sharp dialectical argumentation, in his commentary to the Pentateuch he adhered to a strict literal interpretation, beyond that applied by his grandfather. Tradition has it that as a young man Rashbam argued with his grandfather on the meaning of biblical passages. He continued these arguments in a rather outspoken manner in his commentary, composed after his grandfather's death. Rashbam also man-

ifested that same courage and tendency toward total independence when he interpreted biblical passages in a manner contradictory to the normative Halakhah. Curiously, Rashbam evidently was familar with the Vulgate, a phenomenon rather rare
among Ashkenazic sages of that time. Incidentally, he too interspersed his commentary with French words to further eluci-
date the meaning of certain passages.

Rashi's commentary to Scriptures also came to influence
greatly Christian biblical exegesis down to our own times. The
conduit for his influence were the writings of Nicholas de Lyra
(1270–1349), a French monk and one of medieval Christianity's
greatest biblical scholars. With the help of Jewish teachers he
absorbed so much of Rashi's writings that there is hardly a page in
his works in which the great Jewish commentator is not quoted.
Some Christian commentators reacted to this by calling Nicholas
"Rashi's ape."

Abraham ibn Ezra (1089–1164 or 1092–1167) wrote his commentary to the Bible in his later years, after leaving his native
Spain. The unusual interest in biblical exegesis which he found in
France and England may have served him as a stimulus for writing his commentary. Although Abraham's commentary is not
complete, it is likely that originally it covered the entire Bible.
Being one of the most outstanding grammarians of the Hebrew
language, he used his erudition to interpret words and passages in
the Scriptures in an original and independent way. Only passages
which served as sources of the Halakhah did he interpret in con-
formity with rabbinic tradition. And yet the element of biblical
criticism, though veiled, is one of the characteristics of the commentary. Abraham ibn Ezra also believed that chapters 40–66 in
Isaiah are prophecies of a later prophet. Philosophical thoughts
and observations, totally absent in Rashi's commentary, are
found interspersed in Abraham's. Despite attacks directed against
it in later generations for its deviations from the traditional path
of biblical exegesis, the commentary has been eagerly studied by
scholars and enlightened laymen down to our own times. Although Abraham wrote the commentary during his peregrinations in Italy, Provence, France, and England, many scholars consider it the greatest contribution made by Spanish Jewry to the
interpretation of Scriptures.

The biblical commentary of David Qimhi stands somewhere in the middle between that of Rashi and that of Abraham ibn Ezra. Qimhi, who is known as Radaq, was born about 1160 in Narbonne, the great center of Jewish learning in the Provence, where he also died in 1235. He wrote his commentary to many biblical books. We have seen above that Radaq was the author of the major grammatical work *Mikhlol*, the second part of which consists of a dictionary of biblical Hebrew. It is therefore not surprising that he too endeavored first and foremost to interpret the Bible in a simple philological manner. In addition, as a true Provencal scholar, he included in his commentary midrashic material so dear to the North, and philosophical observations so common in Spain to the south. His commentary thus became the great contribution of Provencal Jewry to biblical exegesis. Radaq's commentaries were translated into Latin, and so came to influence later Christian biblical exegesis and translations, including that of the King James Bible.

In the waning years of the Early Middle Ages, a new type of commentary to the Bible was written in Spain, and it greatly differed from those of Rashi, Abraham ibn Ezra, and Radaq. Its author was Moses ben Nahman (Ramban), Spain's greatest talmudic scholar. True, Ramban completed the commentary after his arrival in the Holy Land in 1267, but practically all the work on the commentary was done by him prior to his emigration from Spain. Unlike Rashi, and to a much greater degree than Abraham ibn Ezra and Radaq, he used the commentary as a vehicle to expound his theological and philosophical ideas. There is in his commentary a perpetual endeavor to fathom the deeper meaning of the Bible's laws and narrative. In fact, the thoughts interspersed in Ramban's commentary add up to a complete set of views on God, the universe, and Judaism. Another innovation in the commentary was to connect biblical passages with the then nascent kabbalah. But whenever Ramban interpreted a passage in the manner of the kabbalists, he simultaneously provided a simple philological interpretation, too. All this made Ramban's commentary one of the most popular until our time. It was printed many times in the standard popular editions of the Bible and a number of supercommentaries were composed of it.

Hebrew Poetry and Belles-Lettres

The widespread knowledge and use of the Hebrew language and the interest in grammatical studies provided a basis on which a serious poetical endeavor could have developed. And yet a Hebrew poetry outside of the realm of religion practically did not exist. Its emergence was precluded by the overwhelming devotion to talmudic and biblical studies in the older communities and by the incipient nature of Jewish culture in the new communities. The pietistic trends so strong in Germany and France in the twelfth century, and in the last decades of the period also in Spain (see below, Chap. 10), likewise turned away interest from non-religious poetry. A small number of poems other than *piyyutim* were written in Italy and the Provence. It is not surprising that they were written on the model of the secular Hebrew poetry cultivated in Muslim Spain.

The most important Hebrew secular work written in Italy, the chronicle of Ahimaaz of Capua and Oria, was composed in well-structured rhymed prose. The influence of Spanish Hebrew poetry also penetrated farther north. No doubt Abraham ibn Ezra's long sojourn in the northern countries greatly contributed to the spread of interest in, and the use of, poetical forms created in Muslim Spain. Whenever Rabenu Tam wrote Hebrew verses other than *piyyutim*, he followed the style and manner of Spain's Hebrew poets. Curiously, there were among the minstrels in Germany, France, England, and the Provence some Jews who composed their verses in the vernaculars and presented them to a non-Jewish audience.

Western Jewry seems to have manifested more interest in the short story. Quite a number of them survived in *The Book of the Pious*, a great collective moralistic work, which will be discussed in a later chapter. Many of the short stories had as their heroes biblical figures. However, the deeds attributed to them were not those found in the Bible but rather invented by the authors. Their warfare too was non-biblical but clearly resembled the chivalrous deeds of the contemporary feudal knights. The stories and anecdotes were also full of elements borrowed from non-Jewish demonology, and rather devoid of elements from the *aggadah*. The number of stories which led the reader to a life of piety is, however, impressive. To the same category belong the over 100 animal tales contained in Berakhiah the Punctuator's *Mishle shualim (Fox Fables)*. Berakhiah wrote this book either in northern France or England late in the twelfth or early in the thirteenth century. He took the material from Jewish, pagan, Muslim, and Christian folklore, but added to each fable the moral teaching which he expected the reader to derive from it.

Chronology and History

Western Jewry's historical literature in the Early Middle Ages was much richer and of a broader scope than that of its counterpart in the Muslim world. The Jews of the West encountered more stormy moments on their historical course than the Jewry of the East and therefore had a greater need to express their reaction in the form of historiographical and historiosophical observations. To begin with, the Jews of the West also manifested interest in the chronology of the world of Jewish learning so skillfully expressed in Sherira's *Epistle* (cf. above, Sec. XIII, Chap. 5). Not only do we find Rashi repeatedly quoting in his commentaries the old chronicle *Seder olam (The Chronology of the World)*, but Sherira's *Epistle* too attained widespread circulation in the Ashkenazic lands. Furthermore, Franco-German Jewry made its own important contribution in the form of the gigantic biobibliographical work *Seder tannaim weamoraim (The Chronology of the Tannaim and Amoraim)* by Judah ben Kalonymos of Spires in the twelfth century. But the historical interest of Western Jewry went far beyond the chronology of the scholars.

Despite the chasm which had opened between Jew and Gentile in the period of the Crusades, there was a remarkable parallelism between Jewish and Christian historiography in the Ashkenazic lands. As among the Christians, Jewish historiography here began early in the eleventh century, with short descriptions of mostly contemporary, episodic, local events. This genre reached its peak about the middle of the twelfth century when the three extant chronicles of Jewish martyrdom during the First Crusade were compiled, all from descriptions of local happenings. The shock of the unexpected attack on the hitherto tranquil Rhine communities called both for an attempt to understand the role of the Jew in a world seemingly adverse to God (cf. above, Chap. 5) and for the immortalization of the memory of the martyrs. The same holds true of the single chronicle which described the events which took place during the preparations for the Second Crusade. The elegiac tenor of the chronicles, written in a blend of biblical and rabbinic Hebrew, served as a fitting expression of the feelings of that Jewish martyr generation. Another category of historical literature, the theme of which was Jewish martyrdom, were the penitential poems which described the Crusades or tragic events like the blood libel of Blois in 1171. These historical poems also had their parallel in contemporary Christian historiography. Common to Jewish and Gentile historiography were, finally, the many descriptions of the lives of great spiritual leaders in which their saintliness and piety were stressed to a much greater degree than their biographies.

Western Jews also manifested interest in world history. The main source from which they drew their information was *Yosippon*, which, as we have seen (cf. Vol. I, Sec. VIII, Chap. 2), was possibly written in Germany in this very period. A sort of world chronicle is also the work of Jerahmeel ben Solomon composed in northern Italy in the twelfth century. Southern Italy supplied the above-mentioned family chronicle, *The Scroll of Ahimaaz*, composed in 1054. This chronicle, written in beautiful Hebrew rhymed prose, abounds in fantastic stories about the author's ancestors. The boundless credulity of the author made him a poor historian. His chronicle nonetheless can serve as a good mirror of Jewish life in a period when Jewish historical literature was generally rather scarce.

In the second half of the twelfth century a Spanish Jew also made a major contribution to Jewish historiography. True, Abraham ibn Daud was born about 1110 in Muslim Spain and was educated in its great cultural center, Cordova. However, it was not until 20 years had passed after his immigration to Toledo, the capital of Christian Castile, that he wrote his historical work *Sepher haqabalah*. A translation of one of Avicenna's works into Spanish ascribed to him indicates that he had undergone the process of integration within the Jewry of Christian Spain. The fact that *Sepher haqabalah* was composed in Hebrew and not in

Arabic, as was most of the Jewish prose in Muslim Spain (cf. Sec. XIII, Chap. 5), clearly indicates that it was meant to be read by a Jewish public that did not know, or did not read, Arabic.

Sepher haqabalah (The Book of Tradition) was written in the years 1160–61, and was the first part of a tripartite work which also contained a treatise on the rulers of Rome and an abridgement of *Yosippon.* As the title indicates, the author's foremost aim was to establish the validity of the religious tradition. We have seen above (cf. above, Sec. XIII, Chap. 7), that in the twelfth century Karaism made an attempt to penetrate Spain, and that the Jewish leadership took severe measures to neutralize it. *Sepher haqabalah* was probably designed to aid the actions of the Jewish leadership. It is therefore not surprising that a part of the work consists of mere lists of sages which demonstrate the continuity of the chain of tradition. The book, however, also contains narratives which describe Jewish life in Muslim Spain colorfully and with a high degree of readability. It is also understandable that *Sepher haqabalah* was composed in the rhetorical vein of Muslim historiography known to the author from his years of study in Cordova. It is doubtful whether Abraham ibn Daud knew the chronicles of the First Crusade composed in the Rhineland only a decade or two before he wrote *Sepher haqabalah.* And at any rate, the martyrological mode of the northern Jewish historiography was of little use for his descriptions of Jewish intellectual life in Muslim Spain, where anti-Jewish riots were mere episodes. The fact that Abraham ibn Daud attempted in a sense to picture Jewish history against the backdrop of general history adds to his work a quality then still rare in Jewish historical literature.

Geography and Travel

Western Jewry's practical interest in geography was even greater than in history. The major role Jewish merchants played in international trade in the Carolingian period and beyond made travel and familiarity with conditions in distant countries a matter of course within the Jewish community. The Jewish expectation for the "ten lost tribes" to reveal themselves prior to the coming of the Messiah also contributed to geographic knowledge, distorted and unrealistic as it may have been. More realistic and accurate geographic information was, to be sure, disseminated by the immigrants from the South and the Near East who came to the Ashkenazic lands in the early centuries of the Early Middle Ages and by the emigrants who at the end of the period initiated Ashkenazic Jewry's great expansion to Eastern Europe. The opening chapters of *Yosippon* also contributed to interest in, and familiarity with, geography.

Western Jewry also had to solve a specific geographic problem: to find Hebrew names for all new states that emerged in Europe on the ruins of the Roman empire. Apparently, the best solution was to adapt for them biblical geographic names, no longer identifiable. Why Ashkenaz (Genesis 10:3 and Jeremiah 51:27) came to be identified with Germany, Zarephath (Obadiah 1:20) with France, and Sepharad (Obadiah 1:20) with Spain is a matter of speculation. Phonetical considerations may have been the main motif. Canaan, clearly identical with the Holy Land to every Jew reading the Pentateuch, nevertheless became the medieval Hebrew name for the Slavic lands. Some scholars believe that these lands, the main suppliers of slaves in the early Middle Ages, earned the name Canaan because of the frequent identification of Canaan with slavery, both in the Bible and Talmud (cf., e.g., the verse: "And let Canaan be their servant," Genesis 9:26). England was mostly called by its French name *Angleterre*, but also *Erets hayi*, the island country, or *Kenaph haarets*, the end of the world, because of the literal interpretation of the word *angle*, end. Names of localities were often simply translated into Hebrew from their meaning in the vernacular. Names of towns which had a Christian religious connotation were often translated or twisted to assume a derogatory character. As we have seen, rivers and those towns that had existed in Roman times were called by their Latin names—for example, *Rhenus* for Rhine, *Colonia* for Cologne, and *Eborwakh* for York, the Latin name of which was *Eboracum*.

The travels of western Jews to distant lands were quite remarkable. Few caravans of merchants made trips like those of the Radhaniya, one of whose headquarters was in northern France (cf. above, Chap. 8). With the opening of the Mediterranean to western travelers in the period of the Crusades, Jewish immigrants and pilgrims to the Holy Land greatly increased in number. Some of the pilgrims reported what they had seen, and especially about the holy shrines and sepulchres of the prophets and other holy men. The catalogue of holy sepulchres kept on growing and ultimately contained as many as 500 sites. But far beyond those of the pilgrims were the achievements of two Jewish travelers, one from Christian Spain and one from Germany, who undertook years-long travels to the Near East and with their travelogues made a lasting contribution to the geographic literature of the Middle Ages.

Benjamin of Tudela, about whose life practically nothing is known, began his journey either in 1159 or 1167. He first visited a number of cities in his native Spain, and then crossed the border into southern France. He then embarked in Marseilles for a sea trip to northern Italy. After visiting many towns, including Rome, he boarded another ship in Otranto for mainland Greece and various Aegean islands. From there Benjamin went to Cyprus, Syria, and the Holy Land. After a prolonged stay there, he returned to Syria whence he went to Iraq and Persia. Some scholars are of the opinion that Benjamin visited India as well. The exact route of Benjamin's return trip to Spain is not fully known. We know that he was in Egypt and Sicily, from where he probably returned directly to Spain in 1172 or 1173.

Benjamin's report, known as *Massaoth Binyamin (Benjamin's Travels),* is a partly inaccurate abridgement of his probably much more ample travelogue. Nonetheless, the data it conveys belong to the most valuable and precise geographic information which has come down to us from the Middle Ages. Benjamin was a keen observer, and since he stayed everywhere for weeks or months, he was able to bring back to the West accurate details on political, economic, social, and cultural conditions. He is said to have been the first to report about China, under the name "China," a century prior to Marco Polo's journey. It was only natural that Benjamin's information about the Jewish communities he visited was comprehensive and detailed. It is not surprising that Benjamin's travelogue was translated into most western languages. There is hardly a modern work on the history of geography that does not include a chapter on Benjamin and his travels.

Less spectacular but still remarkable was the journey of Pethahiah of Ratisbon undertaken several years after Benjamin's return to Europe. Pethahiah's point of departure was Prague, the capital of Bohemia. While Benjamin traveled to the East mostly by ship, Pethahiah went there on the overland route. He first went to "Russia," the name then used for today's East Galicia. From there Pethahiah proceeded to the southern Ukraine and the shores of the Black Sea. His next destination was the Caucasus, whence he went to Armenia and Iraq, as far as the border of Persia. Here he turned back westward and went to Syria and the Holy Land. Pethahiah, too, did not tell clearly by what route he returned to Germany possibly as late as 1190, but there are some indications that he visited Greece on his return trip.

The report of Pethahiah's journey, known as *Sibuv haolam (A Trip Around the World)*, was not written by him but by an anonymous contemporary. This travelogue too presents only a part of the traveler's original notes or oral reports. What is left in the travelogue deals mainly with the Jewish aspects of the journey: holy shrines, graves of holy men, and miracles connected with them. But information on the Jewish communities and their leaders is also quite ample. Pethahiah was not unmindful of the problem of the "ten lost tribes" and he believed that when he reached the frontier of Persia only ten days' journey separated him from the country in which they were "hidden." It is obvious that Benjamin of Tudela was a much keener observer that Pethahiah and that he was also less credulous than his Ashkenazic counterpart. But Pethahiah's observations and report are basically no different from those of most medieval travelers and their travelogues. Pethahiah and his experiences are also given ample attention by historians of medieval geography.

Philosophy

In no field of the cultural experience were the differences between the Ashkenazic and Sephardic flanks of Western Jewry as deep as in their attitude to philosophy. No philosophical work was produced during the entire Early Middle Ages by Jews in Germany, Northern France, and England. Rashi's commentaries to the Bible and the Talmud do not contain any philosophical discussions. It is possible that Abraham ibn Ezra formulated the numerous philosophical remarks in his commentary to the Bible in an enigmatic and cryptic way in order not to offend the Ashkenazic Jews among whom he wrote a considerable part of the work.

The situation was different in the Provence and Christian Spain. Here philosophy occupied a place of major importance among the Jews. To begin with, in nearby Muslim Spain philosophy was an integral part of the culture of the Golden Age and its influence could not help but spread to the northern, Christian part of the peninsula. In the first half of the twelfth century the famous astronomer and mathematician Abraham bar Hiyya (ca. 1065–ca. 1136) composed, probably in Barcelona, a philosophical work, *Hegyon hanephesh (Reflections of the Soul)*, in which he discussed practically the same issues which were central to Jewish philosophy in Muslim Spain. The interest in philosophy intensified even more by the middle of the century, when Almohade persecution in the south drove many philosophers, Jews, Christians, and Muslims to Christian Spain. Here even Muslim thinkers felt more at home than in fanatical, fundamentalist Almohade Andalusia.

Among the Jewish refugees was the historian Abraham ibn Daud, whose work *Sepher haqabbalah* was discussed above. Years after his arrival in Toledo he wrote in Arabic, still used by refugees from Muslim Spain as an instrument of literary expression, a philosophical work which survived in a Hebrew translation under the name *Haemunah haramah (The Sublime Faith)*. *The Sublime Faith* offers a strong defense of the idea of revelation and of the tenets of Judaism in general. More than any other philosopher, except for Maimonides, Ibn Daud attempted to achieve a reconciliation between the religion of the heart and the religion of the intellect. One wonders why no other major philosophical works were written in Christian Spain at a time when so many philosophically trained refugees settled there.

Equally strong, if not stronger, was the interest in philosophy in the Provence. A process of major significance was unfolding here. The average Jewish intellectual in Southern France did not know Arabic, the language in which practically the entire Jewish philosophical literature had been written hitherto. Nor was he familiar with Latin, the scholarly language of the Christian world. Two objectives were thus called for: to make available to him in Hebrew the great Jewish theological and philosophical works composed in Arabic; and to provide a literature which discussed in Hebrew general philosophical issues mostly left untouched in the works of Jewish philosophers in Muslim Spain. The Jews in Arabic-speaking countries learned about such issues from the writings of the Muslim philosophers. Jews in the orbit of Western Christianity, who mostly abstained from studying Latin, "the language of the priests" (*leshon galahuth*), needed a general philosophical literature in Hebrew. Various scholars in the Provence engaged in the translation of general and Jewish philosophical works from Arabic into Hebrew, but they were all outdone by two members of the Tibbon family, Judah and Samuel, father and son. Judah ibn Tibbon (1120–90), a refugee from Granada, translated Saadiah's *Beliefs and Opinions*, Bahya ibn Paquda's *The Duties of the Hearts*, and Judah Halevi's *Kuzari*.

His son Samuel (1150–1230), himself an author of a variety of works, dedicated his entire skill as a translator to the works of Moses Maimonides. While working on the translation of *The Guide of the Perplexed* he took his work so seriously that he offered to travel to Cairo in order to be able to consult with the author on problems of the translation. He also provided the reader of the Hebrew version of the *Guide* with a dictionary of the "strange" words in the work. The dictionary contains an elaborate commentary on many of the concepts and terms employed by Maimonides. In addition to the *Guide*, Samuel also translated the *Eight Chapters* and some other minor treatises of the great master. The translators and other Provençal authors also composed a variety of philosophical writings of their own. Characteristically, authors of Rabbinic works, too, unlike their Ashkenazic colleagues, showed interest in, and inclination to, philosophical speculation.

The difference in the attitude to philosophy manifested itself fully during the first controversy on the writings of Maimonides which raged in the 1230s (cf. above, Sec. XIII, Chap. 5). While the northern rabbis uncompromisingly rejected the philosophical writings of the Great Eagle and banned their study, the opinions were divided in the Provence, where a deep chasm existed between the attitudes of the pietists and the adherents of allegory. The approach of Moses ben Nahman in Spain was conciliatory. As a Sephardi with no mean philosophical erudition, he could not help but implore the Ashkenazic rabbis to rescind their ban. But, deeply imbued with the pietistic ideals coming from the North, he was also aware that the allegorists and secularists were using Maimonides' writings to the detriment of the normative Jewish faith. This diversity in the attitude to philosophy continued to dominate the Jewish religio-cultural scene in the later decades of the thirteenth century, with the advent of the Late Middle Ages.

It must finally be stressed that what was happening on the Jewish cultural scene was not unparallel to contemporary phenomena in Christian society. Here scholasticism dominated the scene, more broadly affecting thought and life than is popularly believed. Scholasticism, in fact, had a noticeable, though subtle, impact on Jewish philosophical thought, too. And despite the growing alienation of Jew from Gentile in the period of the Crusades, Jewish thought also fructified to a certain degree the philosophical trends among the contemporary Christians.

The Sciences

The sciences, everywhere companions to philosophy, were also represented to a much greater degree among the Spanish and Provençal Jews than among the Ashkenazic. There was interest among the Ashkenazim in the sciences, as is indicated by the presence of Hebrew scientific works in libraries of northern Jews, as well as by the geometric figures included by Rashi in his commentaries to illustrate certain interpretations. No doubt Abraham ibn Ezra found among the Ashkenazim, as well as in Italy, an atmosphere of interest in the sciences, if he chose to write most of his many scientific treatises in these countries. But Ashkenazic Jewry's interest in, and hospitality for, the sciences was not sufficient to forge local creativity in this branch of knowledge. The Jewish scientists in Spain and Provence were aware of the situation among the northern Jews and looked down upon the Tosafists as men lacking erudition in the sciences and method in their way of thinking.

The Jewries of Christian Spain and of the Provence were indeed much more creative in the sciences. During the first decades of the thirteenth century the above-mentioned philosophical author Abraham bar Hiyya of Barcelona wrote what may be termed a whole scientific library. Most of his writings were in the fields of mathematics and astronomy. Being by profession a surveyor in the service of the state, it is not surprising that he authored in Hebrew a book on geometry, which was translated into Latin a few decades after his death and was for generations a standard textbook in Western Europe. Significantly, in this book he coined a number of geometrical terms hitherto unknown in Hebrew. His other works are mostly in the field of astronomy, and include an encyclopedia of astronomy, mathematics, optics, and music, of which only a part has survived. Some scholars consider Abraham bar Hiyya the greatest Jewish mathematician and astronomer of the Middle Ages. Like many other medieval astronomers, Jewish and Gentile, Abraham bar Hiyya considered astrology a legitimate part of astronomy. In fact, he practiced astrology in the royal court of Aragon and among its nobles. To justify his practice, he attempted to prove the legitimacy of astrology from sources in Rabbinic literature.

Astronomy was probably the most popular science in those times, and Jewish translators translated various astronomical works from Arabic into Hebrew, Latin, and Spanish. The most important of such translations was that of the work known in the Middle Ages under the name of *Almagest,* written by the second century C.E. Alexandrine astronomer Ptolemy. It was translated into Hebrew by the Provencal scholar Jacob Anatoli in the first half of the thirteenth century. Jacob Anatoli, incidentally, was invited to Sicily by Emperor Frederick II for the purpose of translating scientific works for him.

Abraham ibn Ezra's scientific writings were also in the fields of mathematics and astronomy. In a series of treatises he discussed various mathematical and chronological issues. He was also first to use letters of the Hebrew alphabet as digits. In one of his treatises he described a new astrolabe, the instrument used by navigators to calculate the altitude of stars. He and other Jewish astronomers of that period prepared astronomical tables which were used a century later when the famous Alphonsine (planetary) Tables were made for King Alphonso X of Castile. Probably Abraham ibn Ezra's astrological writings were as numerous as his astronomical works. He wrote a series of astrological treatises which in their totality can be considered an encyclopedia of this pseudo-science. True, his scientific works, written during the decades of his peregrinations, often lack thoroughness, but they all are original works and not translations of the works of others.

Jewish involvement in the science of medicine and in the practice of medicine was probably as great in this period in the Western countries as in the orbit of Islam. Jews played an important role in the development of the school of medicine in Montpellier in southern France. Although the story that Jews were among the founders of the famous medical school in Salerno in southern Italy is probably legendary, there are many indications that Hebrew played a certain role there as a language of instruction. Various physicians translated, or wrote, treatises on medicine and drugs. Despite recurring bans against the employment of Jewish physicians, issued by various Church bodies, and the popular belief that Jews were sorcerers and poisoners (cf. above, Chap. 6), Jewish doctors continued to be consulted by Gentiles, including the nobility and the clergy. Names of Jewish doctors are frequently found in the sources, but it is clear that their actual number was much larger.

Especially numerous were the Jewish physicians in Spain. Members of the Tibbon family, whose historical fame rests on their achievements as translators of philosophical works, were by profession physicians. The 18 Jewish physicians whose names are documented in England for the period 1190–1290 are surely only a few of the many who practiced medicine there in this last century of the existence of the Jewish community. Of greater importance, however, is the testimony of England's philosopher-monk Roger Bacon (died in 1294) that the Jewish physicians were more learned than their Christian counterparts. In a period when most medical training was conducted on a private basis, Jews, with their knowledge of languages and access to the many Hebrew translations of medical works from Arabic, indeed had better opportunities to learn the medical profession in a thorough manner. The fact that Jews were untouched by the Christian belief in miraculous cures through relics of saints also promoted among them the art of medicine. Jews, as international traders, also played a major role in the importation of drugs from the Muslim East to the Western countries.

Chapter 10

The Religious Life

Although the Middle Ages are described as the "Age of Belief," Western Jewry's religious life was at first by no means monolithic. As on the cultural scene, great differences existed between its Sephardic and Ashkenazic components in the sphere of religion as well. The Italianic component also had its own ways of religious experience. By and large, Ashkenazic Jewry was more rigorous and fundamentalist than its Sephardic counterpart. Complaints about religious laxity were much more often heard in Spain than in the Ashkenazic countries. The situation was similar in Provence, where the religious practice sometimes had only a symbolic character, and where some considered the biblical narrative a mere allegory. Curiously, while religious laxity in Spain was mainly rampant among the upper classes of Jewish society, in the Ashkenazic countries the wealthy leaders of the communities promoted a way of life totally dedicated to the service of God. Late in the period, Spanish Jewry, now living in its majority under Christian rule, was increasingly exposed to influences coming from Ashkenaz. As a result, religious differences between the two parts of Western Jewry became less conspicuous, and Ashkenazic piety found adherents in Spain.

The Question of Religious Authority

Western Jewry, and especially its Ashkenazic component, had to struggle from its very inception with the problem of religious leadership and authority. In the Near East the authority of the geonim was only rarely challenged, since they were universally considered to be legitimate heirs of the Amoraim. Hence, there was no need for rabbinic ordination, which fell into oblivion some time after the conclusion of the Mishnah (cf. Vol. I, Sec. VIII, Chap. 6). Nor did the geonim see themselves as obligated to prove to inquiring communities or individuals the validity of their decisions; they could therefore write concise, and sometimes even curt responsa. In the West the situation was different. Here, where new communities came into being as a result of immigration from different directions (cf. above, Chap. 2), no authority such as that of the geonim could develop. Here, the Talmud, the main repository of the Jewish law, became the source and basis of all religious authority.

To be sure, Rabenu Gershom, the first major leader of Ashkenazic Jewry in its formative years, harkening back to Babylonian Jewry and its institutions, attempted to regulate Jewish life by issuing ordinances (the most famous, the one banning polygamy), so imitating a procedure of the geonim. He thus in fact introduced into the West the law-making function of the Rabbis common in the Near East. But he, as well as Rashi in the following generation, wrote responsa in a novel way. These were neither short nor concise, since their authors had to justify their decisions by summoning supportive arguments from the Talmud. The responsa thus became a forum of dialectical reasoning in the interpretation of the Talmud.

Maimonides, who lived in the Near East at a time when claims were still made in Babylonia that the geonic period was not yet over, could write *Mishneh Torah,* a code of laws, without referring to talmudic sources. In the West, however, Rashi had to write a *commentary* to the Talmud, to open it and make it operational as a source for practical decisions and their validation. The need was also felt here to re-introduce ordination, in order to invest the individual rabbi with the formal authority to make decisions in matters of religion. And so Ashkenazic Jewry restored ordination, probably some time in the eleventh century. Once ordained, each rabbi felt authorized to decide and adjudicate in matters of religious law. Rabenu Tam, the most outspoken religious leader of Ashkenazic Jewry during the Early Middle Ages, expressed this unequivocally when he demanded recognition for his court similar to that accorded in the Antiquity to the Sanhedrin.

Ritual and Prayer

Little is known of the daily religious life of the Jew early in the period when most of the area was controlled by the Frankish rulers. Some historians are of the opinion that the few Jews who survived the turmoil of the Germanic invasions, as well as the early new arrivals, sacrificed many Jewish customs on the way to their integration in general society. This view is probably exaggerated, since we learn from Christian sources that Frankland's Jews of the ninth century observed the Sabbath and listened to sermons in the synagogues.

Jewish religious life greatly intensified beginning with the tenth century when Rabbinic learning began to occupy an ever-increasing place in the life of the individual. We shall see later that in the period of the Crusades a new, extraordinary piety developed among the Ashkenazic Jews, which accompanied their martyrdom (cf. above, Chap. 5) and became known as Ashkenazic Hasidism. Significantly, this heroic piety found its way even to such a young community as that of Poland. To be sure, the religious behavior of western Jewry during all this time was in a state of fluctuation. English Jewry, for example, although following generally in the footsteps of Franco-German Jewry, disregarded a variety of religious customs common on the continent. The approach of Rashbam and Rabenu Tam to a variety of religious precepts was sometimes drastically different from that of their grandfather Rashi, even though Rashi was one of the main molders of Franco-German Jewry's religious life. Even the order of the pentateuchal passages in the *tephillin* became a matter of controversy between Rashi and Rabenu Tam. Strange as it may sound, Rabenu Tam's older brother Samuel (Rashbam) interpreted Genesis 1:5 in a manner that could suggest that the right time to begin the Sabbath should be at dawn Saturday instead of Friday at sunset, as practiced since times immemorial. To repudiate such an interpretation, Abraham ibn Ezra possibly wrote his *Iggereth hashabath (The Epistle on the Sabbath)*, in which he strongly defended the traditional way of observing the day of rest. These differences, it should be noted, were by no means detrimental to the role of religion in the life of the average Jew. They rather manifested the vitality of the brand of Judaism unfolding in Western Jewry.

The daily religious experience of the Jews of Provence and Christian Spain was less intensive. Religious laxity, widespread in the upper classes of the Jewish population, was also not uncommon among the masses. Often this was a result of sheer ignorance of the most elementary aspects of the ritual. Most neglected seems to have been the precept of laying *tephillin* (phylacteries), which was also to a certain degree neglected in the communities north of the Pyrenees. Violation of the Sabbath and the holidays was also widespread. And yet, it was precisely at this time, the first half of the thirteenth century, that signs of a change began to appear. Ashkenazic modes of piety found followers, and the saintly Rabbi Jonah of Gerona, author of the popular work *Shaare teshuvah (Gates of Penitence)*, was greatly revered. It is thus not surprising that when in 1236 Moses of Coucy undertook a trip to Christian Spain for the distinct purpose of promoting a more strict observance of the religious practice, his mission was crowned with success. Spanish Jewry on the threshold of the Late Middle Ages was obviously turning toward a greater devotion to God and His service.

The center of religious life in all Western Jewry was, as everywhere, the synagogue. The responsa and the *Scroll of Ahimaaz* make it clear that services were held on a daily basis, mornings and evenings. Since prayerbooks were rather expensive and scarce, the cantor often recited the entire service aloud. Most localities had more than one synagogue. A town in Italy with a Jewish population of only 200 had 4 synagogues. A rabbinic ordinance demanding free access for every Jew to synagogues located in private homes also points to a large number of places of worship. The tendency of newcomers to continue praying according to their own rite also added to the number of places of worship in those times of steady migratory movements. Only in the outgoing years of the period did the Catholic clergy begin to insist successfully that the number of synagogues be limited.

Different orders of prayer were followed in the Western Jewish communities. The debate which has been going on between historians as to the origin of the Sephardic and Ashkenazic orders of prayer and their relationship to the Palestinian and Babylonian rites, has not yet led to final conclusions. Some historians believe that *minhag Ashkenaz*, the Ashkenazic order of prayer, originated in southern Italy. A historian of Jewish religious music has shown that melodies common to Ashkenazic synagogues were known in Central Italy in the tenth century. Whatever the origin of the Ashkenazic rite, it is beyond doubt that it took very much from the *siddur* of Amram Gaon (cf. Sec. XIII, Chap. 6).

This is also evident in the *Mahazor* (holiday prayerbook) *Vitry*, compiled in the eleventh century by Rabbi Simhah of Vitry in France. This prayerbook, which represents the order of prayer of northern France and of Rashi and his school, is only slightly different from the basic Ashkenazic prayerbook. The Ashkenazic prayerbook was followed with only slight local variations also in England and in the new communities in Central Europe. It has become the most widespread order of Jewish prayer. The communities of the Burgundy region also had their own prayer book, which varied from the French rite only to a limited degree.

As in the area of culture, a special situation with regard to Halakhah and ritual was prevalent in Provence. Originally, its Jewry adhered exclusively to the halakhic patterns of the Ashkenazim. However, Palestinian influences came in and made their impact on the religious practice. Close to the middle of the twelfth century, when many intellectuals from Almohade Spain sought refuge here, the influence of the geonim and of the code of Isaac Alfasi (cf. above, Sec. XIII, Chaps. 5 and 6) appeared as well. All these—sometimes conflicting—factors created within the religious life of Provencal Jewry characteristics typical of a transitional area. Curiously, nearby Catalan Jewry followed the Provencal rite instead of the Sephardic. The Sephardic order of prayers is basically not very different from the Ashkenazic, and it is not unlikely that both these major orders of prayer had as their sources the old Palestinian as well as Babylonian rites. The Italianic order of prayer is, however, very different from both the Sephardic and Ashkenazic rites.

The *piyyutim*, the religious hymns and poems, occupied an increasingly conspicuous place in the holiday prayerbooks of all the rites. The Ashkenazic Jews did not hesitate to use in their services *piyyutim* written by the great poets of Muslim Spain. But, in the center of the Ashkenazic holiday services stood the hymns written by northern *payyetanim*, among whom Ephraim ben Isaac of Ratisbon, who died in 1175, was the greatest. The foremost religious leaders of Franco-German Jewry, Rabenu Gershom, Rashi, and Rabenu Tam also made a weighty contribution to the *piyyutic* literature. The Ashkenazic *piyyut* resembled the old Palestinian religious hymns and was distinguished from the Sephardic by its somber tone and lack of stylistic elegance so common in the latter. How important the *piyyut* was to Ashkenazic Jewry can be seen from the fact that one of its scholars, Abraham ben Azriel of Bohemia, wrote in the first half of the thirteenth century a voluminous commentary to the *piyyutim* under the title *Arugath habosem (Bed of Spices;* cf. Song of Songs 5:14).

Many a liturgical poem was written in the spirit of the Pious Men of Ashkenaz. Foremost among these were the *Shire hayihud (The Hymns of Unity)* by Samuel the Pious and the *Shir hakavod (Hymn of Adoration)* by his son Judah the Pious. The latter poem attained immense popularity, and countless synagogues in our own times conclude their Saturday morning services with it. Italian Jewry too made a major contribution to the *piyyut*. One gets the impression that the religious hymns constituted the bulk of Hebrew poetry then written in Italy. In Christian Spain, too, Moses ben Nahman mostly used his considerable talent as a poet to compose *piyyutim*.

The Pious Men of Ashkenaz

Alongside the stream of normative religious life, certain trends developed which aimed at satisfying the religious needs of men whose devotion to God was more than the usual encountered even in those times when people were "breathing" religion. One group of such devotees became known as *Haside Ashkenaz*, the Pious Men of Ashkenaz. The movement of the hasidim came into being in the twelfth century and was centered in the Rhine communities in the north and in Ratisbon in the south. Some of the major leaders of the group belonged to the family of the Kalonymi, members of which were among the ranking communal leaders and talmudic scholars. The ideals of the group came to fruition in post-Crusade Germany with its heated religious atmosphere. Its members, never too numerous, created for themselves a heroic way of Jewish life worthy of a period in which so many of their contemporaries sacrificed their lives for the sanctification of the Holy Name. They aspired to perform the *mitswoth* in a manner above and beyond what was required by the law. Their social and economic behavior, too, was to be of a higher quality. They believed that above the *din Torah*, the normative Jewish law, stood the *din shamayim*, the Heavenly law, which represented a higher form of devotion to God and of ethical behavior.

Some historians believe they have detected in German Hasidism similarities to the Franciscan movement in Christianity. If there were any significant similarities between the two movements, they did not result from mutual influences but rather from a parallel reaction of Jewish and Christian pietists to conditions and ideas common at the time. The hasidic movement began in Germany prior to the appearance of Saint Francis of Assisi, and its main leader, Judah the Pious, was his older contemporary. Be it also noted that the idea of poverty as a virtue, so central in the Franciscan movement, was unknown among the Pious Men of Ashkenaz.

The German hasidic movement produced a literature of its own. This literature aimed at teaching the adherents of the movement how to reach the double goal of fulfilling the *mitswoth* in an extreme devotional way and of behaving in everyday life with uncompromising morality. This placed the hasidic writings within the category of what is called *musar*, moralistic literature. However, a comparison between as classical a musar work as Bahya's *The Duties of the Hearts* and the major work of the hasidim of Ashkenaz, *Sepher hasidim (The Book of the Pious)*, shows the vast differences between the teachers of morality in Muslim Spain and in the Ashkenazic lands. The former described systematically and in the manner of the philosophers the various areas of the relationship between the Jew and his God. The latter is a collection of about 2,000 chapters, some very short, some long, in which a multitude of issues are discussed. Here and there a group of chapters does discuss various aspects of one and the same issue. But in vain will the reader of *The Book of the Pious* look for a systematic and broad discussion of the general principles of ethics and morality. He will find instead instructions, admonitions, and directions presented with much vigor and enlivened by tales and parables often bordering on the fantastic and supernatural. *The Book of the Pious* as we have it is a great anonymous collective work which attained its form (in a shorter and a longer version) probably late in the twelfth or early in the thirteenth century. It is quite likely that Samuel the Pious (twelfth century) and his son, Judah the Pious (ca. 1140–1217), had a major part in the compilation and redaction of the work.

Another major work produced by the hasidic movement is the above-mentioned *Roqeah (A Compound of Spices)*, by Eleazar of Worms (born in the 1160s, died in the 1230s). This is a typical Ashkenazic law book, most of which is dedicated to a description of ritual and prayer. What makes *Roqeah* a unique religious work are its first two sections. The first section is called *Hilkhoth hasiduth (The Laws [guiding the Jew to true] Piety)*. The author discusses here such concepts as the unity of God and the love of God, as well as the ways to attain humility and to avoid envy and hatred. The second section is dedicated to the idea of penitence, so important in the life of medieval man. All in all, the first two sections charted for the Jew a way of total and uncompromising dedication to God and of just and ethical behavior toward his fellow man. One gets the impression that by writing this "philosophical" prologue to the rather customary description of the ritual in the rest of the work, Eleazar of Worms imitated his older contemporary, Moses Maimonides, whose *Code of Laws* is prologued by the Book of Knowledge, describing the philosophic foundations of the Jewish law.

The movement of the Pious Men of Ashkenaz reached its peak about the year 1200. To be sure, some opposition to the movement showed up in Germany, which can partly be attributed to the radical nature of its teachings, and partly to the similarity it displayed to contemporary pietistic trends within Christian society. But despite this and the limited number of people who could live up to its ideals, the hasidic movement prevailed and survived into the early times of the Late Middle Ages. It even expanded geographically into France, England, and Poland. It gave the Jew a meaningful way of reacting to the experience of the Crusades and to his ever-growing isolation from his Gentile neighbor.

Mysticism and the Mystics

Another group of people not satisfied with routine observance of the *mitswoth* were the mystics. The mystics were men who aspired to an immediate awareness of God in addition to serving Him. These aspirations led them to introduce mythological elements into Jewish theology. Sometimes their ideas became so antinomian that they expressed contempt for normative and fundamentalist Rabbinism. It is not surprising that mysticism, possibly more than any other trend in Judaism, encountered rabbinic opposition. And yet there were periods in the Jewish past when the mystic way had a mighty attraction to rabbinic as well as lay pietistic circles. Mystical trends were known within the Jewish people already in the Antiquity. The mystics were usually reluctant to expound their teachings in public, and preferred to hand them down to small selected groups of disciples. For this reason the teachings of the Jewish mystics came to be called "kabbalah" [the teachings] received [by the chosen]. Scholars who have researched the kabbalah have found in it elements akin to gnosticism, which appeared in the Near East in the late Antiquity.

It is likely that among the Jews of Frankland kabbalistic books were known as early as the ninth century. German Jewry probably encountered the kabbalah a century or so later, when members of the Kalonymos family brought its ideas from their former home in Italy. But it was again, as with the Pious Men of Ashkenaz, that in the twelfth and thirteenth centuries the mystics became a distinguishable group in Western Jewry and their teachings in a sense came out into the open. The same heated religious atmosphere which produced people ready to serve God in extraordinary ways provided in Germany and northern France the proper climate for men who sought a deeper meaning in the Scriptures and were yearning for an experimental knowledge of God.

Often a hasid was at the same time a kabbalist, and Samuel the Pious and his son Judah rank equally high as mystics and leaders of the hasidim. How deep the belief in the possibility of experiencing Heaven entrenched itself among the Franco-German mystics may be fathomed from the fact that Rabbi Jacob of Marvege (late twelfth and early thirteenth century) was addressing halakhic inquiries to Heaven and receiving from there the proper solutions. He attained his visions in dreams following seclusion, prayer, and the recitation of Holy Names. The collection of his responsa is, indeed, known as *Sheeloth utheshuvoth min hashamayim (Responsa from Heaven)*.

While in Germany the Jewish mystical trends were somewhat overshadowed by the impact of the Ashkenazic *hasiduth*, they emerged more vigorously and unmuted in the Provence. Near Eastern spiritual trends, Jewish as well as non-Jewish, always reached it more easily than far-off Rhineland. In addition, the Provence was the classical place for non-conformist ideas. Here the radicalism of the Jewish allegorists was beckoning for reaction, and the extreme rationalism of many drove others to mystical speculation.

It is not surprising that the first truly distinguished kabbalist there, Isaac the Blind, was the son of Rabad of Posquieres, Maimonides' most articulate critic. Isaac is called "the father of the kabbalah." He was so revered as a mystic that some believed that his kabbalistic teachings came down to him over the generations from Moses himself, who received them at Mount Sinai. It is still a matter of debate whether Isaac was the author of *Sepher habahir (Book of the Bright Light)*, or only its popularizer. But the possibility should not be dismissed that the title *Book of the Bright Light* euphemistically hints at his authorship, since he was generally called Isaac *saggi nehor*, Isaac [who possesses] *much light*. Be this as it may, the appearance of the book *Bahir* was a milestone in the emergence of the mystical movement in the Provence and of its literature.

Some of Isaac's pupils wrote important kabbalistic works, and one gets the impression that the kabbalists in Provence were no less numerous and no less influential than the allegorists. From the Provence, kabbalistic influences moved into Christian Spain. As we have seen (cf. above, Chap. 9), there Nahmanides introduced kabbalistic elements into his commentary to the Pentateuch, so popularizing the kabbalistic ideas more than anybody else. The Jewry of Christian Spain was thus prepared for one of the kabbalah's greatest triumphs, the appearance of the *Zohar (The Book of Splendor)* at the beginning of the Late Middle Ages, only a short few years after Nahmanides' departure from Spain.

Facing Christianity

We have seen (cf. above, Chaps. 3, 4, 5, and 6) to what degree Jewish destiny in the orbit of Western Christendom depended on attitudes promoted by the Church. But Jewish destiny also depended on the Jewish attitude to Christianity as a religion. The talmudic law, which increasingly entrenched itself as the main basis of Jewish existence, developed in countries (Judaea, Babylonia) where the Gentile population was largely pagan. The creators of the Talmud thus had a very clear task set for them: to fully isolate the Jewish people from the surrounding idolatrous atmosphere. In the Near Eastern countries, where the Jews lived in compact masses, such isolation could be conceived without causing any serious economic harm to the Jewish communities. In Western Europe, where the Jewish communities were small in size and widely scattered, such total isolation from the Gentile neighbors could render Jewish existence nigh impossible. The question of the attitude to Christianity as a religion thus became a major issue for the religious leadership and the individual Jew.

A perusal of the existing information indicates that no clear solution to this problem was found until the very end of the Early Middle Ages. It is obvious that the thousands of martyrs of 1096 in the Rhineland and the many who died in York in 1190, mostly by their own hand, considered Christianity a pagan religion, due to its belief in a man-God and reverence for images. In times of relative tranquility, however, the religious leaders could not help but see the striking differences between Christianity and the idolatry of the Antiquity. Furthermore, they faced a situation in which Jew and Christian maintained economic relations on an uninterrupted basis. Such relations could not readily be abolished, since the small Jewish communities were by no means self-sufficient, and the Jew needed the Gentile as a client or supplier no less than the Gentile needed him. Thus, a middle-of-the road attitude developed, represented by Rashi and his grandsons, as well as by other Tosafists. They never came out with a clear-cut statement exonerating Christianity from the guilt of idolatry. They nevertheless tacitly permitted, or at least did not prohibit, Jews dealing with Christians in all areas of economic endeavor. The Pious Men of Ashkenaz, who in every respect attempted to act with extreme honesty, extended this principle with much emphasis to the area of Jewish-Christian economic relations. Once such relations were sanctioned as legitimate, these too had to become an act of sanctification of the Holy Name. Thus, a sort of "truce" with the rival religion was achieved, leaving the way open to reconsideration and new solutions for the coming period of the Late Middle Ages.

Jewish society and its religious leaders also had to formulate an attitude to Jews who converted to Christianity. The conversionary pressures were always present and they were manifold. To begin with, a Jew could escape all his political and social disabilities once he submitted to baptism. In addition, beginning with the second half of the twelfth century, the Church Councils were pressing for increased missionary activities among the Jews. The Catholic clergy found many ways to implement the wish of the Councils, and in the tense religious atmosphere of those times such conversionary efforts enjoyed a degree of success. The sources make it clear that there were indeed Jews in the Ashkenazic countries as well as in Spain, who succumbed to the religious or social lures of Christianity. Rabenu Tam personally knew about 20 such converts. The attitude to converts-opportunists was unequivocal. They were treated with scorn and their names, whenever possible, were twisted to express disdain and condemnation. The Jews of those times were strengthened in their negative attitude to converts by the fact that some of the latter turned informers and slanderers of their former faith and co-religionists. Such a convert, for example, was Nicholas Donin, who brought upon the Jewish community the calamity of the Paris Disputation of 1240 and the subsequent burning of the Jewish books.

Much more numerous were Jews who converted to Christianity under duress. Quite often conversion was the only way to save one's life and not everyone had the courage and strength to die for the sake of his faith. An attempt to forcibly convert Jews was made in Germany and France as early as the first decade of the eleventh century. True, only few Jews then submitted to baptism, and more probably chose flight or death over conversion. Ninety years later, during the First Crusade, more Jews converted, although their number was insignificant in comparison with those who chose to die.

The attitude to the forcibly converted was divided. The rabbis, beginning with Rabenu Gershom, manifested compassion and understanding. Many, if not most, of these forced converts sooner or later found a way to return to Judaism. We have seen (cf. above, Chap. 5) that when the storm of the First Crusade abated, Emperor Henry IV permitted all those forcibly converted to return to Judaism. Their number must have been large, and they became a problem in the Jewish communities. The rabbis insisted that the tragic Christian episode in their life should be forgotten, and that they should be treated on an equal basis with all other members of the community. The rabbis specifically demanded that they should be called to the Torah in the synagogues and that they should be permitted to fulfill all their other religious duties.

Public opinion in the Jewish communities did not, however, always agree with the rabbis. Many felt that a Jew who did not have the strength to die for his God when challenged to do so was not a good Jew, and should upon returning to Judaism be considered a sort of second-class Jew. It is not surprising that this attitude could be found among the Pious Men of Ashkenaz. In their scheme of extreme devotion to God and of fulfilling the precepts in a heroic way, there was no place for Jews who wavered in the moment of the great trial. The repeated calls of the rabbis for compassion indicate how deep and stubborn was the resentment towards those who did not stand up for their God.

There were also Christians who converted to Judaism. Their number was small, however, due to the danger involved in such a step. There was possibly some truth in the complaint of Bishop Agobard of Lyons that Jews were conducting missionary propaganda in the very court of Emperor Louis the Pious of Frankland. The Jewish count William of Toulouse is also said to have religiously influenced some noblemen at the same court to the point that they converted to Judaism. Nevertheless, when Bodo, a clergyman at this court, decided to embrace Judaism in 839 he had to flee to Muslim Spain to go through with his plan. An eleventh-century clergyman (possibly archbishop) of Bari also had to flee, first to Constantinople, and then to Egypt when he decided to become a proselyte. Another convert, a south-Italian Norman knight, who as a Jew became known as Obadiah the Proselyte, also lived in the Muslim Near East after embracing Judaism, but not all proselytes had to escape, and there were some who stayed in Germany to perish in the holocaust of the First Crusade. The number of proselytes, though not large, was probably more than negligible.

INDEX

Geographic names which appear very
frequently have not been indexed.

A

Aaron ben Joseph (the Elder), 93-94
Aaron of Lincoln, 192
Aaron ben Meir, Gaon of Jerusalem, 44, 48, 82
Abassids, dynasty, 8, 10, 13-14, 42, 81
Abd al-Malik, caliph, 9
Abd ar-Rahman, Umayad prince, 14
Abraham ben Azriel of Bohemia, 229
Abraham ben David of Posquieres, also Rabad, 60, 207, 233
Abraham bar Hiyya, 219, 222
Abraham, son of Maimonides, also Abraham Maimuni, 34, 53, 78
Abraham Maimuni. See Abraham, son of Maimonides
Abraham, patriarch, 151, 170
Abu Bakr, caliph, 2
Abu Isa. See Obadiah
Acre, 54, 61, 167-68
Aden, 5, 15, 18, 23, 27, 33
Aegean Islands, 165
Afghanistan, 7, 88
Aghlabid, dynasty, 14
Agobard, bishop, 139, 152, 186, 188, 237
Ahai of Shabha, Rabbi, 51
Ahimaaz of Capua and Oria, 212
Ahmad ibn Tulun, ruler of Egypt, 14
Ahwaz, 7
al-Adeni, David ben Amram, 52-53

Alans, 117
al-Balkhi, Hivi, 87
Alconstantini, family, 181
Aleppo, 6, 23, 32
Alexander II, pope, 160
Alexander III, pope, 145
Alexandria, 10, 27, 73, 118, 173
Alfasi, Isaac, 39, 50-52, 82, 228
Algeria, 2, 17, 20, 33, 50, 96
Al-Hakim, sultan of Egypt, 22, 23
al-Hariri, 75
al-Harizi, Judah, 58, 68, 74-76
Al-Muizz, sultan of Egypt, 14, 33
Alphonso VII, king of Castile, 138
Alphonso X, king of Castile, 223
al-Qumisi, Daniel, 89-90, 94
Alroy, David, 10
Amalfi, 159
Amittai ben Shephatiah, 111
Amram, Gaon, 83-84, 112, 228
Amulo, bishop, 152
Anan ben David, 89, 92, 95-96, 115
Anatoli, Jacob, 222
Andalusia, 16, 32, 67, 122, 196, 219
Andrew II, king of Hungary, 149
Angleterre, 216. See England
Anjou, 123, 126, 141
Antioch, 166
Antiochus IV Epiphanes, 173
Aphendopolo, Caleb, 99

Apion, 173
Arabia, *also* Arabian Peninsula, 1, 26
Arabs, 2, 3, 11, 73, 77, 121
Aragon and Aragonians, 122, 128-29,
    138, 176, 181, 195, 222. *See also*
    Spain
Armenia, 107, 218
Arpad, dynasty, 126, 132
Asaph, 78
Ashdod, 105
Ashkelon, 6, 166-67
Ashkenaz, 216. *See also* Germany
Astrakhan, 114. *See also* Atil, Itil
Asturia, 121, 128
Aswan, 17
Aterno, 174
Atil, 14, 117. *See also* Itil, Astrakhan
Atlas mountains, 50, 96
Augsburg, 172
Augustine, Father of the Church, 155
Austria, 131, 143-44, 173, 192, 204
Avencebrol, Avicebrol. *See* Ibn
    Gabirol, Solomon
Avicenna, 214
Avignon, 154
Aymeri. *See* Theodoric, duke of
    Toulouse.
Ayyubid dynasty, 15, 23

B

Babenberg, 144
Babylon, 82
Babylonia, 3, 5, 7, 16, 29, 32-33, 35,
    36-41, 47-49, 51-52, 61-62, 64, 78,
    80, 82, 95, 98, 118, 127, 168, 206,
    234. *See also* Iraq
Bacon, Roger, 223
Badis, king of Granada, 19
Baghdad, 7-10, 12, 14-15, 27-28, 31,
    42-44, 48, 59, 76, 81, 88, 115
Bahutsim, 96
Bakhchiserai, 100
Balearic Islands, 122, 128-29
Balkan peninsula, Balkans, 107, 108,
    111, 162
Barcelona, 122, 129, 138, 140, 195,
    204, 219, 222

Bari, 202, 237
Bashyatchi, Elijah, 91
Basil I, Byzantine emperor, 109
Basra, 7, 51
Bavaria, 122-23, 131, 163
Bedouins, 23
Bela IV, king of Hungary, 149
Belgium, 131
Benjamin of Tudela, 108, 217
Berakhiah the Punctuator, 213
Bernard of Clairvaux, 164
Beziers, 165
Black Sea, 99, 118, 218
Blois, 171, 214
Bodo, 237
Bohemia, 124, 126, 132-33, 144, 148,
    162, 164, 166, 173, 186, 199, 203-4,
    218. *See also* Moravia
Bohemians, 126, 162
Boleslaus I, king of Poland, 126
Boleslaus III, king of Poland, 126
Boleslaus V, grand duke of Great
    Poland, 149
Bologna, 145
Boris I, czar of Bulgaria, 108
Brabant, 131
Brussels, 131
Bulan, ruler of Khazars, 115-16
Bulgaria, 107, 111-12, 115
Burgos, 129
Burgundy, 123
Bury St. Edmunds, 165
Byzantines, 22, 125
Byzantium, 3, 26, 41, 67, 76, 84, 94,
    98-100, 107-8, 110, 112, 114-15,
    118, 127, 150, 162, 174, 194

C

Caesarea, 167
Cahorsins, 193
Cairo, 14, 22, 24, 54, 58, 73, 82, 220
Calatrava, 138
Calixtus II, pope, 156
Canaan, 119, 216
Canossa, 124
Capet, Hugh, king of France, 123
Capetians, dynasty, 123

Carolingians, dynasty, 123-24, 129-31, 134, 139-42, 145
Caspian Sea, 114
Castile, 16, 97, 121, 128-29, 137-38, 176, 181, 195, 214. *See also* Spain
Castilians, 122
Catalonia, 122, 128, 138
Catherine II, empress of Russia, 101
Caucasus, 6, 85, 113-14, 116-18, 218
Champagne, 195, 203, 205
Charlemagne, 122, 124, 139-40
Charles the Bald, king of France, 123, 139-40
Charles Martel, king of Frankland, 2, 122
China, 26-28, 184, 217
Chiquatilla, Moses, 66
Chufut Kale, 100
Clermont, 159-60
Cluny, 159
Cologne, 129, 143, 161-62, 165, 179-80, 216
Constantinople, 98, 108, 110, 114, 165, 237
Copts, 22
Cordova, 9, 16, 19, 21, 50, 53, 67, 73, 79, 82, 122, 214-15
Cornwall, 187
Corsica, 130
Cremona, 145
Crimea, Crimean peninsula, 99, 100-101, 103-4, 113, 117-18
Ctesiphon, 7, 29
Cyprus, 98, 217

D-E-F

Dacia, 126. *See also* Hungary
Dahya al-Kahina, 2
Damascus, 2, 6, 8, 10, 23, 49
Dan, one of the Ten Lost Tribes, 83
Danube, 162
David, king of Judah and Israel, 28-29, 31, 156
David ben Maimon, 54
David, Maimonides' grandson, 61
David ben Zakai, Babylonian exilarch, 30, 45-46

Derbent, 117
Dnieper River, 113
Don River, 113-14
Donin, Nicholas, 141, 157, 236
Donnolo, Sabbathai, 111

East Galicia, 100, 102, 218
Eboracum. *See* York
Eborwakh. *See* York
Ebro River, 122
Edessa, 163, 166
Edward I, king of England, 125, 148, 187, 193
Egypt, 2, 7, 10-11, 14-15, 17-18, 21-23, 26-27, 32-34, 36-37, 40, 44, 46, 49-50, 54, 58-59, 62, 73, 75, 77, 82, 84, 94-96, 103-4, 116, 118, 168, 217, 237
Elbe River, 122
El Cid, 137
Eldad, "The Danite," 69, 82
Eleazar of Worms, 207, 231-32
Emicho of Leningen, 161
England, 123-25, 128, 132, 146-48, 155, 164-65, 167, 171, 175, 180, 185, 187, 189-90, 192-93, 199, 201, 203, 206, 210, 212-13, 216, 218, 223, 228, 232
Ephraim ben Isaac of Ratisbon, 229
Erets Hayi. *See* England
Erets Israel. *See* Holy Land
Even Shemuel, Yehudah, 64

Fatima, daughter of Mohammed, 14
Fatamids, dynasty, 14, 15, 21, 23, 25, 82
Fayyum, 44
Fez, 7, 17, 21, 49-50, 53-54, 96
Flanders, 148
France, 26, 58, 60-61, 75, 103-4, 122-25, 127-28, 131-32, 140-42, 148, 155, 157, 159-60, 164-65, 167, 171, 176-77, 180, 182, 184, 186-90, 193-95, 197, 200-206, 209-10, 212-13, 216-19, 228, 232-33, 236. *See also* Provence, Zarephath
Frankland, 2, 122, 129, 134, 139-40, 152, 175, 186, 188, 196, 198, 226, 233
Frederick II, Duke of Austria, 144, 173, 190, 192

Frederick I Barbarossa, German
     emperor, 124-25, 135, 143, 164, 176
Frederick II, emperor of Germany,
     124-25, 135, 144, 146, 172, 187,
     196, 222
Frenchmen, 166
Fulda, 143, 172
Fustat, 22, 27, 49, 96

G

Galicia, 218
Galilee, 6, 78, 166
Gaul, 184. *See also* France, Frankland
Gazah, 5, 166-67
Genoa, 145, 159, 185
Germans, 104, 133
Germany, 48, 102-3, 122-27, 130-33,
     141-44, 147-48, 161-64, 166, 174,
     176-77, 180, 182, 184, 186-88, 190,
     194, 199-200, 202-3, 206, 212, 214,
     216-18, 232-33, 236-37
Gerona, 205
Gershom of Mayence, *also known as*
     Rabenu Gershom, 130, 170, 183,
     203, 206, 225, 229, 236
Godfrey of Bouillon, ruler of the
     Kingdom of Jerusalem, 161, 166
Granada, 11, 16, 19, 20, 32, 67, 72-73,
     122, 220
Greece, 107, 111, 165, 196, 217-18
Gregory I, the Great, pope, 155
Gregory VII, pope, 124
Gregory IX, pope, 157, 204
Gozzo, 130

H

Hadassi, Judah, 99
Haifa, 6, 166
Hai, Gaon, 32, 43, 84
Haman, 172-73
Hananel, Rabbi, 49, 52
Hapsburg, dynasty, 124
Harun-ar-Rashid, Caliph, 8
Hebron, 166
Henry II, king of England, 124

Henry III, king of England, 125, 147-48
Henry IV, German emperor, 124,
     142-43, 161-62, 176, 236
Henry VI, German emperor, 124-25
Henry I, king of Germany, 123
Hereford, 147
Hohenstaufen, dynasty, 124, 126,
     143, 145
Holy City, 167. *See also* Jerusalem
Holy Land, 2, 5, 6, 9-10, 21, 23, 27, 34,
     37, 44, 48-49, 54, 64-65, 73-75, 81,
     83-85, 91-92, 95, 98, 101, 123,
     159-60, 162, 165-68, 211, 216-18.
     See also Palestine
Hungary, 118, 126, 132, 144, 148-49,
     173. *See also* Pannonia, Dacia
Huozmann, Ruediger, 130, 142
Hushiel, Rabbi, 49

I-J

Ibn Abitur, Joseph, 66, 85
Ibn Adret, Solomon, *also known as*
     Rashba, 61
Ibn Daud, Abraham, 19, 65, 71, 82, 97,
     214-15, 219
Ibn Ezra, Abraham, 66, 74, 77, 85, 97,
     201, 208, 11, 219, 221-23, 227
Ibn Ezra, Judah, 97, 138
Ibn Ezra, Moses, 39, 67, 69-73, 76, 85
Ibn Ferrizuel, Joseph, 97
Ibn Gabirol, Solomon, 62-63, 69-71,
     77, 85
Ibn Hayyuj, Judah, 39
Ibn Janah, Jonah, 39
Ibn Labrat, Dunash, Adonim, 39, 69
Ibn Nagrela, Joseph, *also known as*
     Yehoseph Hanagid, 19, 32
Ibn Nagrela, Samuel, *also known as*
     Samuel Hanagid, 19, 32, 37, 70-71
Ibn Paquda, Bahya, 63, 68, 196,
     220, 231
Ibn Saruq, Menahem, 39
Ibn Shamun, Joseph, 57
Ibn Shaprut, Hisdai, 18, 19, 32, 37, 67,
     71, 76, 78-79, 109, 116-17
Ibn Tibbon, Judah, 39, 47, 58, 63-64,
     220
Ibn Tibbon, Samuel, 58, 60, 75, 220

India, 26-28, 54, 184, 217
Innocent III, pope, 154, 156
Innocent IV, pope, 173
Iran. *See* Persia
Iraq, 6-10, 13, 30-31, 75, 80-82, 95-96,
    103-4, 107, 127, 217-18.*See also*
    Babylonia
Ireland, 125
Isaac the Blind, 233-34
Isaac ben Moses of Vienna, 207
Isaac, patriarch, 170
Isaac. *See* William-Isaac
Isfahan, 7, 88
Israel, 63, 74, 104-5
Israeli, Isaac, 62, 79
Israelites, 116
Italy, 37, 41, 49, 52, 79, 98, 107, 111,
    125, 127-130, 132, 145, 148, 161-62,
    174, 186-88, 190, 194-96, 201-3,
    208, 210, 212, 214, 217, 221, 223,
    227-28
Itil. *See* Atil, Astrakhan

Jacob of Marvege, 233
Jacob ben Meir, *also known as* Rabenu
    Tam, 163, 177, 187-88, 200, 202-3,
    206, 208, 213, 226, 229, 236
Jaffa, 166
James I, king of Aragon, 181
Japan, 28, 184
Japheth ben Ali, 90
Jaroslaw, 180
Jerahmeel ben Solomon, 214
Jerusalem, 2, 5-6, 44, 48-49, 81-82, 89,
    95, 98, 105, 141, 159, 163-64,
    166-68, 173. *See also* Holy City
Jesus, 150-51, 153, 157, 174
John Lackland, king of England, 125
Jonah ben Abraham of Gerona,
    204, 227
Jordan River, 5
Joseph, king of Khazaria, 116-17
Judaea. *See* Judah
Judah, Judaea, 34, 136, 166, 168, 234
Judah Halevi, 47, 50, 63-64, 67-69,
    71-74, 85, 87, 91, 94, 97, 158,
    196, 220
Judah ben Kalonymos, 213
Judah the Pious, 229-31, 233
Judith, empress of Frankland, 139
Justinian I, Byzantine emperor, 110
Justinian II, Byzantine emperor, 109

K-L

Kairuwan, 7, 11, 15, 17, 21, 25, 33,
    49-50, 64, 82
Kalmanowicz, Seliq, 104
Kalonymos family, Kalonymi, 230, 233
Kenaph Haarets. *See* England
Kertch, 117
Khaibar, 6
Khayyam, Omar, 72
Khazaria, 113-18, 133, 194
Khazars, Khazarians, 63, 100, 108,
    113-14, 116-18, 133
Khorasan, 7, 30, 87-88
Kiev, 113, 117-18, 184
Kohen Zedeq, Gaon, 45
Korea, 28, 184
Languedoc, 141
Las Navas de Tolosa, 21, 122
Latvia, 103
Lebanon, 49, 166
Leibnitz, 58
Leo III, Byzantine emperor, 109
Leo III, pope, 122
Leon, region in Spain, 128
Libya, 2, 7, 14, 22. *See also*
    Tripolitania
Lincoln, 165
Lisbon, 129
Lithuania, 100-104, 180.
    See also Poland
Lombards, 125, 193
Lombardy, 122-23, 193
London, 147, 164, 171
Lorraine, 123
Lothair, king of Lorraine, 123
Louis V, king of France, 123
Louis VI, king of France, 123
Louis IX, king of France, 123, 141-42
Louis I the Pious, Frankish emperor,
    122-23, 139, 186, 237
Lublin, 180
Lucca, 130, 202
Lucena, 8, 16, 50, 67
Lunel, 60, 202
Luzzato, Samuel David, 58
Lynn, town in England, 165
Lyons, 186
Lyra, Nicholas De, 210

M

Magdeburg, 142
Magyars, 126, 132
Maharam of Rothenburg. *See* Meir of
  Rothenburg
Mahoza, 29
Maimon family, 54
Maimon, father of Maimonides, 20,
  53-54, 78
Maimonides. *See* Moses ben Maimon
Majorca, 188
Makhir. *See* Theodoric, Duke of
  Toulouse
Malaga, 19, 71
Malta, 130
Mameluks, 168
Marranos, 20
Marseilles, 128, 217
Masadah, 169
Mayence, 143, 161-62, 165, 180,
  203, 205
Mazovia, 182
Meir of Rothenburg, *also known as*
  Maharam of Rothenburg, 158, 170
Meiri, Menahem, 61
Mendelssohn, Moses, 58
Merovingians, dynasty, 189
Metz, 142, 161
Mieszko I, king of Poland, 126
Milan, 145
Mizrahi, Elijah, 209
Mohammed, 1-5, 53, 56, 87
Mongolians, 100
Montpellier, 195, 202, 223
Moravia, 126, 132, 199. *See also*
  Bohemia
Morocco, 7, 17, 21-22, 26-27, 49-50,
  53, 96, 128, 132, 184
Moses, 233
Moses of Coucy, 158, 207, 227
Moses ben Hanokh, 50, 82
Moses ben Maimon, *also known as*
  Maimonides, Rambam, 20, 23-24,
  33-34, 47, 49, 52-62, 64, 75, 77-80,
  83, 86-87, 94, 196, 202, 207-8,
  220-21, 225, 232-33
Moses ben Nahman, *also known as*
  Nahmanides, Ramban, 167-68,
  204-5, 207-9, 211, 221, 229, 234
Mosul, 31
Mount Sinai, 233

Muawiya, Caliph, 2
Mushka, 88

N

Nahawendi, Benjamin, 89, 90
Nahmanides. *See* Moses ben Nahman
Naples, 130
Narbonne and Narbonnaise, 2, 139-40,
  194-95, 197, 202, 211
Nathan ben Jehiel of Rome, 208
Natronai. *See* Theodoric, duke of
  Toulouse
Navarre, 121-22, 128
Negev, 5-6, 166
Netherlands, 131
Netira, 12
New Jersey, 104
New York, 104
Nicholas I, Russian czar, 102
Nile Delta, 17
Nissim ben Jacob, 49, 68
Normandy, 123-24, 132, 141, 146,
  161, 163
Normans, 21, 123, 125, 145, 166. *See
  also* Vikings
North Arabia, 3, 5, 6
Norwich, 146, 164-65, 171

O-P

Obadiah, *also known as* Abu Isa, 88
Obadiah, king of Khazaria, 116, 117
Obadiah the Proselyte, 237
Olmuetz, 133
Oporto, 129
Orleans, 123
Otranto, 202, 217
Otto I, German emperor, 124

Palermo, 130
Palestine, 1, 3, 6, 10, 14, 23, 32, 49, 73,
  81-83, 166. *See also* Holy Land
Palmyra, 6
Paltiel, Nagid of Egypt (?), 33
Paltoi, Gaon, 50

Pannonia, 126. *See also* Hungary
Papal States, 125
Paris, 61, 123, 142, 154, 157-58, 197, 203-4
Pavia, 130, 145
Pepin the Short, king of Frankland, 122, 139-40
Persia, *also* Iran, 7, 29-30, 38, 42, 67, 88, 95, 217-18
Persians, 3
Pescara, 174
Peter of Amiens, *also known as* Peter the Hermit, 161
Peter of Cluny, 163
Peter the Hermit. *See* Peter of Amiens
Pethahiah of Ratisbon, 48, 100, 218
Philip II, Augustus, king of France, 123, 132, 141
Philip III, king of France, 131, 142
Philip IV, king of France, 142
Piast, dynasty, 126
Pilsen, 133
Pirqoi ben Baboi, 81
Pisa, 145, 159, 185
Poitiers, 2
Poland, 100-104, 117, 126, 132-33, 144, 148-49, 162, 173, 180, 182, 187, 199, 226, 232. *See also* Lithuania
Poles, 126
Polo, Marco, 217
Pomerania, 133
Portugal, 122, 129, 138, 180
Posquieres, 60
Prague, 132, 162, 218
Premysl Ottokar II, king of Bohemia, 126, 149
Provençe, 58, 60, 123, 141, 194-96, 200, 202, 204, 207, 210-12, 219, 221-22, 224, 227-28, 233-34. *See also* France
Ptolemy, the astronomer, 222
Pumbedita, 29, 40, 42-45, 48, 50, 64, 80-82, 84
Pyrenees, 2, 140, 177, 227

Q-R

Qalir, Eliezer, Eleazar, 84
Qayyara, Simon, 51
Qimhi, David, *also known as* Radaq, 201, 208-9, 211

Qirqisani, Jacob, 90

Rabad. *See* Abraham ben David of Posquieres
Rabenu Tam. *See* Jacob ben Meir
Radhaniya, 77, 184, 216
Ram Bam. *See* Moses ben Maimon
Ramban. *See* Moses ben Nahman
Rameru, 203
Ramleh, 6, 49, 105, 166-67
Rashbam, *See* Samuel ben Meir
Rashi (Solomon ben Issac), 90, 170, 188, 200, 202-3, 205-6, 208-11, 213, 218, 221, 226, 228-29, 235
Ratisbon, 162, 184, 230
Rhenus. *See* Rhine
Rhine, Rhine River, Rhenus, 169, 214, 216
Rhineland, 129, 131, 162, 166, 170, 179, 186, 195, 203, 215, 233, 235
Rhodes, 108
Rhone Valley, 131
Richard the Lionhearted, 147, 164
Romanus I, Byzantine emperor, 109
Rome, 130, 136, 138, 154, 158, 174, 180, 202, 215, 217
Russia, 101-2, 113, 117-19, 133, 184, 194, 218
Russians, 117, 133
Rouen, 161, 163

S

Saadiah, 30, 36, 40-41, 44-47, 52, 56, 62-63, 65, 70, 80, 82, 84, 87, 93-96
Saint Gilles, 180
Saladin, 34, 167
Salerno, 79, 223
Salonica, *also* Thessalonica, 98, 108
Samaritans, 6, 33
Samuel ben Ali, 43, 48, 59
Samuel ben Hananiah, 33
Samuel ben Meir, *also known as* Rashbam, 206, 208-10, 226
Samuel the Pious, 229, 231, 233
Sana, 5, 15, 18
Saracens, 160
Saragossa, 16, 18, 67, 71, 79, 129, 171, 195
Sardinia, 130

Sarkil, 117
Sassanians, dynasty, 40
Saxon dynasty, 145
Saxony, 123
Scotland, 125
Seljuks, 9, 10, 14, 49, 159. *See also* Turks
Sepharad, 216. *See also* Spain
Septimania, 2, 140
Seville, 8, 11, 16, 21, 67, 122
Shemariah ben Elhanan, 49, 66
Shemaryah of Negro-ponte, 94
Shephatiah ben Amittai, 111
Sherira, Gaon, 43, 64, 213
Sheshna, Gaon, 9
Shiraz, 7
Sicily, 15, 17, 21, 24, 27, 36-37, 107, 125, 128, 130, 145, 155, 187-88, 190, 195-96, 199, 217, 222
Silano, 111
Silesia, 117, 126, 133, 186
Simeon, czar of Bulgaria, 108
Simhah of Vitry, 228
Solomon ben Issac. *See* Rashi
Solomon, king of Judah and Israel, 89, 101
Solomon, opponent of Maimonides' writings, 61
Spain, 2, 4, 7-8, 10-11, 13-16, 18, 20-22, 25, 27, 32-33, 35-36, 38, 50-51, 53, 65-67, 73-75, 82-83, 85-86, 94, 97, 107, 111, 121-22, 127-29, 132, 137-39, 148, 152, 154, 160, 165, 177, 182, 185-90, 194, 196, 198-200, 202, 204-5, 207, 210-12, 214-17, 219-24, 227-29, 231, 234, 236-37. *See also* Sepharad, Aragon, Castile, Leon, Asturia, Balearic Islands, Catalonia
Spanish March, 122, 140
Speyer. *See* Spires
Spinoza, 58
Spires (*in German,* Speyer), 135, 142, 161, 176, 180, 213
Stamford, 165
Swabia, 123
Sura, 7, 29, 40, 43, 45, 48, 51, 80, 81-83
Syria, 3, 6, 10, 14, 22-23, 27, 32, 34, 49, 62, 73, 75, 78, 82, 98, 107, 166, 217-18
Szapszal, Seraiah, 104

T

Tartars, 100, 126
Thebes, 108
Theodoric, duke of Toulouse, 140
Theodosius II, Byzantine emperor, 110
Thessalonica. *See* Salonica
Thomas Aquinas, 58
Thrace, 165
Tibbon family, 75, 196, 223
Tiberias, 6, 48, 54, 65, 80, 167
Toledo, 11, 16, 20, 72-75, 97, 122, 129, 137, 195, 204, 219
Toulouse *and* Toulousaine, 123, 140, 197, 202
Tours, 2
Trani, Isaia da (the Elder), 208
Transjordan, 2, 166
Treves (*in German,* Trier), 161
Trier. *See* Treves
Tripoli, 6, 17, 166
Tripolitania, 2, 14, 17. *See also* Libya
Troki, 100-102, 104
Troyes, 180, 203, 205
Tudela, 72
Tulun, dynasty, 14
Tunis, 25
Tunisia, *also* Ifriqiya, 2, 7, 11, 15, 17, 21, 26-7, 32-3, 49-50
Turkestan, 7, 88
Turkey, 94, 98, 103-4
Turko-Mongols, 104
Turks, 9, 34, 159. *See also* Seljuks
Tyre, 6, 23, 49, 166-68

U-V-W

Ukraine, 99-100, 108, 113, 184, 203, 218
Umar I, caliph, 2, 4-6
Umar II, caliph, 9
Umayyads, dynasty, 2, 8, 10, 14, 18, 42
United States, 103-5
Ural mountains, 104
Urban II, pope, 159

Valencia, 122, 128-29, 137
Venice, 145, 159, 185
Verona, 130, 145, 202
Vespasian, Roman emperor, 136
Vichy, 104
Vikings, 117, 123, 131-32. *See also*
    Normans
Vilna, 100, 102, 104
Vishehrad, 162
Vladimir, Grand Duke of Kiev,
    115, 118
Volga River, 113-14, 117
Volhynia, 100

Wales, 125
William I, The Conqueror, *also known*
    as William, Count of Normandy,
    123-24, 132, 146
William II, King of England, 163
William, Count of Toulouse, 140, 237
William-Isaac, count of Toulouse, 202

Worcester, 180
Worms, 142-43, 161-62, 165, 175-76,
    180, 205
Wuerzburg, 163

X-Y-Z

Yarmuk River, 2
Yehiel of Paris, 158, 167-68
Yehudai, Gaon, 51
Yemen, 5, 15, 18, 23-24, 32, 33, 56, 77
York, 132, 147, 165, 168-69, 192,
    216, 235
Yudgan (Judah), 88

Zarephath, 216. *See also* France
Zuta, Nagid in Egypt, 33
Zydowo, 133